THE TASTE OF PLACE

The publisher gratefully acknowledges the generous support of Carol and John Field as members of the Publisher's Circle of the University of California Press Foundation.

CALIFORNIA STUDIES IN FOOD AND CULTURE

DARRA GOLDSTEIN, EDITOR

THE TASTE OF PLACE

A CULTURAL JOURNEY INTO TERROIR **AMY B. TRUBEK**

UNIVERSITY OF CALIFORNIA PRESS   BERKELEY LOS ANGELES LONDON

University of California Press, one of the most distinguished university presses in the United States, enriches lives around the world by advancing scholarship in the humanities, social sciences, and natural sciences. Its activities are supported by the UC Press Foundation and by philanthropic contributions from individuals and institutions. For more information, visit www.ucpress.edu.

Parts of this book were previously published in different form and are reprinted here by courtesy of their original publishers: a section of chapter 1 in Carolyn Korsmeyer, ed., *The Taste/Culture Reader: Experiencing Food and Drink* (New York: Berg, 2005); parts of chapter 2 from Amy B. Trubek, "Incorporating *Terroir*: L'Affaire Mondavi Reconsidered," *Gastronomica: The Journal of Food and Culture* 4, no. 3 (summer 2004): 90–99, and "Wine Is Dead! Long Live Wine!" *Gastronomica* 6, no. 2 (spring 2006): 88–90; part of chapter 4 from Amy B. Trubek, "Tasting Wisconsin," *The Art of Eating*, no. 68 (2004); and part of chapter 5 from Amy B. Trubek, "Food from Here: Struggles and Triumphs at the Farmer's Diner in Vermont," *Expedition Magazine* 45, no. 2 (summer 2003): 22–25.

University of California Press
Berkeley and Los Angeles, California

University of California Press, Ltd.
London, England

Library of Congress Cataloging-in-Publication Data
Trubek, Amy B.
    The taste of place : a cultural journey into terroir / Amy B. Trubek.
        p.   cm.—(California studies in food and culture)
    Includes bibliographical references and index.
    ISBN 978-0-520-25281-3 (cloth : alk. paper)
    1. Diet—United States.   2. Diet—France.   3. Food crops—United States.   4. Food crops—France.   I. Title.
TX360.U6T79   2008
641.3—dc22   2007008839

Manufactured in the United States of America
17 16 15 14 13 12 11 10 09 08
10 9 8 7 6 5 4 3 2 1
This book is printed on New Leaf EcoBook 50, a 100% recycled fiber of which 50% is de-inked postconsumer waste, processed chlorine-free. EcoBook 50 is acid-free and meets the minimum requirements of ANSI/ASTM D5634-01 *(Permanence of Paper)*.

FOR BRAD, AND FOR KATHERINE

CONTENTS

ILLUSTRATIONS

PREFACE

IS THERE A RELEVANT AND POSSIBLY EVEN VITAL CONNECTION TO BE MADE between food and place? On average, any food eaten in the United States has traveled at least fifteen hundred miles on its long, often winding journey from farm to table. Could it conceivably be important to know where your food comes from in an era when even our most quotidian meal—a dish of two pieces of bread with a ground-meat patty in the middle, served with the condiments of mustard and ketchup, and perhaps also lettuce, tomato, and onion—has come from unknown surroundings and traveled far before it is served at an American table? When our supermarkets are filled with thousands of processed foods but only hundreds of raw whole foods? When the average American eats one out of five restaurant meals in his or her car? This book says yes.

However, the relevance of the connections between food and place outlined in *The Taste of Place* may not echo the prevailing sentiments of food activists or parallel the popular analyses of journalists and scholars. Much of our present debate on the state of the contemporary food system (not just locally but globally)—and as a result the fate of farming, cooking, and eating—is grounded in two powerful American cultural values: first, that talking and caring about food above and beyond its mere sustenance value are improper (a legacy of our Puritan ancestors), and second, that every American deserves a chicken in his or her pot. Any effort to influence our food culture must therefore embrace these values or be labeled as elitist. These assumptions, based on moral values, can make other values— concerning food practices, food tastes, and food origins—appear trivial. But what if concerns about practices, tastes, and origins in fact can help create alternative cultural values about place, about community, about agriculture, and about hospitality? And what if these alternative values allow us to see our contemporary food system and shape our food future in new ways? The intersection between taste and place organizes such values and practices.

How does this happen? Well, take the potato, like the hamburger, a quotidian food for Americans. A closer look at the humble spud illuminates the making of the taste of place in the United States. The average American consumes more than seventy pounds of potatoes per year, of which the majority are eaten as French fries. Maine farmers, as it was reported in a 2005 *New York Times* article, want to move beyond the hegemony of the French fry. These farmers and their allies want to make people realize the array of flavors and textures available from potatoes. Since the eighteenth century Maine has been a fertile ground for growing potatoes, but there has been a steep decline in the number of potato farmers over the past eighty years, from six thousand in 1940 to just under six hundred today. Over time, the distinctiveness of potatoes being from Maine has been lost to the larger world, but a number of farmers are trying to change that: "To distinguish their potatoes, these farmers have embraced a raft of ideological labels: organic, local, sustainable, heirloom, slow, artisanal, gourmet and farm to table. Instead of growing an industrial potato suitable for long-term storage, the farmers say they grow a culinary potato," the article states.[1]

The culinary potato? The industrial potato? In the more than two hundred years since the potato was first planted in Maine, what has happened to food in America? In the first decade of the twenty-first century, we apparently

categorize our potatoes not simply according to variety—Yukon Gold, Car-
ola, Russet—but also according to process and intent: culinary or industrial.
The article reveals that the culinary potato is used in Portland chef Rob
Evans's roast potato soup with bacon and sour cream for an annual potato
dinner dedicated to celebrating the tastes of Maine potatoes. The industrial
potato, on the other hand, is grown by contract. It is then shipped to the new
McCain processing plant in Easton, Maine, and ultimately transformed into
precut, precooked French fries for any number of chain restaurants
throughout the United States. Fifty years ago the industrial potato appeared
to be the spud of the future in Maine, but now potato farmers there want to
celebrate the uniqueness rather than the sameness of potatoes from this
place, a land of loamy soil and cool northern climate. These farmers and
their allies, such as chefs in funky restaurants in Portland, Maine, are helping to build the taste of place, or what the French call *le goût du terroir*.

The classic nineteenth-century French dictionary, Pierre Larousse's
Grand dictionnaire universel du XIXe siècle, defines *terroir* as "the earth considered from the point of view of agriculture," and clarifies with *le goût de
terroir*: "the flavor or odor of certain locales that are given to its products,
particularly with wine." The ability to trace a connection between the symbolic and practical definitions of the earth and the tastes of food and beverage defines French food culture: as the dictionary elaborates on the
definition, *"Ce vin a un goût du terroir; Je n'y trouve pas le parfum de terroir."*[2]

Anthropologist Claude Lévi-Strauss famously said, "Food is good to
think." The French have long thought about the relationship of food and
beverage to place and linked place to taste, developing values and practices
and making such thinking a type of cultural common sense. Here in the
United States such thinking is also in play, and the taste of place could
emerge as part of our cultural ways of knowing about food and beverage. My
aim is to examine carefully the taste of place in France and the United States
as a set of values, practices, and aspirations.[3] My hope is to reveal how such

thinking *and* doing may be a "middle way" for navigating between the increasingly relevant but beleaguered categories of local and global when we consider farming, cooking, and eating in the twenty-first century.

The Taste of Place uses stories—ethnographic descriptions and explanations of how this idea works in the everyday practices of people in France and the United States—to explore the contemporary genesis of goût du terroir. This book looks at numerous modern stories of farming, cooking, and eating, stories in which people embrace the culinary over the industrial, incorporate ideas about the importance of process and intent into growing plants, raise animals, make wine and cheese, and create meals. Such stories need to be considered together, as if they were individual squares of a quilt stitched together from coast to coast and from continent to continent, for only from their combined weight and impact does the entire pattern emerge.

Each chapter follows a main story, a certain road to the taste of place, but along the way I follow some side roads too, perhaps in the form of a historical discussion, a description of a place or a meal, or a short discourse on the many possible definitions of terroir. Chapter 1 situates the story in the past, focusing on the development of the *appellations d'origine contrôlée* and the founding of the Institut National des Appellations d'Origine in 1935. This chapter also explores the French cultural focus on the link between place, taste, and agriculture. Chapter 2 closely examines l'affaire Mondavi, the attempt by the Robert Mondavi Winery to create a terroir-style grand cru wine in the Languedoc region. Exploring the story of why the Mondavi family wanted to go there, what happened, and why they ultimately abandoned their efforts creates a more nuanced understanding of the cultural importance awarded to place by the French and introduces the many implications of globalization for any contemporary understanding of terroir. The scene shifts to California in chapter 3, which explores how terroir and goût du terroir are understood and used in the United States. The chapter focuses on Randall Grahm, an innovative winemaker from Santa Cruz who has dedicated his life to capturing terroir on

American soil. California is also a point of origin for the countercuisine movement in the United States, a movement that has fully embraced the taste of place as an organizing principle, as fully revealed in the organization of the Ferry Building Marketplace in San Francisco. Chapter 4 looks closely at the importance of chefs and restaurants in the modern American version of the taste of place by telling the story of Odessa Piper, who owned and operated L'Etoile restaurant in Madison, Wisconsin, for almost thirty years. The restaurant continues to adhere to a philosophy of a Midwestern *cuisine du terroir*. The importance of agrarian values, both old and new, to the taste of place in Vermont, and an in-depth consideration of the Vermont Fresh Network, a small nonprofit partnership between farmers and chefs, form the center of chapter 5. This chapter also examines the importance of the back-to-the-land movement of the 1960s for the creation of an American version of the taste of place. The possible future of the taste of place, and the intersection of such a framing mechanism with the modern fascination with brands and branding, shapes chapter 6. This chapter moves between the United States, France, and Italy, focusing on the place-based foods maple syrup and goat cheese as the main lenses for the intersecting yet paradoxical notions of goût du terroir and, as the French say, "le marc."

In a restaurant review in the same *New York Times* food section as that delineating the difference between the industrial and culinary Maine potato, reviewer Frank Bruni remarks on the ways food is good to think today: "To appreciate how far eating has evolved from a matter of survival to a statement of values, take a trip to Cookshop and look at its chalkboards."[4] Bruni somewhat ambivalently excavates the connections between taste and place instrumental to the restaurant's vision: "Cookshop, you see, is selling more than Montauk squid, Catskill duck, and a cornucopia of lettuces, legumes, root vegetables, and fruits that dutifully obey their seasons. Cookshop is selling virtue."[5] As the review progresses, the tone becomes more favorable, for the restaurant's "theology [also] incorporates the pleasure principle."[6] For a restaurant to have values about food practices, tastes, and origins is acceptable, it appears, as long as those values are not too, well, puritanical. As these two short pieces, written for the same newspaper at the same time, reveal, the increased investment in food as the intentional result of unique processes and places is being taken seriously. However, the taste of place has yet to become part of our cultural common sense, for it continues to simultaneously engender sentiments of engagement and uneasiness. But there has been progress. Ultimately, after judging various dishes quite favorably, Bruni concludes that Cookshop is "a place where eating well and doing good find common ground."[7] If these articles can serve as our Rosetta stone, helping us to unlock mysteries of meaning and action, we can see that the taste of place might be very good to think as we look into our globalized future, and might unite Americans, French, and others in how we farm, cook, and eat. And to begin, I will follow Salman Rushdie's exhortation in his novel *Shame* that "in order to unlock a society, look at its untranslatable words." Rushdie talks of Takallouf, "a member of that opaque, world-wide set of concepts which refuse to travel across linguistic frontiers." We, though, will take a journey into *terroir*.

ACKNOWLEDGMENTS

THE FERTILE SOIL OF THE NEW ENGLAND CULINARY INSTITUTE NURTURED ANY crop, culinary or intellectual, I have been able to harvest. Many colleagues sparked my curiosity and shaped my questions about the taste of place. Thanks to everyone, and above all to Mark W. Davis, my mentor in all matters related to *terroir*. My tenure as a Food and Society Policy Fellow sponsored by the W. K. Kellogg Foundation was a true gift, allowing me to travel around the United States (and beyond) and learn of all the great ideas, people, and places where the taste of place matters. Vermont Fresh Network allowed me to dig deep with my questions; thanks to all the members who shared their stories and ideas. None of my work at Vermont Fresh Network would have been possible without the enthusiastic support of Meghan Sheradin. More recently, the Nutrition and Food Sciences Department at the University of Vermont was a wonderful source of support, both intellectual and administrative, as I developed many scattered ideas into a finished manuscript. Thanks to Jean Harvey-Berino, who supported my research in ways big and small. Alyssa Nathanson has been a truly wonderful research assistant, cheerfully helping with all the details involved in researching and writing a book. Eva Antczak was a great help, too.

Many, many people graciously and generously shared their time and thoughts with me during my travels to understand the taste of place. One of the great pleasures of this project has been listening to people passionately explaining what they do and why it matters. Thank you to everyone who took the time to talk to me. Of course, any errors are my own.

Numerous friends and colleagues have read and commented on various sections and versions of the book over the years, and their involvement helped me write more clearly, more thoroughly, and more thoughtfully. John Feffer, Ritty Lukose, John Elder, Melissa Pasanen, Chris Keathley, Jacob Tropp, David Sutton, Carolyn Korsmeyer, Arlin Wasserman, and especially Kyri Claflin and Priscilla Parkhurst Ferguson deserve many thanks for comments along the way. Vanessa Wolff was the best first reader of the entire manuscript I can imagine, giving me the confidence I needed to finish. Krishnendu Ray, Mike Hamm, and Lisa Heldke were also generous and thoughtful readers of the manuscript. Darra Goldstein supported this project from the beginning and has been an exemplary colleague, both for her commitment to my work and, more generally, for her dedication to the growing field of food studies. Sheila Levine, Randy Heyman, Laura Harger, and Sharron Wood at University of California Press have been supportive colleagues as well.

Kitty Cowles listened to my very first incoherent ideas, cajoled me to "tell lots of stories," worked with me every step of the way, and then graciously let me finish and publish on my own. I cannot thank her enough for her commitment and generosity. Ed Behr made me think harder and write better about terroir, and for that I will be eternally grateful (and so will you, dear reader).

My husband, Brad Koehler, has been my companion and helpmate on this journey since I first started to think about food, wine, and *goût du terroir*. His work creating the taste of place inspires me every day. I am truly blessed to share my life with him and our daughter, Katherine. This book is for them.

INTRODUCTION

WHEN I WAS IN MY EARLY THIRTIES, JUST FINISHING MY DOCTORAL DISSERTA-
tion in cultural anthropology, I moved to Vermont to teach at a culinary school, the New England Culinary Institute. I had worked as a cook for many years, and my dissertation looked at the history of the culinary profession. Working at a culinary school, then, was really a form of fieldwork, allowing me to be a participant-observer in the making of contemporary American food culture, especially the subculture of people earning their living making, selling, and serving food in restaurants. Soon after I arrived at the school I met Mark W. Davis, a trained sommelier who taught all of the wine courses. The students revered Mark for his depth of knowledge and his sophisticated palate (not to mention his fashion sense). Eventually Mark and I ended up sharing an office, and our close collegiality continued for many years. When writing classic ethnographies, anthropologists like Ruth Benedict, Margaret Mead, and Clifford Geertz relied on native informants, cultural insiders that provided the naïve anthropologist with an entry into their complex world, a web of cultural meaning, symbols, values, and practices. Mark was *my* native informant, if you will.

From my own experience and research I knew a lot about the culture and history of professional chefs. However, I knew little about evaluating wine, or analytically pursuing the sense of taste more generally, and I was extremely curious. With Mark as my guide I was able to use our shared experience as a way to recognize a certain worldview not solely related to wine, but to the very way people *taste* wine and food, and how they evaluate those tastes. He first introduced me to *terroir* and *goût du terroir,* glossed in English as the taste of place, the central focus of this book.[1]

So sharing an office with Mark started my informal, and then ultimately my formal, education in the appreciation and discernment of wine and food. Simply by overhearing Mark's conversations with students, and then through our own conversations and shared meals, and ultimately by taking some of his courses, I learned about viticulture and viniculture, about the aroma wheel and tasters and super-tasters, about distinguishing between New World and Old World styles of winemaking, and, most importantly, about terroir, the notion that the natural environment can shape the taste of wine. This last idea really took root in my thinking, as it encapsulated so much of what I was learning in my everyday work life. Was *terroir* a word familiar to me before I spent my days at a desk three feet away from a sommelier? Probably, since I had traveled often to France, including on recent research trips to explore the country's food culture. But sitting in our office was where I realized that *terroir* was not simply a word but a *category* for knowing and discerning wine.

Over time, as my participant observations of the culinary school became subtler, my understanding of terroir shifted from an incidental result of sharing an office with Mark to the focus of my own scholarly inquiry. As an insider with the classic outsiders' stance, always trying to understand how the various individual actions and underlying assumptions fit together, I began to recognize themes, such as certain standards about what constitutes a "good worker," or what is needed for a dish or a glass of wine to "taste good," or what it meant to be a technically proficient chef or sommelier.

In the course of a workday I taught culinary students, talked to farmers, and attended faculty meetings at which at least ten working chefs were frequently in attendance. I also often talked to Mark about our teaching strategies as we shared stories about our students. At this school, most of the courses were taught in a professional setting. Students learned to bake, for example, by arriving at the school's bakery at 5 AM, ready to mix doughs and shape breads. Chef-instructors ran restaurant kitchens, building the menus and executing the dishes with students, who rotated through various kitchens as part of their education. In this environment people discussed taste and the taste of things every day: the blackberry notes in the merlot, the crispness and purity of a freshly picked organic carrot, the best ways to pair wine with a sole dish served with lemon and ginger. I became fascinated by these conversations for what they *revealed* about what mattered in this community, but also for how they *informed* everyday choices.

Above all, I was intrigued by the thread that stitched together all these conversations: the connection between the *taste* of the wine and food and their origins. By *origins* I mean what happened before the food and beverages came to the loading dock of the school's central purchasing facility: the region where the wine was made, the method used for pressing the olive oil, the style of the cheese maker. Besides their shared explanations of why food and wine have certain tastes, clear differences existed among the people having such conversations: the wine sommelier lean and elegant in his Hugo Boss suit swirling and sniffing; the local organic farmer fit and tan in a scuffed Carhartt jacket and work boots discussing compost and Roundup pesticide; the compact and intense chef from France passionately discussing the pitfalls of too much garlic in a sauce. But for all of them, the taste—the sensation when the wine and carrot and sauce were brought into the mouth, when the products of the earth were incorporated into the human body—is what mattered most. And for everyone, any attempt to explain the experience in the mouth and articulate a sense of discernment (the mellowness of the wine, the sweetness of the carrot) led back out of the mouth into the surroundings and settings. The *place* where the wine and carrot came from and the methods used in their creation, according to the sommelier, the farmer, and the chef, created *distinctive tastes*.

When Mark taught his students about terroir, he emphasized the "Old World" or European origins of the association between taste and place. Students learned about methods of using labels of origin to differentiate wines in much of Europe, especially France's Appellation d'Origine Contrôlée system, Italy's similar Denominazione di Origine Controllata system, and, more recently, the European Union's protected denomination of origin. Most Old World wines, he explained, are made to best express the unique aspects of the grape's environment (geology, climate, farming methods), but the labeling system helps people appraise a wine's final quality as well. Understanding such internal referencing between the taste of a wine and how and when it was made was instrumental to the students' appreciation of European wines.

From my first engagement with terroir, the result of my own conversations with Mark and overhearing his discussions with students, I was struck with how this idea seemed at once particular (students learned about a French concept and a European set of practices) and universal (shared by the sommelier, the chef, and the farmer, as well as by the French and Italians). This dynamic between the universal and the particular was fantastic food for thought for me, someone with an anthropological imagination and a trained cook's palate, and so it became my central research subject. Initially, I spent much time just trying to clearly define *terroir* and the frequently used phrase *goût du terroir,* and the role of both in the French system of labels of origin.

Anthropologist Pradeep Jeganathan describes his own research in Sri Lanka as "travers[ing] the basic problem of anthropology, which is to make the particular available through the categories of the universal."[2] I came to realize that our many specific conversations about the taste of food and wine and their origins could be heard around the globe as well.

The complexities (and contradictions) of the particular and universal qualities of terroir and goût du terroir became very apparent early on in my research, when I still worked at the culinary school. I was asked to speak to a group of professionals who run the food service at an Ivy League university. I discussed the importance of thinking about food from a cultural and historical perspective. As an introduction to the next event, a port tasting led by the maître d'hôtel (the manager of the front of the house) of the school, I spoke briefly about my early research considering terroir, focusing on the French AOC labels of origin. The director of the university food service, savvy to the importance of marketing in America to create market niches for certain products, looked at me skeptically and said, "They are just trying to sell the sizzle and not the steak." I stayed for the tasting and sat next to the director. The sommelier led us through a tasting of four different ports. (Though produced in Portugal, ports are subject to a control system similar to that of the French Appellation d'Origine Contrôlée. In fact, some consider the system used for port to be the historical precursor of that in France.) He began with two fairly inexpensive blended ports produced in large quantities. He explained that the third port was a vintage port, which means it was created from an unusually good harvest. Every year could be labeled "vintage"; however, a year is not declared a vintage year unless conditions are considered favorable for producing high-quality wines. All the grapes came from a single vineyard (most ports are made from grapes picked in a number of vineyards), and only a very small quantity, 39,000 bottles, was produced. After tasting two blended nonvintage ports, we could truly discern a difference when we tasted the third port. There was greater clarity and depth to the flavor. The director looked at me, laughed, and said, "Okay, it's not just the sizzle. This port simply tastes better." His comment haunted me as I continued my research.

The director's initial skepticism but ultimate acceptance of the taste parameters I outlined reflected my central concern: How could I figure out both the sizzle *and* the steak? Ultimately I moved beyond the assumption that the taste of place is a preoccupation of professional "foodies" and began to think about taste more broadly, realizing I was looking at tastes whose origins were ultimately about both culture and nature. The universal elements of the taste of place came to inform my consideration of all the complex particulars I examined through archival research, interviews, and participant observation. From that time on I wondered how could it be that thousands of miles away from where the port was made, two people in another culture tasted how place intersects with unique flavors?

THE CULTURE OF TASTE

In the act of tasting, when a bite of food or a sip of wine moves through the mouth and into the body, culture and nature become one. Universally, eating and drinking are processes of bringing the natural world into the human domain. Thus, these everyday events are by no means culturally neglected; eating and drinking are powerful and meaningful throughout the world in ways that extend far beyond pure sustenance. Incorporating the natural world into the physical body can signify so much. Consider the globally varied list of taboo foods: grasshoppers, for example, are considered unacceptable as food in the United States, but they are enjoyed in Mexico. And this cultural attention encompasses what, where, when, how, why, and with whom you eat or drink.

Taste is the difference between food as a mere form of sustenance and food as part of life's rich pageant, a part of sociality, spirituality, aesthetics, and more. Taste unifies the myriad means humans have devised to make food so much more than what makes us able to move, to survive as a species. Human eating habits are paradoxical. On one hand, unlike almost every other animal species, we are omnivores: we eat animals, vegetables, grasses, grains, and fruits. But we don't really eat everything; in fact, we eat very little of what is available to us. Some of us eat ants; some turn in disgust. Some eat sea urchins and octopus and squid, while others embrace squid in the form of fried calamari at T.G.I. Friday's but reject it everywhere else. Ideas about what tastes good or is even appropriate as food vary immensely among nations, cultures, religions, and peoples. And the reasons we refuse to eat certain foods are not arbitrary, but mediated by cultural beliefs and practices.[3] In Oaxaca, a taco filled with fried *chapulines*, or tiny grasshoppers, tastes wonderful and also helps define the taste of Oaxacan cuisine. In south India, fresh coconut and red chili, used in any number of dishes, is a deeply loved taste combination, and for many Keralites living abroad, it tastes like home. For an observant Jew or Muslim, the consumption of pork is an affront to God, although the consumption of beef or lamb is not. For many Americans, the smell of powdered cheese combined with a Styrofoam-like crunch harkens back to the most wonderful days of childhood, while the smell of liver can bring back the worst dinner table memories. Our cultural tastes frame our physiological taste experiences.

Judging the sensory quality of any food or drink is complex. All human beings do share certain physiological aspects of taste, thanks to the taste buds located on everyone's tongue. These hundreds of small papillae that dot the tongue's surface enable us to distinguish between salty, sweet, bitter, and sour, and even the most recently identified taste, umami. The taste buds at the front of the tongue are considered most sensitive to sweetness, the ones at the edges to saltiness, and those toward the back to bitterness. Smell is as important as the taste buds in the ability to taste, since flavors and aromas are perceived by the human brain with the olfactory bulb. However, taste remains profoundly subjective because the taste experience can never be physiologically shared. Instead, taste evaluations must occur through language, through a shared dialogue with others. The complexity of discerning taste, therefore, lies in how that dialogue develops, and what factors shape both the conversation and the final sensory evaluation.

My participant observations at the culinary school led me to realize that the *origins* of food and beverage determine prevailing notions of taste. Taste—this unbelievably vital, complex, amorphous, physiological, cultural, undoubtedly elusive, and probably evasive notion—kept being *located*, both in geographical terms (in the gravel, schist, or clay; on the hillsides, in the valleys, or by the river) and by name (Joey's strawberries, Bill's lamb, Laini's cheese, Helen's wine). As soon as I first heard of this locational philosophy of taste, my curiosity was piqued. I borrowed this notion from the world of wine aficionados and began to look at taste as if it were produced by a locality rather than by a technique or in a certain social setting. Once I changed my worldview with regard to taste, numerous questions arose: If taste is produced by place, how does it work? Can the earth, air, sun, and water really make such a powerful imprint on my mouth? Is the link between taste and place particular to certain cultures or a universal human phenomenon? Why is this coupling so potent right now?

Although the social structure understood by sociologists such as Pierre Bourdieu to be determined by social and economic class may influence what we believe is in good taste, other involved processes shape what we think *tastes good*. Working at a culinary school I witnessed every day a dynamic tension between a set of structural constraints and individual and professional aesthetic and creative ideals when it came to the taste of food and drink. Students learned how to cook while making food for the locals and tourists that came to the restaurants run by the school. The restaurant menu had to reflect the expectations of consumers: yes to hamburgers and French fries, but no to fermented yak butter and calves' brains. At the same time, chefs wanted to demonstrate their mastery of culinary techniques and sensory evaluations and students aspired to such mastery. As a result, each menu item became an opportunity to transcend the often static assumptions about what the customer expected with surprising ingredients or unusual presentations. Every day the interplay between social expectations about what would sell and the desire to express aesthetic values and skills was worked out. Making sense of such an interplay requires an analysis of growing, cooking, and eating food and drink based on *practice*. Exploring how the physiology of taste is elaborated by those who grow, make, and eat food every day allows a more nuanced analysis of the culture of food, and also the larger cultural assumptions we enact every day.[4]

FRENCH TASTE

As someone who takes a decidedly historical approach when attempting to answer broad questions, I first wanted to understand the origins of this idea—the taste of place—which means I had to consider France, for that is where the idea originated. It is difficult to translate *terroir* from the French in a way that encapsulates all its meanings; in fact, some say *terroir* can never really be translated from the French at all. When it is attempted, the word is translated alternately as soil, locality, or part of the country.[5] Among the reasons the term is so difficult to translate is that the word's meaning is embedded in French culture. It is part of people's everyday assumptions about food; it is as fundamental as our assumption that the first meal of the day should include coffee and orange juice but not miso soup. The French are unusual in the attention they place on the role of the natural world in the *taste* of food and drink. When the French take a bite of cheese or a sip of wine, they taste the earth: rock, grass, hillside, valley, plateau. They ingest nature, and this taste signifies pleasure, a desirable good. Gustatory pleasure and the evocative possibilities of taste are intertwined in the French fidelity to the taste of place.

By now this French orientation has moved far beyond France, and it has become a method for people like Mark to explore and explain taste experiences. According to Mark, if I want to understand the unique terroir found at Mas de Daumas Gassac in the Languedoc (one of Mark's favorite vineyards), I need to be where the grapes are grown and the wine is made. I need to go to France. I first tasted the robust red wine from this vineyard in a comparative wine tasting Mark hosted for a group of students interested in French wines. As Mark expounded on the vineyard's unique terroir and the other students and I tasted the wine in a small, dark classroom, I had another epiphany about the existence of the taste of place, and its importance to the French.

So, to truly understand what my colleagues were discussing so passionately, and to be able to tell the story of the importance of the natural world to our ideas about taste, I went to France. I found terroir in many places and guises, although capturing it was often as difficult as describing taste experiences. The first section of this book details the important events, people, and institutions that have been instrumental in developing terroir as a powerful category for tasting food and wine. I also explore why terroir has been such an important cultural category for the French, tracing it back to the celebration of the peasant and agrarian life so central to French identity.

People are a large part of the story of terroir and goût du terroir, even if rock, soil, slope, and sun may seem to be the central characters. Many French people are dedicated to championing the connection between taste and place: the dynamic dialogue that happens when we evaluate what we eat and drink has long been shaped by tastemakers and taste producers. The term *connoisseurship* is often used to describe discriminating tastes when it comes to wine, cheese, chocolate, and other foods; the dictionary definition of a connoisseur is someone "with a thorough knowledge and critical judgment of a subject, especially one of the fine arts; an expert in any matter of taste (e.g., wines, foods)."[6] Although during my research I often engaged with people who could be understood to be connoisseurs, in the end *connoisseurship* doesn't cover all of the meanings and activities involved in understanding terroir and the goût du terroir. Other interpretations more convincingly capture the taste of place. To better capture the entire universe of possibilities when considering the taste of place, I use the word *discernment* instead.

Michel de Certeau and Luce Giard argue for a close analysis of food and drink embracing contingency, context, and aspiration and not simply assuming our choices are shaped by a static social structure. Such an approach requires a consideration of a constellation of features ultimately shaping taste experiences, for "the food that is reserved, authorized, and preferred is the place of a silent piling up of an entire stratification of orders and counterorders that stem at the same time from an ethnohistory, a biology, a climatology, and a regional economy, from a cultural invention and a personal experience."[7] A study of the quotidian activities of how people grow, cook, and savor needs to incorporate de Certeau and Giard's ideas of "the *truant* freedom of practices" involved in making and tasting food and drink, and then, in turn, what such daily activities bring to the making of culture.[8]

Inherently a comparative project, this book explores how, why, where, and when terroir arrived on the shores of North America. The historical particulars of the "production of locality," using anthropologist Arjun Appadurai's felicitous phrase, as well as the tremendous cultural commitment to the notion, are certainly unique to the borders of France. But when it comes to the idea that quality of flavor is linked to certain origins, ultimately found in locally based farming and cooking practices that pay attention to natural conditions, I wonder if the French have captured and bottled, so to speak, a powerful sensual dimension of taste. Such a cultural vision of the taste of place is increasingly becoming part of contemporary notions of discernment for food and drink around the globe. This is happening now; the connection is being made every day, in ways both big and small.

My investigations became much deeper and broader than I ever imagined they would in those early days of wine and food talk and tastings at the New England Culinary Institute. Above all, achieving a nuanced picture of how the taste of place works and what it ultimately accomplishes took me into unfamiliar territory. Much of this book navigates the many different possible paths leading to and from the taste of place, for above all I know now that to tell the story of terroir requires more than a simple narrative of cause and effect. The concept can never be captured in a linear fashion: first comes rock, then soil, then plants, then sun, and so on. As I was completing this book, I met the French food scientist Yolande Noël, who in her employ-ment by the French Institute for Agronomic Research has thought long and hard about how to define terroir, and how to capture its essence in order to help farmers and winemakers use it in practice. In one wide-ranging dis-cussion about the taste of place, I asked, "How do you envision it?" She replied, "The best way to think about terroir is as a double helix; all the strands work up and around each other. Each aspect is necessary for the fi-nal result." What a perfect analogy: it is an evocative image that also refers to a modern scientific discovery, a key to unlocking many secrets of who we are and how we live. The spiraling, interdependent, and universal double helix truly evokes terroir.

DISCERNING TASTE

Taste of place ultimately transcends France: terroir and goût du terroir have become transnational categories for discerning taste. This book investigates *why* the taste of place has become part of a global dialogue about taste. Plac-ing or localizing food and drink is our bulwark against the incredible (and in-creasingly menacing) unknowns of our interdependent global food system. Locating food makes it ours, and it can also train us to appreciate it in new ways. This sensibility is beginning to inform people everywhere: we are in-creasingly a global community of concerned consumers and producers. By comparing France and the United States, I can look at all the different ways food is being localized, for reasons of economics, politics, and aesthetics.

These two nations are under similar pressures related to the supply of food. They are both subject to a shrinking agricultural sector, greater globalization of markets, and increased consolidation of distribution systems and retail food sectors. Especially over the past century, farming has shifted away from being a localized activity that spurs economic and culinary activity in home communities toward becoming a sector of a larger industrialized portfolio based on distant trade. But what does this shift mean? How should it be understood? How broad and how deep are these changes? And, finally, how are people responding to such changes in their everyday lives? Analyses of the economics of globalization tend to rely on metaphors of forward movement—a juggernaut, a fast-moving train—and these images reinforce an underlying assumption of inevitability, to "like it or lump it." However, not every place on the globe has responded in the same manner to an increasingly globalized economic system. A poll published in *The Economist* in 2006 asked people from a number of nations to agree or disagree with the following statement: "The free-enterprise system and free-market economy is the best system on which to base the future of the world." Seventy-three percent of the people polled in the United States agreed, but in France the number was significantly lower, with only 40 percent in agreement.[9]

At the same time, tastes are always changing, and the way these changes occur can ultimately reveal much about the larger structures that do shape our daily lives. A fine wine and an organic carrot may appear to represent very different creations in the taste hierarchy. It may be hard to imagine that a discussion of the finer points of the wines grown by Château Mouton-Rothschild could be related to a discussion about the variations in flavor between Nantes and Chantenay carrots grown on Joey's farm. One seems so fancy, the other so, well, plebeian. But why is that so? Perhaps this assumption has more to do with how we think than with what we taste. Our contemporary thinking about the physiology of taste is increasingly mediated by modern capitalism, an economic system that values food like it values any other commodity, thus putting tremendous pressure on any other cultural sensibilities and distinctions. Food and beverages continue to straddle the gap between a good and a commodity, between known and unknown objects, even though consumption of commodities—including food and drink, the only ingestible commodities—now functions as the primary marker of social status.

Many in France perceive globalization as a threat, but in the United States we apparently do not share their fears. The persistence of the French agrarian tradition means that France as a nation and a culture has responded to globalization quite differently than the United States has. Even though there are fewer and fewer French peasants, the idea of the peasant looms large in the cultural imagination. Certain decisions that are considered common sense in France are thought elitist or strange in the United States. The French habit of shopping for food daily, for example, is quite foreign to Americans, who tend to shop only weekly. Similarly, the Americans' more nonchalant attitude toward the agrarian world and landscape is difficult for the French to understand.

In America as a whole, we have embraced a fully industrialized and globalized food system as well as a more open acceptance of economic globalization and free markets more generally, and this level of acceptance certainly influences our everyday diet. However, acknowledging the globalization of food and drink, and accepting that this phenomenon may influence the culture of taste, does not necessarily mean that all local differences have been lost. This book could be read as a foodie version, if you will, of a number of recent ethnographies that consider the importance of globalization to our everyday cultural beliefs and practices.

The new cultural term *foodie,* however, is often used pejoratively or with a dismissive tone. Those who use it often mean to suggest that a focus on ingredients, their origins, and their quality is an elitist set of practices, or is aimed at capitalizing on the desire for distinction (in the Bourdieuian sense) among elite groups. Such dismissals, which I encountered often over the course of my research, reveal the American foodview, or our dominant way of thinking about and making food. Our foodview is not informed primarily by taste, or by place, but by the ability to purchase a consistent product, or, even more generally, a commodity. Commodities are not perceived as sensual objects, capable of evoking pleasurable and meaningful moments. Rather, our approach is quite dour. In the United States, preparing, cooking, and eating food (or drinking wine or other beverages, for that matter) is often no different a process than getting gas and driving our cars. Discernment in our commodity culture relies on external information, not personal knowledge: choices revolve around numbers—cost, rankings, popularity. Taste is defined chiefly in relationship to status; the sensory element is generally neglected, and if you pay too much attention to what happens in your mouth, you are readily dismissed as a "foodie."

Why is caring about food, drink, and taste so suspect in the United States? Perhaps it is our Puritan heritage, but maybe this suspicion is of more recent vintage. Until relatively recently, the values that shaped people's taste preferences in the United States revolved around abundance and accessibility:[10] we wanted to know we could have plenty of food. Many people think our quest for quantity comes from our immigrant past. Most of our ancestors, whether Irish, German, or Laotian, fled dire circumstances, and others were brought here under duress, so once on the shores of the New World they needed to make sure there was plenty. Perhaps this history explains the preponderance of the all-you-can-eat buffet throughout the country. When we want to dine fancy, however, the sophistication of the food is more important. We want to eat food that seems impossible for us to make ourselves. What better way to demonstrate our sophistication than to eat an exotic dish like caviar and blini, or a complicated one like *tournedos de boeuf* with a truffled Madeira sauce?

Thus can the French definition and embrace of terroir be transmitted, or perhaps invented anew, in the United States? A close examination of how terroir and goût du terroir are seen in everyday values and practices related to food and drink in several regions of the United States reveal a strong connection to what Warren Belasco aptly called a "countercuisine," the response to our fully industrialized food system that began more than thirty years ago. Throughout this book I explore the myriad places where the taste of place intersects with definitions of authenticity. The uses of authenticity when related to food and drink rest on assumptions about the superiority of traditional practices; historical persistence somehow guarantees higher-quality food and drink. However, the American definition of terroir may need to be more entrepreneurial.

There remains a paradox in terroir as a practice, for we have the ability to reach across the globe for desirable foods and drinks. Globalization has changed the landscape of food forever. As anthropologist Ted Lewellen points out, "The easy categories of the past seem oddly out of place in a world that is fragmented and in which space and time have imploded."[11] When we fly at thirty thousand feet, the changes humans have made to the earth can seem permanent, the scars on the land as deep and disturbing as strip mines. The story can seem to revolve solely around irrevocable loss. However, there are countless stories of continuity and invention to be told, stories that are necessary for any nuanced analysis of how people think about food, and how they make and taste it as well. And for the tastemakers on the ground just trying to figure out what to do, their everyday decisions force them to engage with desires for continuity and changing realities, and to attempt to make sense of the past as they move toward the future. Keeping these as my primary considerations, I do not abandon the local versus global framework, but perhaps it gets bent in a slightly different direction.

And so the taste of place, like food and drink, may end up being a universal phenomenon with very localized stories, practices framed by particular cultural memories, meanings, and myths. I wonder now if I *experienced* the taste of place many times before (and since) I came to work with Mark and others at the culinary school: in a small restaurant down a winding road in Vermont where the salad came from the huge vegetable beds just outside the restaurant door; at my friend Ritty's family home in Kerala, where we picked the taro for the evening meal; at the small wine shop in Alsace where, as I sipped my glass of Riesling, I glimpsed through the windows the vineyards where the grapes for that bottle were grown; in my family's heirloom orchard on a cool, crisp October night as I twisted off a newly ripe Esopus Spitzenberg apple, redolent of flowers and honey, and took a bite. In these moments I was blessed with a sensual experience bringing together place, taste, and practice. *The Taste of Place* encourages readers to think about and understand the taste of place, although reading about the concept will never replace tasting it. May you have the opportunity to do both.

ONE

PLACE MATTERS

A REMARKABLE CONSISTENCY EXISTS IN DISCUSSIONS OF *TERROIR* AND *GOÛT du terroir* in France, a cultural sensibility that extends back over several centuries. In historical documents, government treatises, and contemporary conversation, everyone—be they journalists, farmers, vintners, bureaucrats, chefs, or citizens—does not adopt a point of view. Instead they consider terroir and goût du terroir to *reflect reality*. This fundamentalist mode always begins with a defined place, tracing the taste of place back from the mouth to the plants and animals and ultimately into the soil, creating a very Gallic twist on the oft-used American phrase "location, location, location." In France, food and drink from a certain place are thought to possess unique tastes. Thus, more than words, terroir and goût du terroir are *categories* that frame perceptions and practices—a worldview, or should we say a foodview? The agrarian roots of terroir best explain the origins and persistence of this foodview. Terroir and goût du terroir are categories for framing and explaining people's relationship to the land, be it sensual, practical, or habitual. This connection is considered essential, as timeless as the earth itself.

Agriculturalist Olivier de Serres says in his seventeenth-century treatise *Le théâtre d'agriculture et mesnage des champs* that "the fundamental task in agriculture is to understand the nature of the *terroir,* whether it is the land of your ancestors or land recently acquired."[1] Soil and roots are at the heart of French cuisine as well. In his discourse, places make unique tastes, and in turn such flavor characteristics and combinations give those places gastronomic renown. Le Grand d'Aussy, in his 1789 work *Histoire de la vie privée des français,* discusses French cuisine as the natural fruition of provincial agriculture, tracing back at least two centuries the connection between the cuisine and what "nature has seen fit to allow each of our provinces to produce."[2] *Le cours gastronomique,* first published in 1808, includes a map of France that outlines the nation's borders and then charts the inner territory solely with agricultural products. Included are the wines of regions such as Bordeaux and the Rhone; Roquefort and Brie are named, with drawings of cheeses; and many charcuterie items such as sausages and cured hams are shown as well. Jean Anthelme Brillat-Savarin's *La physiologie du goût* (The physiology of taste), first published in 1826, is a catholic exploration of the physiology and culture of taste, replete with scientific, literary, political, and economic commentaries celebrating taste. He characterizes the ability to discern the natural origins of tastes as a "point of perfection": "[The] *gourmands* of Rome distinguished, by taste alone, the fish caught between the bridges from that which had been caught lower down. . . . And have we not plenty of *gourmands* who are able to indicate the latitude under which a wine has ripened, as certainly as a pupil of Biot or Arago can foretell an eclipse?" (emphasis mine). During the same period, Madame Adanson, in her influential and widely distributed book *La cuisinière de la campagne et de la ville,* lists cheeses by place name—Neuchâtel, Brie, Marolles, Cantal—and specifies the flavor characteristics and methods of proper storage of each. The flavor of the *fromage des Vosges,* Adanson writes, "is unique among all cheeses; the method of fabrication is a secret of the locality."[3] In these analyses, the physical environment (soil, weather, topography), not the tiller of the soil,

FIGURE 1. Gastronomic map of France, 1830s. From Horace Raisson, *Le Code Culinaire.* COURTESY OF BARBARA K. WHEATON.

the shepherd, or the vintner, is the primary source of the distinctive tastes of French wine and cheese.

CREATING THEIR OWN DESTINY

A closer examination of historical events tells a different story. The natural environment *influences* the flavors of food and beverages, but ultimately the cultural domain, the foodview, creates the goût du terroir. The taste of place does not originate with the Mesozoic-era collision of the African and European continental plates that defined France's geography and geology. Rather, beginning in the early twentieth century a group of people began to organize around this naturalized interpretation of taste, for they saw the potential benefits of a foodview celebrating an agrarian and rural way of life. French *tastemakers*—journalists, cookbook writers, chefs—and *taste producers*—cheese makers, winemakers, bakers, cooks—effectively shaped how people tasted wine and food. The French terms used to describe those dedicated to food are *gastronomes*, tastemakers, and *les artisans des métiers de bouche,* taste producers; both are highly specific terms that more fully evoke the attention the French pay to food and drink than can be captured in an English translation. These advocates intervened into an everyday occurrence, eating and drinking, and guided the French toward a certain relationship between place and taste.

These tastemakers and taste producers worked hard to shape French judgments of the morsels and liquids that they put in their mouths. These artisans, critics, and commentators elaborated a new language of taste. This language was never purely aesthetic, however, but instead these new translations of taste were part of a dialogue with nature, in this case the agrarian countryside of France. And this was not merely a fanciful dialogue, the sort of raucous food talk that can happen at dinner parties and local cafés and then is all but forgotten the next morning. Nor was this new language merely another version of the utopian food visions characterized by the legend of the medieval Land of Cockaigne, where "cooked food—patés, meat pies, cakes, white bread—grows on trees."[4] This grammar and syntax was built one ingredient at a time, from the ground to the table.

These men and women observed their world and decided to champion certain practices (small farms, regional dishes) and values (tradition, local taste) in order to make sure that they did not disappear. Their cultural and economic investments made the French word for *soil* signify so much: a sensibility, a mode of discernment, a philosophy of practice, and an analytic category. What they *said* may have embraced the timeless and essential notion of mother Earth, but what they *did* was to create a vision of agrarian rural France and convincingly put it in people's mouths. These tastemakers and taste producers cared about taste and place and did not want traditional ways of growing, eating, and drinking to be lost. They made arguments linking place, taste, types of agriculture, and quality that helped protect certain forms of agricultural production and enabled France's modern regional cuisines. These discussions helped shape taste perceptions beyond France as well, for their claims about the taste of place have been adopted throughout the world. The question thus is how did a definition of terroir extending beyond an instrumental explanation of the soil to a more complex category emerge?

Terroir has been used to explain agriculture for centuries, but its association with taste, place, and quality is more recent, a reaction to changing markets, the changing organization of farming, and changing politics. By the late nineteenth century, everyday rural agricultural practices—a reliance on certain crops or livestock because they responded to the local climate and geography, harvesting the bounty of nearby rivers and seas—came to represent the building blocks of regional cuisines. A new connection emerged between how the French farmed, lived, and supped. Some historians examining the emergence of a unified interest in championing the relevance of terroir to French food and farming see geographer Paul Vidal de la Blache, who lived from 1845 to 1909, as a seminal figure.[5] He published his best-known work, *Tableau de la géographie de France,* in 1903, and it has been in print ever since. Geography was in its infancy at the time, and the main influences on the field were ecology, evolution, and nationalism. Trained in history and literature, Vidal de la Blache spent most of his career involved in the field of geography, and at the end of his career he obtained a position as professor of geography at the University of Paris. Perhaps because of his initial training in history, he was interested in the human and social dimensions of geography, and he became deeply involved in developing a regional geography. In doing so, he sought to understand the interaction between humans and their environment, emphasizing the *genre de vie*, or cultural dimensions.

In his introduction, Vidal de la Blache states, "What one hopes to explain in these pages concerns how can the history of a people be (or must be) incorporated in the soil of France? The rapport between the soil and the people is imprinted with an ancient character that continues through today." This essentialist argument, so powerful in early anthropology, geography, and other disciplines, can be interpreted negatively for its nationalistic and racist underpinnings that helped to justify oppressive and regressive policies during the late nineteenth and early twentieth centuries. In the case of food and drink, however, this book, with its focus on the specific and unique geographical conditions of different regions of France, served a different purpose by becoming an important cornerstone of attempts to affirm regionally based agriculture and cuisine.

Underlying Vidal de la Blache's analysis is the assumption that "environment determines the way of life *[genre de vie]*, that is, the enduring features of existence in any particular locality."[6] His book examines the geography of France region by region, focusing on the underlying geologic structures but also celebrating differences in regional character, including food and drink, along the way. Jean-Yves Guiomar sees Vidal de la Blache as a naturalist and romantic: "For Vidal, the characteristics of a way of life include the manner in which people situated themselves in a particular location, the type of dwelling they chose, and the design of their homes, all interpreted as a direct reflection of the nature of the soil."[7] He created a timeless and essentialist portrait of the relationship of people to the land, affirming the already powerful cultural belief in the importance of the *pays* and *paysans* by focusing on the impact of geology (biological and physical) on regional economic and cultural life. Vidal de la Blache was also supported by the French state to create good maps of all the regions of France. This project, sponsored by the Minister of Public Education, Jules Simon, resulted in the Cartes Murales, larger maps of France and its regions that were distributed to schools throughout France.

Vidal de la Blache's scientific treatise did not directly address the economies of the regions. However, taste producers and tastemakers of the same period translated his geographic analyses into daily practices. The agrarian activism of the *vignerons* of Champagne, the AOC regulations and the regional movements of the early twentieth century, and the atlases and guides of Curnonsky were all influenced by his work. They used the timelessness of Vidal de la Blache's *genre de vie* and made it central to their argument for protection and preservation. Exploring their efforts explains the emergence of goût du terroir as a French cultural category.

TASTE, TERROIR, AND THE FRENCH STATE

Grapes for wine historically have been one of France's largest agricultural products, and apparently *vignerons* were the first group of taste producers to realize the possibilities inherent in promoting the link between place and quality; they were the first to take this foodview and use it to their economic advantage. The 1855 Bordeaux wine classifications are considered the first attempt by those involved in wine production and sales to promote the quality of wines by their place of origin. They were developed internally by those involved in the Bordeaux wine industry, particularly wine brokers, to be used at the 1855 Exposition Universelle in Paris. These classifications, however, were not monitored by the French state. The use of ideas about place to make arguments about quality became increasingly important in the late nineteenth century, and it became part of a serious sociopolitical movement to protect French agricultural products in the early twentieth century, culminating with the founding of the Institut National des Appellations d'Origine in the 1930s and laws that supported the idea of *appellations d'origine contrôlées*.

Historian Kolleen Guy elegantly documents the initial efforts to create state-sanctioned and -supported controlled delimitations, establishing that terroir and the system of controlled appellations have a particularly French genealogy, beginning with champagne. By the belle époque era, champagne was an international commodity that symbolized France and Frenchness to elites around the globe, and the connection between commodity and nation was instrumental in initial justifications for the protection of champagne by the French state.

Guy's work, focusing on the period between 1890 and 1914, concerns both competing and allied interests of *vignerons* and *négociants* in the Champagne region at the turn of the century. Even at that time champagne was a beverage endowed with symbolic power and cultural capital. Historically, sparkling wines were an unintended product, the result of carbonic gas emerging from a secondary fermentation of yeasts. Many wines are capable of "sparkling," but champagne producers began to realize the upmarket potential of their sparkling beverage and worked hard to promote its distinctiveness. This was done with the creation of aristocratic genealogies and myths of patrimony, linking the drink, the place, and the producers to a storied past. Guy argues that by the belle époque, to drink champagne was to stake your claim to the civilized life. Champagne became a national brand in an international market, a commodity with tremendous symbolic and cultural capital. But who was reaping the rich rewards of the allure of champagne? As the eloquent *vigneron* René Lamarre states in the beginning of his editorial "Where Industry Meets Terroir," "I cannot repeat it enough: with the way that [wine] lists are drawn up today, within ten years people will no longer be acquainted with the name Champagne but with those of Roederer, Planckaert, Bollinger and it will not matter from which [grapes] these wines are produced."[8]

The elevated status of champagne among the international bourgeoisie in fact did little to contribute to the livelihoods of the laborers in the fields and much to threaten their identity. The local response was to turn to terroir, to fight for champagne as a product of the soil rather than a placeless pretty label. The *vignerons* wanted to retain some proprietary rights to the name champagne, now used all over the globe, so they turned to the soil. The agrarian roots of the movement to create protection for place and products situate the history of terroir. The need to valorize the soils and grapes was particularly acute for growers in this region, since champagne is a blended wine, and large family estates dominated as *négociants,* responsible for crushing, blending, aging, and marketing the wines. Grapes and soil were the growers' only means of controlling the appropriation of champagne. A series of events, especially the phylloxera epidemic of the 1860s, which threatened *vignerons* and *négociants* alike, helped legitimate the idea that Champagne as a defined region was fundamental to the identity of cham-pagne as a beverage, nationally or internationally.

As the link between taste and place evolved in the early twentieth century, taste producers, particularly the *vignerons,* involved the French state, arguing that legal and political means were needed to protect unique French products from international competition. They succeeded. The *vignerons* of the Champagne region were the first to use the legal system to create delimitations on production related to locale. The fundamental goal of the first law (initially passed in 1905, and then amended in 1908) was to protect against fraud; those who "falsely attributed the location of origin of the merchandise as a way to sell their goods" could be punished by law.[9] This legal decree, however, did not deal with what made certain locations unique. By 1908 the law was made more specific, stating that a delimitation could concern a wine that had an association with a region that was "local, loyal, and constant,"[10] and Champagne was granted that status of "the first recognized regional delimitation."[11] Certain areas were judged to be in the "Champagne region," and only wines produced in those areas could be sold with the "Champagne" label. This was the beginning of a system that protected and promoted French wine and would ultimately be extended to cheese and other products.

This initial attempt to define legal boundaries for the production of wine, however, did not take into account notions of quality; no specific parameters were established for how wine was made, nor how much could be produced and sold in the marketplace. Thus one chronic problem for winemakers, overproduction and the resulting price depression, was not addressed. As a result, a series of protests was staged against initial government efforts to protect the wine industry. During the Champagne revolt of 1911, for example, many complained that the decisions about where the boundaries should be drawn for different wines, including Champagne, were politically manipulated.

Joseph Capus, a trained agronomist who worked on grapes and wine, was an instrumental figure in the development of the initial laws promoting delimitations and the subsequent refinements that led to the 1935 law creating the Institut National des Appellations d'Origine (INAO).[12] A professor in the Gironde region, home to many vineyards, he eventually became the commissioner of agriculture there, and then finally the president of the INAO from its inception until his death in 1947. At the end of his life he wrote a report explaining the evolution of the *appellations d'origine contrôlées*. The main flaw of the early legislation, he felt, was that it concerned only provenance. Only in the revised legislation, first in 1919 and then in 1935, do "uniqueness" and "quality" come into play as important parameters.[13] Capus outlines the barriers to creating a law that can adequately capture the true nature of the taste of place, saying that in the thirty-year period between the first and last law, an ongoing struggle occurred between the "theorists" and the "realists." The theorists, he argues, had the upper hand in the 1905 and 1919 versions of the law, and "the legislature considered place solely as a jurisdiction. They did not want to see the human dimension, or the technical dimension."[14] In order to create a powerful link between wine and place, the guarantees must extend past place of origin to include "guarantees of authenticity as well."[15] He expands on this notion, saying, "It is not sufficient simply to guarantee the product's authenticity, but also to assure the *quality* insofar as it can be measured by soil and grape variety."[16] By 1935 terroir no longer functioned primarily descriptively, but it now also determined quality and authenticity.

In 1930 Capus became a member of the French senate, representing the Gironde, and he became a primary author of the legislation that finally linked taste, place, and quality, legislation that far surpassed previous regulations that focused on provenance. The 1935 law created a new regulatory agency within the French Ministry of Agriculture, an agency that would oversee all aspects of determining, monitoring, and promoting wines awarded the Appellation d'Origine Contrôlée designation. This was a first in French agricultural history: "Viticulture understood [before any others] the importance of collective organization in order to understand specific aspects of production, to research, maintain and promote quality, and also to protect and promote these products to consumers."[17] No other collective of producers came up with a similar integrated endeavor for some time, although the AOC system ultimately came to include cheese as well. In 1990 a new law was passed to give the opportunity for AOC status to any agricultural product, and so there are now AOC olive oils, lentils, and potatoes, to name just a few foods.

The Institut National des Appellations d'Origine has been part of the French Ministry of Agriculture since its inception. Despite the activist legacy behind its creation, the direct result of the organizing efforts of vintners and others, the institute's goal is to "protect terroir." As the official literature states:

> It has been known from ancient times that certain lands are made more suitable to the creation of products that retain, and in fact draw out, the specific flavors of that place.
>
> Due to this phenomenon, at the beginning of the century the idea was born to create the notion of the *appellation d'origine,* to acknowledge and protect it under the rubric of the Appellation d'origine contrôlée.[18]

Further on, the link between taste and place is elaborated: "The INAO was initially charged to *identify* wines and eaux de vie, *to codify* their usage for protection in France and abroad against all encroachments" (emphasis mine). Awarding a wine or cheese or any other food product the status of Appellation d'Origine Contrôlée put the official stamp on the connection between taste, locale, and quality.

Rural sociologist Elizabeth Barham analyzes the French AOC system and the link to terroir as an example of Karl Polanyi's theory of economic embeddedness, which argues that markets have always operated within environmental and social constraints. She sees label of origin systems as an example of "translating" nature by focusing on the production process, and she examines how this translation system becomes socially legitimized and reinforced. As she points out, "The legitimation process, to be effective, must be carried out not only within the territory of production but nested within multiple levels of coordination from the local to the global."[19] She goes on to argue that terroir (which she says is a cultural concept) is used to create the legitimation for these place-based products. At another point she says that "what there is in nature to be known" is the basis of the AOC system, "rather than viewing nature as an obstacle to be overcome or controlled for production."[20]

From its very inception, the AOC system has rewarded the alliance of producers. The ability to get AOC status for a certain wine or cheese, or now an olive oil or another product, has always been based on a collective process. Individuals or corporations may not submit an application for AOC status. Instead, a group of producers must submit a dossier of required information, which goes first to a regional committee of the Institut National des Appellations d'Origine and then, if approved, to a national committee. The national committee then appoints a review committee that includes professionals from the submitting region, and this committee ultimately makes a recommendation to the national body. If the producers' dossier is accepted, the Ministry of Agriculture then fixes the boundaries of the appellation and makes it into law. As Barham points out, this process, which starts locally, is codified nationally, and also has implications for global markets: "The new appellation is now protected as the collective property of the producers, as well as part of the agricultural, gastronomic and cultural heritage of France."[21] Because of the complex framework of environment, agriculture, and tradition that ultimately defines terroir, many technical consultants must be involved in order to both operate and monitor the AOC system. Geologists, soil scientists, plant scientists, anthropologists, sociologists, and historians all get involved. In addition, tasting panels are organized for all proposed AOC foods and wines to determine their *typicité*, or shared sensory dimensions, and these tasters can have a say in the final specifications for the product. One cannot overemphasize the importance of terroir in every step of the process of obtaining legitimation for place-specific foods and drinks in France. In one study involving INAO agents, those who oversee the processes of both getting AOC status and maintaining it, terroir was selected as the most important concept used in their everyday work.[22]

In an explanation of the Appellation d'Origine Contrôlée system and the management of terroir, the INAO states that the AOC system provides the tools growing regions can use to fully take advantage of their resources: "With the extraction of the specifics [or characteristics] of their *terroir*, and the search to value and protect the agricultural possibilities in a geographic zone, AOC products can be genuine instruments for managing and supporting territory." But the consumer also needs to be involved in order for the system to work. Whereas "standardization leads to delocalization . . . [the AOC system] supposes that the consumer takes the initiative, recognizes the superiority of a strongly identified product and agrees to pay the price."[23] The INAO therefore oversees how food and wine is made locally, but it also encourages the consumer to find and appreciate those items. The award of AOC status provides producers in the growing region with the economic, political, technical, and marketing support of a government agency. And as Barham points out, the process of obtaining AOC status is heavily subsidized by the French government.[24] From the point of view of the INAO, places create distinct tastes. The mission of the institute, which uses an essentializing definition of terroir, is to be a steward of the relationship between locale and flavor, and to encourage everyone to agree that they can taste place.

With the AOC laws and the founding of the INAO, in effect, a sensibility, or a foodview, became the rationale for laws and government policy that shaped people's approach to growing food and wine for the entire twentieth century through today. Now part of the Code de la Consommation, the rules and regulations of the AOC system *guarantee* the possibility of local control, thus keeping the knowledge and the power in the hands of the growers, the vintners, and others in each agricultural region. As one legal scholar puts it, the "effects of the AOC system are both *célebré* and *célèbre* in France, that is 'celebrated' in the sense of 'famous' and in the sense of 'revered.' "[25] He also points out that the AOC laws protect *both* the natural and human elements involved in the creation of these distinctive foods and wines, and give farmers "claims of entitlement" and government support far beyond anything available in the United States.[26] The implementation of the AOC system guaranteed that food and wine in France could, and would, stay connected to place. When discussing the French preoccupation with memory, identity, and heritage across many cultural arenas—including cuisine, but also museums and heritage sites—several social scientists concluded that "it could be argued that *appellation contrôlée* is a notion that has spread to the whole fabric of France."[27] Fixing practices to a certain time and place, and then creating value for these practices, they argue, is now a larger cultural undertaking.

THE GASTRONOMY OF PLACE

During the same era that *paysans* and others hoped to define the taste of place, gastronomes like Curnonsky and his colleagues prodded the French to go out and taste the countryside, to experience the unique regional *saveurs* (tastes) firsthand. Before the French Revolution, French cuisine was organized primarily by social status: high and low. In a pattern reflective of all of Western Europe, the wealthy were able to command ingredients from near and far, whereas rural peasants and urban laborers were confined to locally available foods.[28] The cuisine of the courts, where conspicuous consumption helped prove the power of the rulers, set the tone for luxurious food. French haute cuisine thus rested on the principles of complexity and scarcity. Dishes were time-consuming to prepare, and many of the ingredients were hard to procure and expensive. *Le Viandier,* a cookbook written by Guillaume Tirel, a royal cook in the fourteenth century who worked in the courtly kitchen of Charles V, includes a recipe for a swan that has been skinned and roasted before the skin is put back on the cooked bird. The roasted and dressed swan is then decorated and put on a platter to bring to the royal table. Tirel also uses gold and silver leaf to garnish many dishes.

Antonin Carême, born in 1784, is famous for his dedication to combining the use of costly and rare ingredients with spectacularly complex preparations in his quest to prove that cooking was an art. His cookbooks, such as *Le pâtissier royal parisien,* contain drawings, directives, and some recipes, but nary a one would fit the "dinner in sixty minutes or less" bill we contemporary users like to find. The hard-to-procure spices of the Middle Ages have been replaced with caviar and truffles. And the creation of each dish is an exercise in aesthetic refinement: "Almost every recipe involves the use of sieve and cheesecloth, straining, extracting, concentrating, reducing."[29] The desired result was almost always a monumental structure, a three-dimensional edifice representing mastery and majesty. By the late nineteenth century swans had disappeared, but in their place were dishes such as *saumon à la Humbert 1er,* celebrating the Italian ruler with a poached and bejeweled fish on a pedestal with a crown made of kohlrabi and garnished with crayfish.

On the other hand, from the Middle Ages through the French Revolution, most of the French were still involved in a subsistence style of cooking. For most, cereals comprised the bulk of their diet well into the nineteenth century: "in some regions galettes (a kind of pancake made of coarse grains like rye); or starchy slops like oaten porridge; or barley, chestnut, or buckwheat gruel reinforced in spring and summer by vegetables such as cabbage, beans, onions."[30] A soup in medieval France was most often a large piece of stale bread in the bottom of a bowl with broth and a few vegetables poured on top. Famine was constantly perceived as a danger for the majority of the French population during this period: "Much depended on where one lived, but cereals were ubiquitously considered the staple diet, and a hunger was popularly identified with their insufficiency."[31]

During the nineteenth century, two other culinary approaches emerged in France, one related to class *(cuisine bourgeoise)* and the other to location *(cuisine régionale). Cuisine bourgeoise* assimilated aspects of haute cuisine, particularly the techniques and basic principles of what makes a meal, but with a greater focus on expediency and sustenance. It was considered the provenance of middle-class women and their female domestic servants living in French towns and cities. *Cuisine régionale* subsumed traditional peasant fare, taking the agricultural variations of different French regions and then elevating the traditional notion of "making do with what was on hand" to a uniquely important way to cook, one that represented the best of France as an agrarian nation. Priscilla Parkhurst Ferguson argues that models of cuisine should be understood as "the possibilities of practice." What happens on the ground refers to these models, but slippage is constant and boundaries and definitions are in fact fluid and often under negotiation. She says that *"peasant cuisine* is less constrained by the social class of its practitioners than by the context of that practice. . . . Peasant cuisine is the ultimate traditional cuisine defined by place, and regional cuisine is not far behind."[32]

The codification of *cuisine bourgeoise* and *cuisine régionale* was very much a response to the increased urbanization and industrialization of society, and truly a product of the epoch. Beyond the organization of agriculture, the written word—cookbooks, food journalism, and regional food guides—was instrumental in developing French regional gastronomy and celebrating the taste of place. Madame Pampille says in her charming book *Les bons plats de France: Cuisine régionale,* first published in 1913, "Only in France do you find good game," and goes on to assert, "And don't talk to me about the German and Hungarian hares that have infested the markets over the past few years: these are large hares, stupid and without flavor."[33] In the "National Dishes" chapter, her dictums on the quality of game—that it needs to come from France and be raised in certain environments—disclose an emerging vocabulary and grammar of taste. She describes partridges grown in confined spaces and fed rapeseed as "having a taste that is faded and dim," whereas the wild or free partridges roaming the plains, which feel hunger and thirst, have another taste entirely.[34]

This book is full of recipes, certainly, but perhaps it should also be considered a gastronomical treatise, a new physiology of taste in the manner of Brillat-Savarin, whose *La physiologie du goût* has not been out of print since it was first published in 1810. Here, quality of flavor is linked to where the partridges come from and how they were fed. And writing of the glory and splendor of France and French cuisine alone is not sufficient for Pampille; distinct geographic regions also provide specific taste experiences. The Savoie and Dauphiné are lauded for their river trout, whose delicate flesh can be appreciated only when you eat it there. She has even stronger views about bouillabaisse: "The triumph of Marseille, it is only good when eaten in Marseille. Don't try to eat it in Paris."[35] Place matters.

THE CASE OF CURNONSKY

Curnonsky was an instrumental figure in the development of regional gastronomy, publishing inventories of regional dishes and guidebooks of stores and restaurants highlighting regional cuisine. The "Prince of Gastronomes," Curnonsky, born Maurice-Edmond Sailland in 1872, was the author of numerous books on food and gastronomy in France, publishing in every decade of the twentieth century until he died in 1956. His life and career spanned a period that witnessed great changes in French cuisine and gastronomy, and he helped make them. Curnonsky linked the physiology of taste to the particularity of place, taking the everyday practices of locals in various regions of France and creating encyclopedias, guides, and atlases that enabled this local knowledge to become nationally and internationally celebrated.

Early in his career Curnonsky made his living as a journalist, a critic, and a ghostwriter for many books (he collaborated with Colette on quite a few). He was always a bon vivant, a larger-than-life figure in bohemian Parisian circles. It was inevitable that he became part of the long French tradition of gastronomes, dedicated men of leisure commenting on (and participating in) the form and content of French food and wine, beginning with Jean Anthelme Brillat-Savarin and Alexandre Grimod de la Reynière in the early nineteenth century.

Curnonsky (he changed his name as a young man, perhaps inspired by his youthful fascination with Russia) turned almost exclusively to gastronomic writing after World War I. He was at times employed by various organizations, state agencies, and businesses whose goal was to promote automobile tourism. This led him to many years of exploring the French countryside and exhorting the French people to get out and enjoy the gastronomic bounty of rural France. Even though many of his books aimed to get the urban French out of the cities, his philosophy was based on rural preservation rather than rural development. For Curnonsky, the French countryside possessed many gastronomic treasures, and he wanted to make sure that they were not lost or ignored as France moved further into the twentieth century, a century that embraced all manner of technologies in the name of progress.

Curnonsky loved all of France's culinary bounty. He called France "the gastronomic paradise of the universe," and he took great care to describe the different styles of cooking contained within its borders. He asserted there were four major cooking styles. Haute cuisine, the domain of chefs, could be found in premier restaurants; *cuisine bourgeoise,* or French family cooking, strove to retain the "total taste of things as they are"; regional cooking contained all the ingredients and dishes that were based on local practices; and, finally, there was "impromptu cooking, or making do on a potluck basis."[36]

Included in his more than fifty works are *La France gastronomique* (with Marcel Rouff), published in the 1920s; *Le trésor gastronomique,* an inventory of regional dishes written with Austin de Croze in 1933; *Eloge de Brillat-Savarin,* published in 1931; and *Bon plats, bons vins,* published in 1950. In *Recettes de provinces de France* he says, "This work celebrates, in a very artistic fashion, the alliance between tourism and gastronomy I have promoted for fifty years and which is only possible in France, because this is a land of tremendous diversity."[37]

Curnonsky lived during a period when many in France, from those representing small chambers of commerce to members of corporations, became very interested in the development of rural tourism, in part as a result of the growth of urban areas and an expanding bourgeoisie. Curnonsky, along with his colleagues Austin de Croze and Marcel Rouff, helped develop regional gastronomy partially to support car and rail travel to the French countryside. Between 1910 and 1930 a gastronomic literature emerged that extols the various regions of France, declaring them part of the glory of the

French nation. Some of these publications were initially part of a larger set of marketing initiatives by Michelin, the tire company, which was interested in developing ways to get people to use their cars to journey into the countryside for leisure.[38] These are the earliest versions of what became the red Michelin guides, the reference works on dining and lodging throughout France that became powerful arbiters of taste for tourists, French or foreign. The Michelin guides, with their rules of exclusion and inclusion, and their expectations about what made a restaurant great, helped to create an elite cadre of restaurants throughout France that ultimately reinforced a national haute cuisine. In a book of reminiscences, *Curnonsky et ses amis,* published in 1979, Joseph Rameaux commented that Curnonsky preferred female home cooks, "the real cordon bleus," to male chefs. According to Rameaux, he felt that elite chefs too often "ignored the [culinary] rules that had reigned in our *appellations.*"[39]

Curnonsky's goals were quite different then those of the red Michelin guides: he wanted to educate cooks, chefs, and diners about the riches of the regions. In *Le trésor gastronomique de France,* Curnonsky and his collaborator Austin de Croze created a regional repertory. Curnonsky boasts that "this thick book doesn't contain a single recipe. It is simply a complete list of the dishes and wines of France. . . . It contains 380 pages!"[40] This was a book for professionals: Curnonsky and de Croze wanted chefs, restaurateurs, and hoteliers throughout France to have an inventory of regional ingredients and dishes to give them ideas for their menus. The book starts with Alsace and visits all the French provinces. Each chapter starts with a map and then a two-page description of the landscape, the history of the region, and a brief description of the regional cuisine. Then there are lists: fish, meat, vegetables, typical menus.

His books are notable for their breadth, with lists of hundreds of recipes or regional dishes or restaurants. Depth, on the other hand, is another matter. You never hear the experiences and stories of the people responsible for these recipes, restaurants, or dishes, nor their histories. In his writings the taste of place is made timeless.

For Curnonsky and his contemporaries to convince people to leave the cafés and bistros of Paris, Lyon, and Marseille, they needed to create a destination and have a celebration in mind. What could be better than wonderful food and wine? Another gastronome of the period, Edmond Richardin, devotes the introduction of his book *L'art du bien manger* to a "gourmet geography of the regions of France." In what is essentially a prose poem that starts in Flanders and ends in Béarn, Richardin lists the gastronomic wonders of France, region by region: "the andouillettes of Cambrai, the trout of Dunkerque, the triumphant asparagus of Argenteuil, [and] onward to Brittany . . . with its Cancale oysters, lobsters and langoustines of Roscoff." In Bresse, Bugey, and the land of Gex: "poulardes de Bresse, Belley sausages, Feillens apples, the cheese of Passin, a rival to the best Gruyère, and the blue cheese of Gex."[41] He ends by exhorting gourmets to open their minds to the vast gastronomic possibilities of the French provinces.

These previously humble ingredients and dishes, the results of many combined efforts of "making do," became immortal. Thanks to the efforts of gourmands such as Curnonsky, de Croze, Richardin, and others, Camembert cheese, Argenteuil asparagus, and *poulardes de Bresse* became celebrity foods. Ingredients and dishes came to represent their regions, ultimately guaranteeing their permanence, for they came to signify more than a dish using the locally available ingredients (bouillabaisse in and around Marseille, cassoulet in and around Carcassonne), but also to represent the taste of that place, wherever the dish may be consumed. Madame Pampille's admonition to only eat bouillabaisse in Marseille notwithstanding, bouillabaisse, for example, became the iconic dish of the French Mediterranean the world over. In the spirit of Proust's madeleine, these ingredients and dishes became iconographic, the *lieux de mémoire* of certain places, their tastes symbolizing France's rich and diverse geography.

Curnonsky, Austin de Croze, and their compatriots also worked with the French state in their efforts to preserve regional gastronomy. If one looks carefully at *Le trésor gastronomique,* reading not just the list of regional dishes, the *choucroute aux escargots* and the bouillabaisse, but the preface and introduction as well, the calculation of their efforts becomes obvious. Here, de Croze's position is stated to be "president of the French Office of Gastronomy," and under the auspices of his official position he convened a meeting on "the general state of gastronomy." After doing a survey of all the available gastronomic publications, the participants decided there was one major lacuna: "an *impartial* and *complete* repertory of all the regional foods and dishes of France" (emphasis in the original).[42] *Le trésor gastronomique* will thus be extremely useful, they claimed, for "ministers of agriculture, commerce, fisheries, and public works, as well as tourist organizations, chambers of commerce, trade unions, business interests [related to food and drink], and, finally, gastronomes and tourists." *Le trésor gastronomique,* like the AOC system, was a culinary intervention, for those involved felt that "France resembles a bit those beautiful women who are simply too modest and don't take compliments seriously, content to simply be pretty. . . . We must jealously guard our riches."[43]

A newer version of this style of culinary inventory, started in the 1980s, is *L'inventaire du patrimoine culinaire de la France,* sponsored by an inter-ministerial organization, the Centre National des Arts Culinaires, a joint effort of the ministries of culture, agriculture, health, national education, and tourism. In many ways similar to Curnonsky's *Le trésor gastronomique,* this collection of books, one for each of the twenty-two *départements* of France, goes into more detail about each *produit du terroir,* providing contact information and recipes representative of each region. Anthropologist Marion Demoissier sees this newer incarnation of the regional inventory to be "the result of a conscious state policy aimed at both the protection and the promotion of a rural cultural heritage."[44] Curnonsky and de Croze wanted to get the new urbanites back out into the countryside. Now, with the majority of the French living in the cities, the goal is to get them to remember the countryside.

THE PLACE OF THE *PAYSAN*

The attention placed upon regional cuisines may have been particularly strong in France because agriculture remained a large sector of the economy well into the twentieth century. Early in the twentieth century, Jean Fulbert-Dumonteil, journalist and native of the Périgord region, wrote, "The Alps and the Pyrenees, the Landes, Cevennes, Auvergne, and the Jura send us small goat cheeses which have a marvelous flavor. The Limousin, Poitou, Bourbonnais, and Berry create sheep cheeses with a fine *saveur*."[45] Only the introduction of the Common Agricultural Policy in the 1960s, which pushed for a unified European approach to farming that promoted larger and more industrialized farming, forced changes in France's farming practices. Nevertheless, in many regions agriculture remained small in scale and traditional in practice. Rural areas in the west, south, and east of the country remained populated by small farmers producing diverse agricultural products throughout the twentieth century.

France is intensely cultivated. Usable agricultural land still covers 60 percent, or thirty-three million hectares, of France, and of that number thirty million hectares continue to be utilized for farming.[46] As in many other industrialized nations, there have been significant changes in agricultural regions over the past 150 years, including significant rural migration to urban areas: the rural population of France declined almost 50 percent between 1851 and 1982, with only 4 percent of the total working population involved in farming by 1997. However, over the same period many farming practices remained remarkably resilient: although the tiny farms, or *minifundia*, largely disappeared—subsistence laborers were better off in town—the midsize family farm actually increased. In 1929 the number of farms between five and fifty hectares was 42 percent of the total, but by 1955 that figure was at 60 percent and, of most note, remained at 60 percent until 1983. France continues to be the largest agricultural nation in the European Union, with "23 percent of the total agricultural area of the fifteen EU states."[47]

The small family-owned farm is not simply part of the mythic past, but remains vital to France's economy and landscape. Even if the majority of the French do not farm today, they still retain connections to farms and farming communities, and the French countryside still appears to be comprised of many small, diverse farms. Only the north-central region of France (around Paris), where primarily grains and sugar beets are grown, is engaged in the large-scale and corporate agriculture that characterizes farming in most of the United States. The agrarian view still dominates.

Thus, the nation's geography has long been described as a combination of urban and rural, and little attention is paid to uncultivated lands.[48] People's connection to the landscape has remained through farms and farmers, to the point that many observers have noted the "mythic" qualities of the countryside and peasantry in the French imagination, even as the majority of the population has left both behind in their own lives.[49]

Deborah Reed-Danahy and Susan Carol Rogers, pioneering American anthropologists working in France, noted twenty years ago that certain features of French society were strikingly different than those of the United States, including "the French preoccupation with history and traditions, and the importance of rural life in French thought."[50] Rogers explores the role of the peasant in French culture, arguing that the peasant, or *le paysan*, functions as an important symbolic category. The peasant, like food, is "good to think." The idea of the peasant—the small farmer embedded in rural areas and upholding the French agrarian legacy—often serves as a lightening rod in contemporary debates about what makes France unique and the French people remarkable. As Rogers points out, France has "two often conflicting views of itself. On one hand, France is a highly centralized, modern civilization with a strong sense of national identity. . . . On the other hand, its identity is tied to a long history of deeply rooted traditions, many anchored in French soil."[51] The imagined peasant thus speaks to the benefits of national progress or the pain and loss of cultural change.

French historian James Lehning takes up Rogers's exegesis of the French peasant. He sees the domination of what he terms a "metanarrative" in histories of the nineteenth and twentieth centuries. This metanarrative tells a story of the absorption of the French peasant and regional rural practices and lifestyles into the more powerful homogenizing impulses of the French state.[52] Narrative plots rely on a sense of comedy (the savage peasant tamed) or tragedy (rural culture destroyed).[53] He sees the French interest in the rural landscape as a "metaphor for the culture of the countryside, a space on which individuals make meaning as they live their lives." The power of *le paysan* and *le pays* to readings of the French landscape continues from Vidal de la Blache to contemporary French geographers. As contemporary French geographer Armand Fremont says, "No other major civilization in Europe or elsewhere has ever valued the soil more than the French or associated it more intimately with the good." He argues that, historically, France is but one of the great "peasant civilizations," yet in the contemporary period, when farmers are called *agriculteurs* rather than *paysans,* there remains a cultural, even mythic, preoccupation with, as he eloquently describes it, "the living portion of the earth's husk."[54] Fremont feels that "soil is a focus of all France's thoughts and emotions."[55] A foodview associating taste, soil, and the bounty of the earth has a long history.

The French foodview linking taste and place has been tremendously consistent over the past century, in effect preserving agrarian values and practices now often considered quaint and old-fashioned. Today the INAO's mission could be seen as the preservation of a philosophy of agriculture from an earlier era, before the advent of large-scale production, national and international distribution systems, and global consumption patterns. In France, the AOC system, with its emphasis on artisan methods and locale-specific production, evokes the best of agrarian France. The other possibilities—large-scale industrialized farming, production of food and wines solely for commodity export—are considered problematic and possibly culturally anomalous.

The state plays an important part in the continued possibility of a goût du terroir that remains powerful in an era of agriculture characterized by industrialization of practice and globalization of supply. Ours is a time when McDonald's are not found just on the boulevard St-Germain-des-Prés, but also in rural Cavaillon in southwest France, and the European Union wants to regulate the size of duck cages used for holding ducks raised for foie gras to appease animal rights activists in Britain. French farmers, historically well organized and culturally powerful, protest regularly against the encroachment of regional and global market forces and regulations into their territory. In a 1999 trade dispute between the United States and the European Union, the United States decided to create a 100 percent tariff for imported European luxury goods, including Roquefort cheese and foie gras. In protest, French farmers attacked a number of McDonald's restaurants in southwest France (the region where foie gras and Roquefort are produced) with rotten apples, tomatoes, and manure. A French farmer was quoted in the *New York Times* as saying, "My struggle remains the same . . . the battle against globalization and for the right of people to feed themselves as they choose."[56]

The cultural embrace of France's agrarian legacy and the interest in preserving it means that the taste of place often intersects with notions of authenticity. But what makes an authentic or, for that matter, timeless culinary dish? The Alsatian chapter of Curnonsky's *Le trésor gastronomique* lists four types of choucroute, a dish celebrated today as representative of Alsace and Alsatian cuisine. Many restaurant menus feature choucroute, usually composed of two or three types of pork sausages, braised pork chops or pork shoulder, and sauerkraut. The book's longer list of choucroute dishes is mysterious and tantalizing: *choucroute Alsatienne, choucroute aux escargots, canard à la choucroute, choucroute à la Juive*. The first dish fits into our contemporary assumptions about choucroute, but the other three? In the seventy-five years since this inventory was published, perhaps the authors' fears have come to pass: does anyone make snail choucroute in Alsace anymore? At the same time, without inventories, guides, and atlases to document the choucroute of Alsace, would any versions still be available today, when the logic of preservation (cabbage into sauerkraut and fresh meat into sausage) that helped create this dish in the first place has been replaced with *sous vide* and *à la minute* cooking?

Taste, then, in France resides as a form of local knowledge. The success of the turn-of-the-century tastemakers and taste producers lay in their ability to create an association between place and quality. They appropriated the link between taste and place, and helped create legal and governmental mechanisms to champion location-based food and drink. Local tastes now define superior quality, which means the French are willing to pay a higher price. Burgundy wines are known to have different taste profiles than wines from Bordeaux and Languedoc, though all may be red wines. In contrast, Americans do not associate specific locales with flavor profiles in wine. Instead, they buy and taste wines according to the grape varietal, such as pinot noir or merlot. The French also perceive that goods produced locally on a smaller scale are superior. An AOC wine produced from a single vineyard in Bordeaux is considered better than a blended wine brought in from all over the Languedoc. Wine producers and consumers use terroir as an ordering and evaluative concept when it comes to quality of flavor, to the point that in France terroir is now used to market food and wine, indicating their quality.

LA SEMAINE DU GOÛT

The foodview *situating* taste and also developing a *discourse* about taste combining physiology, agriculture, and environment remains a potent force in France. While doing research on terroir I stayed in Montpellier, a lovely university town in southern France. Located in the Languedoc province, the town is a gateway to a major wine-producing region and also houses the University of Montpellier, which includes several academic departments and institutes devoted to viticulture and oenology.[57] One day I attended the annual Exposition of the Coteaux du Languedoc, an event championing a relatively new AOC wine-growing region (it was awarded AOC status in 1985), representing more than a hundred wineries. This region's western edge is Narbonne and it extends east to Montpellier. There are a number of soil and rock types in this region, and the traditional red grape varietals planted are grenache, syrah, and mourvèdre, with cinsault and carignan as the secondary varietals. All the promotional literature for this AOC region uses the tag line "L'Art de Faire Parler Le Terroir," which can be translated into English as "Fine Art from the Terroir," but a better translation might be "The Art of Expressing the Soil."

The event was held in the Mas de Saporta, a complex of buildings near the major highway that goes through Montpellier. The Mas (a traditional Occitan term for *farm*) is dominated by a large stucco structure that was a winemaking facility in the late eighteenth and early nineteenth centuries. The Mas de Saporta is the *maison des vins* (wine store), featuring Coteaux du Languedoc wines. The upstairs was a large hall filled with a number of wineries offering tastings of their wines. The downstairs consisted of several rooms, including a tasting room. Of the series of tastings held in this room during the exposition, I chose to attend "Eveil des Arômes pour les Enfants." An aroma tasting for children? At a wine expo? I was intrigued.

This was a first for me, perhaps because you would never find such an event in the United States, for beyond our notion that kids love sweets, we do not really consider children capable of discerning taste. By 3:30, the official starting time, the room was almost full with perhaps thirty children and twenty adults, and within half an hour another fifteen children filled it to capacity. Philippe Cabrit, an employee at Mas de Saporta, led the tasting. The entire event was patterned on a traditional wine tasting, but with fruit juice instead of wine.

The tasting reveals a fundamental assumption of the French foodview: when you eat or drink, it needs to be a shared experience that incorporates sensory analysis *and* sensory pleasure. The ability to discern tastes is a cultural imperative. So how did it work? Cabrit began the tasting by pouring two different types of flavored water into the same wine glasses used by adults. He said, "I don't care what you say; just tell me what you taste." As parents and children alike tasted, Cabrit described the different taste receptors found on the tongue, explaining where salt, sweet, bitter, and sour are tasted. He then said, "Taste, then reflect." The first glass of water had sugar in it: "Are you reminded of bonbons?" The second glass of water was a bit salty. He then moved on to juices. There were six different juices lined up at the head table, all covered with tinfoil. This would be a blind juice tasting. The children were excited: would they be able to guess?

Cabrit and his assistants poured the first juice into the wine glass farthest to the right in the lineup of six. After the juice was poured for all the children, Cabrit led them through the tasting, in an manner identical to that of a wine tasting. He told them to look first at the color. Was it translucent? Opaque? Then they were directed to swirl the glass and sniff. Cabrit informed them that much of taste is actually smell, and that the aroma of the juice would help them guess which fruits were used. As the children got to the third and fourth juices, they became more confident and began to contribute their perceptions. Juice number four was purple and looked like grape juice, but many children noted that the taste was more sour. Several said it tasted like cassis, a sweet liqueur flavored with black currants. The juice turned out to be a blend of concord and muscat grapes with some black currant juice blended in. Cabrit asked, "Is this juice more or less acidic than juice number three?" The eight-year-old boy sitting next to me was completely enthralled, swirling, sniffing, tasting, and guessing. By the time juice number five was poured, Cabrit asked everyone to determine which of the fruit flavors was more dominant, and then informed the group about how the orange juice balanced the acidity of the more dominant grapefruit, creating a nice juice "equilibrium." The tasting ended after juice number six, which Cabrit pointed out was notable for its high degree of sweetness and its viscosity, due to the bananas and milk that were combined with raspberry and orange juices. The room was abuzz, the tasting ended, and the parents and children slowly filed out, perhaps to go try their luck upstairs among the wines.

After the tasting ended I spoke to Cabrit to find out more about it. I had been entranced not only by the fact that such a tasting existed in the first place, but also by the clever way it mimicked a traditional wine tasting and the extent to which it engaged both the children and the adults. He said that the Mas de Saporta often hosts school groups who come for this "Eveil des Arômes." He also mentioned that often these tastings were part of France's annual Semaine du Goût, an initiative that began in 1990 to help French children learn how to discover tastes and flavor, or, as the official website puts it, "valorisant le goût, la qualité des produits et les savoirs-faire." I knew of this "week of taste"; tastings such as the one at Mas de Saporta provided more evidence of that uniquely French sensibility toward taste.

Recently tastemakers and taste producers in France, sensing a decline in people's ability to evaluate and appreciate food, especially unique French foods, started to feel that consumers, especially young ones, needed to be taught how to taste and how to develop their sense of discernment. The "week of taste," it was hoped, would "offer clear information and education to all as to food origins, how foods are made, and their quality."[58] Every October in schools throughout France lessons on taste are incorporated into the curriculum. In 2004 such lessons occurred in five thousand classes of primary school students. Such a taste education is disseminated by people the organization call "taste ambassadors," chefs, and other *artisans des métiers de bouche* who go into schools all over France to teach children. One lesson, similar to the juice tasting, introduces children to all the senses, with a concentration on taste and smell, while another explores the "tastes of France." These tastes are mapped onto the geography of France as "thirty terroirs," or regional specialties.[59] At restaurants, hundreds of chefs also provide children and their families special menus emphasizing regional specialties.

Making a link between taste and farmers and farming is another important element of the "week of taste." As the Ministry of Agriculture states in official postings about the 2004 event, "L'agriculture donne du goût" (agriculture provides taste). The organization goes on to say, "What we eat, in the first instance, are the products of agriculture. At the heart of that moment are farmers [or agriculturalists], who provide our diverse and quality food."[60] In this culture, the highly elaborated sense of taste is understood not to be purely physiological but also to encompass the physical and social environment creating the sensory experience. Or, as anthropologists put it, in France taste is a total social fact. Over the course of the "week of taste," as many as sixty sites around France host events to showcase regional foods and wines and educate consumers with educational panels and tastings. During the 2004 week Hervé Gaymard, the minister of agriculture, stated that such interventions will allow the French to have deeper knowledge by creating a fuller understanding of the nation's diverse *terroirs d'origine*.

The original impetus behind the Journée du Goût (which became the Semaine du Goût two years later) was the Collective du Sucre, an industry organization, but other agricultural organizations later signed on, and in 2003 the French Ministry of Food, Agriculture, Fish, and Rural Affairs became a main government sponsor. The 2005 partners included the Ministry of Agriculture and numerous food product companies and lobbying organizations, including the event's founder, Collective du Sucre, as well as Rochefontaine (vegetables), Champion (small grocery stores), Baron de Lestac (Bordeaux wines), Neptune (mineral water), Sel de Camargue (salt), and more. Although this combination of invested parties may appear to resemble those behind the food expositions at American state agricultural affairs, in fact the French attempt to build consumer awareness by introducing pedagogies of taste into public schools is unique. The explicit analysis of taste and the connections between physiology and the environment in France marks a deep cultural difference between that country and the United States. Another difference between the two countries is the level of involvement by the "taste ambassadors." Above all, this community of government agencies, educational institutions, tastemakers, and food companies united around the desire to encourage discerning taste among schoolchildren embodies the unique French foodview, the intersection of taste, place, and agriculture.

Such a foodview in effect frames much of French government policy and practice on food and beverage, not simply the policies of the Ministry of Agriculture. The Ministry of Tourism created a new program, "The 100 Remarkable Taste Sites," promoting tourism to places all around France distinguished by their unique food and wine. A British website on travel and tourism in France has this to say about the program: "A 'site remarquable du goût' is a monument to taste, identified by a real product with a history and a strong identity, the presence of an exceptional heritage defined by its aesthetic value and its link with the product, a welcome area which enables visitors to link place and product and a synergy between the product, the heritage and the welcome—focusing on a name and a strong local organisation."[61] The lyrical language and nested phrasing indicate that this description was translated directly from French. Nevertheless, the basic values are clear. A *site remarquable du goût* celebrates the taste of place.

While staying in Montpellier I visited Bouzigues, one of the one hundred remarkable taste sites. Located south of Montpellier on the Etang du Thau, a saltwater estuary of the Mediterranean, Bouzigues is a fishing village, but it is oyster farming that makes this little coastal town unusual. Historically, the primary activities here have been growing grapes for wine and fishing, along with the harvesting of some oysters. In the early twentieth century, however, a series of aquaculture experiments were conducted to see if oysters could be farm raised. (At the time, oysters were not only very popular in the region but were also an integral part of French haute cuisine.) The Oyster Museum, located at the end of a narrow street full of restaurants selling the town's signature oysters, details the story of local oyster farming, including the discovery that putting oyster seeds on ropes and hanging them off wooden platforms into the water was an excellent method of farming them. Bouzigues went on to become known in France and beyond for its succulent oysters, and one hundred years later it became a remarkable taste site. On the day I visited the little fishing town seemed sleepy and the museum was empty, but the restaurants were busy with people tasting the famed oysters, both raw and cooked.

In 2006 the Institut National des Appellations d'Origine teamed up with the 100 Sites Remarquable du Goût to create the Ateliers du Goût, a series of events highlighting AOC food and drink that come from designated "remarkable sites." The four events were intended to introduce journalists to the special tastes of the chosen food and drink (Chalosse beef and Armagnac, for example) and to promote an agriculture of "terroir and quality."[62] One imagines that Curnonsky, de la Blache, and the *vignerons* of Champagne would be pleased with such an evening, which brought together the French Ministry of Tourism and the Ministry of Agriculture to celebrate France's unique terroirs and the goût du terroir of a steak and a brandy.

LOOKING FOR HOME

As we move into the twenty-first century, however, are all these French efforts to link taste, place, and agriculture and to educate people in taste discernment really an exercise in nostalgia, an attempt to recapture a bygone
era? And if so, does this nostalgia extend beyond a taste memory for the
foods and drinks of a region to encompass a certain way of life? The foodview based on terroir and goût du terroir initially elaborated a century ago as
a means of protecting, preserving, and promoting artisan practices and regional identities allows the French, now primarily living in cities and towns,
to flirt with a lifestyle more representative of the past than the present. But
perhaps this rejection of progress makes perfect sense, for our modern
times demand us to be so flexible and rational, yet we remain a sentient
species. Should we not retain some control over our sensual pleasures?

In France terroir is often associated with *racines,* or roots, a person's history with a certain place. Local taste, or goût du terroir, is often evoked when
an individual wants to remember an experience, explain a memory, or express a sense of identity. People will discuss *sentir le terroir,* to have the qualities (or even defects) of where you were born or live. *Gourmet* magazine
explains to its American audience, "Even the most urbane boulevardier can
become near-maudlin about his *terroir,* acknowledging roots reaching back
to a province, a village, a family vegetable patch. . . . [H]is allegiance to the
land of his fathers remains intact." In this form, taste in France mediates
between the body and culture: the gustatory moment incorporates people's
belief that the very soil, plants, climactic conditions, and animals make
France a unique piece of the Earth rather than a nation among many others.
And for the French, the moment when the earth travels to the mouth is a
time of reckoning with local memory and identity.

Sociologist Barham also points to the French interest in documenting
and preserving the nation's past, a fascination with *patrimoine:* "The taste

for history in the form of 'produits de terroir,' therefore, reflects in part the ongoing construction of a collective representation of the past through food that is perhaps largely unconscious for consumers."[63] The French foodview, this sensibility about food and drink, situates their tastes and celebrates their origins. Such a sensibility, especially since it is reinforced by many individual, collective, and government efforts, means that a piece of cheese or a glass of wine exists as much more than an object to be bought and sold on the marketplace. And as historian Kyri Claflin points out, the French government has a long history of intervening in the provision of food to the French people, creating a "moral" market and exchange system: "From the end of the eighteenth century on, even with the success of the free market in many areas of French life, foods were not considered commodities like any other."[64] There is a long-standing tradition of cultural intervention into the agrarian and culinary economies, making place matter—a lot.

At the same time, the taste of place also reflects the conscious decisions and actions of various invested parties who have a stake in the well-being of rural France—both the countryside and its residents—whose inhabitants often compete with each other in their attempts to use the past to assert a new future. In that light, Barham sees that "AOCs are now clearly recognized as important contributors to the economic and agricultural structure of a region, as well as to its shared identity."[65]

In March 2000 in Castelnaud-la-Chappelle, I interviewed the operators of a small press that prints books related to the Dordogne region, including cookbooks, who argued that the emphasis on terroir has increased in the past thirty years, and that it is primarily a form of nostalgia. People are searching for their *racines,* or roots, as an antidote to their increasingly fast-paced urban lives. Only in the last ten years, they argued, have urban sophisticates begun to embrace *cuisine du terroir.* Earlier it was considered uncomplicated peasant food, heavy, often bland, and of no interest to cosmopolitan French people. The twenty-first-century understanding of the taste of place adopts the long-held view that locations within France create unique flavors, only now celebrating these flavors increasingly involves rejecting the trappings of modernity and returning to earlier ways. In nineteenth-century France, saying a wine had a "goût du terroir" was to label it a *vin de paysans*, not worthy of more esteemed labels, such as *vin noble* or *vin classé*. In the twenty-first century, however, place as much as social position explains French wine (and food). It could be argued that goût du terroir has come to describe an aspect of French identity that is locally defined, but perhaps it is also ultimately part of a national project to preserve and promote France's much-vaunted agrarian past. The "production of locality" through taste helps constitute the meaning of France in the midst of the global flow of ideas, ingredients, and values shaping our tastes for food and drink. Terroir, in all its manifestations, is our key to agrarian and culinary France.

TWO

"WINE IS DEAD! LONG LIVE WINE!"

TERROIR POSSESSES MULTIPLE MEANINGS, BUT THEY ALL REFER BACK TO A system of ordering and classifying a particular place. Anthropologist Mary Douglas, famous for her analysis of religious purity and pollution rules, says in that context, "Dirt is matter out of place." Terroir, however, is dirt *in* a certain place. And as Douglas points out, "Dirt, then, is never an isolated event. Where there is dirt there is a system. Dirt is the by-product of a systematic ordering and classification of matter, insofar as ordering involves rejecting inappropriate elements."[1] The cultural significance of dirt—as soil, as surroundings—motivates all interpretations of terroir, although the signifiers can shift depending on the culture, the person, and the moment in history.

In France people consider location first when they choose a wine. The terms describing the location can be broad (Bordeaux or Burgundy, for example) or narrow (rocky or rich soil). As a wine neophyte and an American, from a culture that places more emphasis on grape variety than on location, I have been trying to figure out why dirt or, more elegantly, terroir is so important to wine in France. No doubt terroir is a provocative concept, and a difficult one to grasp, since this understanding of place is guided by one's sense of taste and smell. Americans, however, are more accustomed to *seeing* places. If I think of the Médoc region, I can find a map and locate it northwest of Bordeaux. If I visit the Médoc region, my eyes can follow the land-scape, the flat plains, the elaborate châteaus, and the rows and rows of grapevines. The taste of place is different. Inside your mouth flavor some-how *evokes* landscape and region. It is a slippery concept, yes, but once you get it, once you taste the gravel in the soil as you sip the Médoc wine, your senses make the connection permanent. Any investigation of taste of place needs to consider wine closely, because no other flavor experience has been defined so long and so well by place. With wine, terroir allows us to "see" the taste of place and ultimately explain how and why a wine tastes a certain way.

Of all agricultural products, wine has retained a uniquely *natural* geneal-ogy. From our contemporary vantage point, automation dominates the pro-duction of most food and beverages, which we understand primarily as packaged commodities (a six-pack of beer, a box of Cheerios) lining the shelves of retail stores. But when we approach the wine aisle, we know the terrain is somehow different. Even when we go to our corner grocery store to buy wine, we know that wine is about more than a brand and the bar code pasted on the bottle. The labels always tell us about either the variety of grape used or the place where the grapes were grown. Can we say the same about beer or cereal?

We know that wine is more than a brand, but what else do we know about it, really? Wine is made from the fruit of the vine, a product of the soil, but humans need to transform what comes from the earth in a certain manner in order to create this particular product. Most people only vaguely understand the process of transformation, the movement from earth to shoot to trained vine to grapes to juice to vats to bottle. Ultimately, wine is a product of our desire, just like a finished dish like cold poached salmon or *coq au vin*, the result of human intervention and intent, is more about cul-ture than nature. Just as when we taste *pommes dauphinoises* we do not gen-erally imagine the lumpy, brown-skinned potatoes pulled from the earth by a farmer with an aching back in rural Maine, when we drink a glass of Côte Rôtie we do not necessarily imagine the rows of espaliered vines draped with large clusters of grapes being picked by Spanish migrant workers. But the wine label does tell us something about the process. It tells us where the wine comes from, which varieties of grapes were used, and often the year it was produced and the name of the individuals (and not just the company) who made the wine.

Distinctive taste profiles are a part of what we purchase when we buy a bottle of wine, revealing to us that we are drinking "not beer" or "not lemonade." Even though selling wine is a global business, and my local grocery store sells wines from three continents, knowing where the wine comes from, the grape varieties it contains, and perhaps the natural environment from which it comes still figures in the way I discern which wine to purchase. In our modern food system, details about the process of making food or beverages are not shared cultural knowledge. With wine, however, the process has remained part of the finished product. The continued ability to make discernments about wine based on the knowledge of place helps explain the importance of terroir to making wine around the globe.

MAKING WINE

Vinification is the technical term for turning grapes into wine. Wine is a fermented liquid derived from fruit, most often grapes. Grapes are classified botanically under the genus *Vitis*. In the United States *Vitis labrusca* is the species that produces table grapes, or eating grapes. *Vitis vinifera* predominates among the sixty *Vitis* species used in making wine, and this particular species encompasses up to ten thousand varieties. The number of varieties regularly used in wine making is vastly smaller, and perhaps only fifteen to twenty—chardonnay and merlot, for example—are familiar to the average American wine drinker. When you drink a pinot noir from Oregon, you are drinking wine made from the pinot noir varietal of the species *Vitis vinifera*, a varietal known for its fruity flavor and finicky vine. However, the story of wine does not end with the choice of the grape variety or varieties. There is much more to the creation of this intoxicating beverage.

The two pivotal steps in winemaking are growing the grapes and making wine from the grape juice. *Viticulture,* the science of cultivating grapes for winemaking, involves everything from selecting the vineyard site, to preparing the soil, to planting, trellising, and pruning the vines. Much of the craft and science of growing grapes revolves around getting as many nutrients as possible to the grape clusters, so every other part of the plant must suffer, must actually be held back. You don't simply sow seeds and watch the plants appear. The vines are perpetually pruned; as much as 85 percent of the shoot growth may be pruned from a plant over the course of a growing year. Once shoots start to appear on the head of the vine in the early spring, they are removed. Some growers also trim bunches of green grapes from the vines in the summer to promote ripening and develop more intense flavors in the remaining clusters of grapes (this method is traditional in France, where it is called *vendange en vert*). The most intensive pruning takes place in the winter, when the shoots and vine become woody.

Vineyards are thus striking agricultural landscapes. In the winter they appear unusually austere, since all that is left of the intensely manicured plants are short, gnarled vine stems no more than four feet high and several inches in diameter. Row upon row of gray stems poke out of the dirt, and often above them are long, horizontal bands of metal, poised and ready to be used to pinch, poke, and shape the vines and leaves of the stems as soon as they appear in the spring. Growing grapes for wine is an exercise in constant restraint. The vista is never of an undulating sea of plants waving in the breeze, like the view of cornfields that many of us are accustomed to. Rather, vineyards tend to look like an army of soldiers with uniforms pressed, marching into battle in perfect lockstep.

Once grown and harvested, the grapes are destemmed and crushed, which produces the pomace, or the solids left after pressing, as well as the grape juice. This is the beginning of the transformation of grapes into wine, called oenology, or winemaking. Fermentation comes next. Simply put, the goal is to convert the sugar in the juice to ethyl alcohol, accomplished with the addition of yeast. To make white wines, the juice is fermented after being separated from the pomace. Red wine is made slightly differently, for fermentation takes place before the pomace and the juice are separated (the skins impart color to the juice). The wines are then stored in large vessels before being aged, blended, bottled, and sometimes aged again in bottles. Each one of these phases can be highly elaborate, and the methods used to crush, ferment, store, blend, and bottle wines contribute to the wine's final flavor profile. For wine aficionados, then, every tiny decision made by the viticulturalist or the winemaker can predict and explain the quality of a wine.

Winemaking has traditionally been considered a separate, though allied, activity of viticulture. Since the winemaking process is complex, there are many moments in its course that could be considered definitive for the flavor and quality of the finished product. In the United States many wine aficionados generally consider the winemaker, or vintner, to be the most important person in the creation of wine. In more recent years, however, as Jancis Robinson, a renowned wine critic and writer, has said, "more people accept that wine is made to a great extent in the vineyard."[2]

In France, the idea that wine is really made somewhere between the fields and the vats has a long genealogy. Jean-Antoine Chaptal, minister of the interior under Napoleon and author of the great treatises on wine *L'art de faire le vin* and *Traité sur la vigne*, both published in the early nineteenth century, said in the former work,

> There are few natural products that man has developed for nourishment that don't need to be altered or modified in some way so that they become removed from their natural state. Flour, meat, fruit, all receive some [treatment or care], the beginnings of fermentation, before they are served as food; and these are not just deluxe objects, items of indulgence and fantasy like tobacco, perfumes,

etc. . . . But it is in the making of beverages that man brings the most wisdom: with the exception of water and milk, all are his creations [works]. Nature never makes spirited liquors; she can only put the grape on the vine, whereas it is the art of converting the juice into a nourishing, enjoyable tonic that is called wine.[3]

Chaptal here points out that wine has a more universal *function* than such sins of the flesh as tobacco, and he even suggests that it has a real *purpose*. (This perspective surely identifies him as a Frenchman. Those involved with the temperance movement in the United States would have seen no such difference between tobacco and wine.)

Chaptal, a chemist as well as a bureaucrat who lived from 1756 to 1832, played an important role in the history of viticulture and oenology. (A post-Renaissance Renaissance man, Chaptal also introduced the metric system to France.) Important not only for his writings on wine, he was also a champion of adding sugar during fermentation as a means of making wine more alcoholic, a procedure now known as chaptalization. He was an advocate of new scientific discoveries and standardized techniques in winemaking, all the while helping to transform winemaking from an intuitive process based on an oral tradition to a more analytic or scientific enterprise. These two, often conflicting approaches—intuitive and scientific—continue to shape the debate on production methods today. Nevertheless, Chaptal was right when he pointed out that wine is more like flour and meat than like tobacco when considered from an agricultural viewpoint. From this perspective, what is important about wine is neither its intoxicating properties nor its role in social (and individual) indulgence, but rather the craftsmanship that allows it to be made in a particular way and develop distinctive flavor characteristics.

In other words, unlike chanterelles and truffles, wine cannot be foraged. Instead, it is the product of human intent and effort at every stage. Emile Peynaud, France's legendary authority on wine, puts it well: "In fact wine is both a reflection of the people who make it and the region that produces it, for it is not one of nature's free gifts. Everyone seems to think of wine as a natural product; but it is a processed product, subject to deterioration, man-made and surviving only as a result of constant care."[4] Peynaud, who for years was the director of the Bordeaux University Center of Oenology, says that wine is both "a reflection of the people who make it and the region that produces it." So although he asserts the man-made nature of wine, he also never really pulls wine away from the soil that much. He seems to suggest that wine might be a product of certain dynamics between the soil and the grape, and the grape and the winemaker. It is never far removed from the natural world, but at the same time it is never truly "natural."

Born in 1912, Peynaud was one of the most important figures in the world of wine in France and abroad during the twentieth century. Author of *The Taste of Wine* (1980) and *Knowing and Making Wine* (1982), he combined in his teaching, consulting, and writing a passion for understanding the taste of wine with an analytic sensibility. He wanted those involved in wine production to see that every step of the process was important to the final quality of a bottle, and he always highlighted the combination of attention to natural conditions and scientific research necessary to good winemaking. Called an *homme de terrain* (well-grounded man) as well as a great scientist, he is for many the oenological standard-bearer for modern wine production. He consulted for dozens of vineyards around Europe, spreading his message about the true sources of wine quality.

So wine, as Peynaud points out, is both natural and artificial; it is from the earth, but also from hands, minds, and technologies. A complex dynamic is constantly at work when wine is made. Where, then, does terroir fit into this push and pull between the natural and civilized worlds? Many define terroir in winemaking as the combined influence of soil, geography, and climate on the final taste of wine. The role of terroir in wine, then, is the presence of *nature* in what you taste. For wine aficionados terroir has long

FIGURE 2. Vineyards and ruins, Saint-Emilion, France.
PHOTO BY AMY B. TRUBEK.

spoken to the dialectic between human intervention and natural conditions. The presence of terroir also suggests the possibility that there is a limit to our influence on wines.

In Europe wines were historically made close to the vineyards, and regions generally celebrated the distinctive flavors of their particular wines.

The "natural history" of winemaking here is a story based on local production with all its signature results. In Europe, preserving and promoting terroir is what many—from the grape growers to the cooperatives, vintners, agriculture ministries, and wine consumers—see as their primary wine-related task.

Many different varieties of grapes can be used for winemaking, and the choice of a single varietal or a combination influences the wine's flavor profile. A chardonnay grape is considered to be fruity, sauvignon blanc grapes are known for imparting a grassy flavor to wine, and riesling grapes are considered floral and sweet. Among red wine grapes, the cabernet sauvignon varietal is known to be dry and astringent (often to the point of being sour), while merlot grapes are softer and fruitier.

If we step away from the bottle sitting on the grocery store shelf, across from the boxes of Ortega burrito dinners and above the cat and dog food, and if we remove the bar code and the price sticker and the warning labels and step toward what is *inside* the bottle, we move closer to wine as the product, in Peynaud's words, of "constant care." Here is where we see the complex interaction of wine as a product of nature and the intentions of culture. Terroir, I think, is the notion that attempts to capture, in a sense, to bottle, this interaction between nature and culture for those involved with wine.

Grapes are grown in the soil, as are corn, soybeans, and other crops. Those who grow grapes share many of the same preoccupations as other farmers: they hope for good weather conditions, battle pests, and search for people to help during the harvest. And for some grape growers, like the corn and soy farmers of America's Midwest, their relationship to the crop ends when the harvest is over. But for many—perhaps most—viticulturalists, the harvest is just the beginning. Most farmers of wine grapes understand that they are actually involved in growing *wine*. Even if they are not winemakers themselves, they need to please winemakers in order to sell their products and make a living. The focus of this particular agricultural activity, therefore, is the finished bottle that arrives at the dinner table rather than a large quantity of raw stuff. Wine is always a value-added product.

Wine's ability to fight off efforts to turn it into a uniform commodity like soda means that many people spend a lot of time exploring and explaining *la différence* between wines. Wines are varied enough that countless books have been written describing the different wine-growing regions, their vineyards, and their wines. In 1999 Oxford University Press published the second edition of *The Oxford Companion to Wine,* edited by the renowned wine writer and critic Jancis Robinson. More than eight hundred pages long, the dictionary has thousands of entries, from a discussion of the alicante bouschet varietal to a profile of Yugoslavia's wine industry. If you are passionately interested in wine, chances are you have been called a "wine snob." You need an education in the taste of wine in order to understand fully the difference between Old World and New World wines, between a 1988 and a 2000 vintage of a Bordeaux cabernet sauvignon, between a terroir-driven wine and one shaped primarily by a winemaker.

TWENTIETH-CENTURY TERROIR:
NATURE VERSUS SCIENCE

Contemporary winemaking covers a wide spectrum of production techniques. Any winemaking method is possible, from the naked men who have traditionally hoisted themselves into a wooden vat of grapes and stomped on them to create the pomace, to the use of the most sophisticated technologies that do everything from harvesting the grapes to monitoring fermentation. And because the *process* of transforming grapes into wine is considered to greatly influence the quality of the finished product, the methods used, man or machine, figure prominently in debates and discussions of winemaking. Certainly the slogan for wine should be "vive la différence" rather than "try the Real Thing." Many of the debates about which style and type of wine *tastes better* revolve around the wine's *production:* machine-picked or hand-picked grapes; stainless-steel or oak vats; terroir or personality. Wine has a natural history, but winemaking is not immune to all the innovations in technology and science that drive the production of many foods and beverages around the globe.

The turn from the nineteenth to the twentieth century signaled many changes in the world of wine, as it did for food. At the time, some wine producers in Europe had long exported their wines around the globe, while others were involved in supplying the larger towns and cities in their region, and still others only made what was to be drunk in nearby cafés and restaurants or by their families. Thinking and talking about wine began to change, however, as markets expanded, people moved from the countryside to the city, and industrial techniques were introduced into winemaking. In France, numerous different constituencies involved in wine (grape growers, winemakers, *négociants,* and wine houses) realized that their interests and practices needed to be protected.

In France, to talk of the soil and its importance to food and wine was a cultural tradition. However, by the late nineteenth century terroir was increasingly attributed by those involved with maintaining the vineyards to concern the natural environment. In part this is due to the efforts of French grape growers to experiment with viticulture in various climatic and geographic regions and then to distinguish a particular relationship among grape variety, location, and flavor. As the organization of wine production became more analytic and systematic over time, the definition of terroir and its relationship to wine became both narrower and broader than its colloquial usage: it went from local folklore to defined practices.

The narrower definition of terroir arose because many turned to an understanding of terroir as a matter of science: the precise characteristics of the natural environment in which grapes are grown. Even in the pursuit of

winemaking, a practice invested in the natural context of growing and harvesting grapes, scientific knowledge has had a powerful impact. When I
first began to investigate terroir by reading contemporary wine magazines
and speaking to wine experts, I would become overwhelmed by the use of
scientific jargon. In a discussion about the rieslings of Alsace, for example,
a place I had visited and could imagine in my mind's eye, I was told to consider soil formations of granite, sandstone, schist, and volcanic sediments;
varying altitudes; and relative humidity. In these discussions the green hills,
narrow valleys, and half-timbered vineyard houses were but window dress-
ing for the supposedly deeper conditions that made wine taste of a place.

The Oxford Companion to Wine defines terroir as "the total natural environment of any viticultural site" and then lists the factors that determine
terroir: "climate as measured by temperature and rainfall; sunlight energy
or insolation, received per unit of land surface area; relief (or topography or
geomorphology), comprising altitude, slope and aspect; geology and pedol-
ogy determining the soil's basic physical and chemical characteristics; hydrology, or soil-water relations."[5] This explanation of terroir assumes that it
is a quantifiable, concretely *knowable* phenomenon. There are many ways in
which science is used to explain terroir, but I would argue that scientific
knowledge helps to quantify and thus legitimize long-held traditions of
grape growing and planting. Such knowledge in turn affirms the intuitive
approaches to winemaking practiced over the centuries in the traditional
wine-growing regions of Europe. The French use the earth sciences to
confirm another empiricist assumption, a belief that their long history of
winemaking has led, through repeated trial and error, to viticulture and
viniculture practices that take best advantage of the natural environment.
Isn't there a certain circularity to the contemporary recourse to science in
order to explain terroir? The earth sciences are modern academic disciplines, and the modern period values the abstract and objective knowledge
created by these disciplines, and so this mode of explanation has power.

However, the information provided by the geologists, pedologists, and others does not necessarily create *new* knowledge. Instead, the data provided confirms what is already known.

The original 1935 French law mandating the protection of the *appellations d'origine* does not mention any specific environmental conditions that are necessary for the creation of the *appellations d'origine contrôlées*. Rather, the law states that "the national committee will determine, in consultation with the interested syndicates, the necessary conditions for production. These conditions will be a geographic area, grape varieties, yields per hectare, and the minimum percentage of alcohol that is necessary."[6] In the official history of the AOC published by the French Ministry of Agriculture on the occasion of the fiftieth anniversary of the founding of the Institut National des Appellations d'Origine, the authors point out that it was in fact difficult to put these principles into action because each appellation is unique, and thus "an in-depth study must be performed to show the criteria creating the surroundings whereby the wine grower and winemaker can use his talent with happiness, intelligence, and success."[7] They go on to say that the solution was to uncover the existence of terroirs, and to define each one in terms of soil, environment, and traditional production practices.[8] Protected places need to have a reason for their protection: unique soils, climates, and other environmental conditions can help make the case. In the AOC official history, this discussion is accompanied with a series of pictures of the dirt and rocks found in different appellations. Apparently the contrast between the smooth, round, multicolored stones of Haut-Brion and the large, square yellow stones of the Côte du Rhône say "unique terroir."

James Wilson, author of the massive tome *Terroir*, which outlines the specific scientific attributes of every wine-growing region in France, defines terroir as the "vineyard habitat." Wilson is a geologist and the former vice president for exploration and production at Shell Oil. Wilson also has always appreciated the fine wines of France. In his book he explores his

FIGURE 3. Bottles in wine shop, Saint-Emilion. PHOTO BY
AMY B. TRUBEK.

theory that France has a history of producing great-tasting wines because
the territory has such a varied geology and landscape. The book is the result
of his quest to explain the relationship between wine quality and the rocks
and soils where the vines emerge. In his discussion of champagne and the
region where this sparkling wine is made, he argues that the presence of
chalk in the soil is what makes French champagne distinctive. Describing

the taste of terroir you experience when you sip Dom Pérignon, he writes, "Somehow, the chalk of Champagne soils imparts an élan to 'true' champagne that is not duplicated elsewhere in the world."[9] Elsewhere in the book he analyzes the geologic structure of other regions to explain why some vineyards have more notable terroirs and produce higher-quality wines than others. In Alsace, for example, he thinks that the more distinctive vineyards are located on the lower slopes of the Vosges mountains, which have a higher incidence of granite in their soil.

Wilson's approach is interesting because he attempts simultaneously to explain terroir and to justify geology as terroir. He takes great pains to show that most renowned wines come from locales within a wine-growing area with soil that has distinctive geological characteristics. For those who are skeptical that soils exclusively produce the "taste of place" in wine, he also tries to educate people to identify soil characteristics as a way of developing discernment about wine.

The book *The Wines and Winelands of France: Geological Journeys* introduces readers to the various wine-growing regions of France by describing the subsoils of each area to explain the flavor characteristics of the wine. The section on the vineyards of Alsace starts this way: "The extension of the vineyard area over the three morphological and structural regions of Alsace is conditioned by the nature of favorable terrain and exposure."[10] According to the views of terroir outlined in both of these books, flavor is knowable (and controllable) if you understand the geological and climatic conditions under which grapes are grown. Such an approach is favored by those interested in proving that the flavors of wine are place-specific and therefore that the wine's quality is innate and permanent. Also, quantifying terroir helps create a definition that travels. When terroir is defined as an environmental parameter, if the right conditions are in place, many people believe taste of place is not only to be found in France, but can occur anywhere.

The Institut National des Appellations d'Origine relies on earth scientists to translate a few lines of legislation written eighty years ago into verifiable and legitimate practices. The existence of traditional winemaking methods and the presence of organized cooperatives of wine growers and winemakers in a region were often the initial impetus for deeming a certain area a "controlled appellation," but people's traditions are not enough. The INAO also insists on determining accurate borders that reflect a unique geographic area: "The geographic area of an *appellation d'origine* is defined in the regulations . . . either by administrative borders or natural borders. The delimited area is made up of all the terroirs found inside the geographic area known to make this AOC wine."[11] So the AOC Faugères region, for example, is known for a soil dominated by schist, and the AOC Pauillac region known for its deep, gravelly soil. The INAO regularly calls on the opinions of scientific experts to analyze soils and determine the parameters of a geographical area.

The broader definition of terroir considers *place* as much as earth. According to this definition, the people involved in making wine, the winemaking traditions of a region, and the local philosophy of flavor are all part of terroir. Unlike the narrower view of terroir, this humanist point of view is not really quantifiable. Terroir speaks of nature and nature's influence on flavor and quality, but here the human attributes we bring to "nature" are cultural and sensual rather than objective and scientific.

In France, the narrow scientific and broad cultural definitions of terroir are often used simultaneously. Those involved in the world of viniculture and viticulture have progressively refined the broader definition. At Château Haut-Brion, a well-known vineyard in the Médoc region, they define terroir as "a veritable ecosystem where natural conditions have been modified and transformed by man, who throughout the centuries has exploited the land to the best of his ability using what nature has given him." Again we see the

dynamic between man and nature in growing grapes, making wine, and explaining quality and flavor. The main variations concern *causation:* Does the
winemaker create the unique area, or does the unique area invent the winemaker? And how does the relationship of the winemaker to the natural environment influence the sensory quality of the wine?

L'AFFAIRE MONDAVI

Competing definitions of terroir, one based on science and the other on culture, recently inspired a transatlantic battle of epic proportions. The forces?
On one side, the United States, whose chief emissary was the Robert Mondavi
Winery. On the other, France, represented by a coalition that included vintners, politicians, citizens, and even a famous actor. Emmanuelle Vaudour, a
French wine researcher, has pointed out that "terroir is often mistranslated,
giving rise to a great deal of further misunderstanding."[12] No other story reveals the problems in translating the French understanding of terroir and the
possibility that it can be misunderstood by outsiders (and even wine experts)
as well as the tale of the Mondavi family's journey to southwest France. In the
late 1990s the Mondavis went to Languedoc-Roussillon to make a premium,
or grand cru, wine on French soil. They appointed a general manager to develop a vineyard and winery, but three years later they left the region without
success. Their decision to withdraw from France and abandon their plans was
the direct result of fierce local resistance. Initially the main antagonists were
individuals involved in making wine in Aniane, the village where the Mondavi
family intended to create their vineyard and winery. Later, however, many
other residents of Aniane joined the fray.

For the French, the term *terroir* possesses a constellation of possible ref-
erents; its meaning shifts from place to place, from person to person, and
from situation to situation. The fluid and multiple meanings of the term *terroir* in France have frequently led to cross-cultural confusion, especially

since across the Atlantic, Americans have tended to interpret the term quite narrowly, often translating *terroir* with a single word, "soil."[13] Less attention has been given to other translations, which attribute to terroir specific cultural and historical genealogies. Neglecting to connect terroir to a region's heritage or France's much-vaunted sense of *patrimoine* got the Robert Mondavi Winery into trouble.

Americans focus on terroir as a material phenomenon because the people transporting the word and its constellation of meanings to these shores were involved in making wine, and their interest was in an instrumental connection between wine and the natural environment. Thus, over the past century, terroir has tended to represent a particular philosophy of winemaking, one that argues that the natural environment is what imparts a distinctive flavor to wine. American winemakers who espouse allegiance to expressing the flavor of the natural environment are often labeled "French-style winemakers." And indeed, many French, especially the producers, critics, scientists, and regulators involved with wine, understand terroir as such. But there are other ways to think about it.[14]

The Mondavi family wanted to create a domaine, a specific location where grapes would be grown, harvested, pressed, fermented, aged, and bottled. Such a domaine would contain vineyards possessing all the conditions—the viticultural terroir—for creating a high-quality wine. The Mondavi family chose Aniane. As Tim Mondavi says, "The site was fabulous, [and] I love the wines from the area."[15] He also wanted to make a wine primarily from syrah grapes, the traditional varietal grown in that locale. Those leading the resistance movement, however, were angry about the place the Mondavis chose, lands owned by the village of Aniane in an undeveloped area called the Massif de l'Arboussas. Aimé Guibert, proprietor of the best-known domaine in Aniane, was instrumental in organizing the Association de Défense du Massif de l'Arboussas. Using all the strategies of a contemporary citizen-advocacy campaign, the combatants marshaled their resources. Founded on May 3,

2000, the association promptly set up a website, contacted the press, and started a local initiative to depose the mayor and the city council members involved in the negotiations with Mondavi. Their sole aim was to "fight against the clearing of 108 hectares of woods and garrigue owned by the commune of Aniane."[16] The association resisted the Mondavi proposal because it was not sensitive to their understanding of the terroir of l'Arboussas.

The group was extremely effective in achieving its goals. In the first municipal election after it was formed, 84 percent of the citizens of Aniane voted, and the mayor and city council members involved in the negotiations with Mondavi to develop l'Arboussas were deposed. The new mayor was opposed to any development of l'Arboussas. Rather than fight the citizens of Aniane, the Mondavi family decided to withdraw their proposal, and they abandoned their efforts to create a domaine in France.

"L'affaire Mondavi," as it was often called in the many press reports, was frequently interpreted as an example of French anti-Americanism writ large. It's true that many people used the rhetoric of "the big, bad American corporate machine" to articulate their resistance or their support of the resistors. Even Gérard Depardieu, an actor now also involved in winemaking, "compared the villagers' fight with the Gauls' struggles against the Romans, saying it was 'an amazing story of this little village that resisted the invader.' "[17] However, a closer examination of the chain of events, the motivations of the key players, and the voices of the villagers reveals that this reading is too narrow: terroir itself is a key factor in this story of resistance. Recognizing the role that terroir played in this dramatic conflict offers new insight into l'affaire Mondavi and broadens our understanding of a powerful cultural category. The response of the townspeople to the news of the deal between the mayor and Mondavi was motivated by a concern for the soil, but people were also mobilized by an understanding of terroir as "the cultural meanings of a geographical place or origin."[18] Terroir is to the

French as freedom of speech is to Americans: meanings are multiple, interpretations vary, and consequences shift accordingly.

Ultimately, this battle over a plot of dirt reveals the profound transformation of food and wine production practices over the past seventy years.
Larousse's *Grand dictionnaire universel du XIXe siècle* defines terroir as "the
earth considered from the point of view of agriculture." The importance of
local practices of farming, hunting, and foraging in a particular place helps
to explain the negative reaction of the people of Aniane to the Mondavi proposal to develop l'Arboussas. The Mondavi Winery, an American company,
wanted to use terroir to make a great wine, saying they would respect
French traditions of winemaking. The people of Aniane, however, wanted to
protect a terroir that is instrumental in defining who they are and to protect
a certain way of life. To understand how the story developed, we must look
at the various players.

THE AMERICAN WINE COMPANY

For the past twenty years the Robert Mondavi Winery has demonstrated
both a commitment to making wine that expresses the natural conditions in
the vineyard and a penchant for roaming the globe to start new wine ventures. The company attempts to balance an artisanal approach to winemaking with ambitions of becoming a major world player in the wine business.
The Robert Mondavi Winery began in 1966, when Robert Mondavi started
his own small winery in Oakville, California. From those beginnings Mondavi has become the fifth largest California winery, a publicly traded corporation that sold more than seven million cases of wine and registered $506
million in sales in 2000. Robert Mondavi has always run the company; he is
now founder and chairman emeritus. His two sons, Tim and Michael, have
long worked for the company, and by the 1990s they had taken on more

responsibility. Their corporate mission is to "become the pre-eminent fine wine producer in the world."[19] To fulfill this mission Mondavi's operations have expanded from that first small winery in the Napa Valley. In 1979 the company bought Woodbridge Winery in order to produce lower-end California varietal wines. In the same year they launched a joint venture with Baron Philippe de Rothschild, proprietor of Château Mouton Rothschild in Bordeaux, France. The intent of the venture was to create a signature ultrapremium French-style wine in the Napa Valley. French and American winemakers were charged with creating the wine, named Opus One. With the 1985 vintage they successfully exported California ultrapremium wine to Europe.

The Robert Mondavi Winery went public in 1993, with the family retaining the majority of voting rights. Their strategy for satisfying their stockholders while achieving the family's mission was to expand their winemaking worldwide in a series of joint ventures. The joint venture with the Rothschilds to make Opus One had shown the Mondavi family the benefits of collaboration.[20] In 1993 they started a joint venture with the Frescobaldi family in Italy, and in 1997 they released the partnership's first wines. In that same year they entered into a joint venture with the Chadwick family of Chile's Viña Errázuriz, introducing the Sena and Caliterra labels. That year they also went to France and began producing the Vichon Mediterranean label from grapes grown in the Languedoc region. (Vichon was a California winery they had bought in 1985; in 1997 they moved the entire operation to Languedoc.) In 2000 they announced their intention to purchase land in the Languedoc region to develop an ultrapremium wine on French soil; they also released news of a joint venture with Southcorp Wines, the major wine producer in Australia.

The story so far sounds like the classic tale of the ever-expanding holdings of a large corporation. But in France the story took a decidedly different turn, highlighting the far greater complexity of producing a commodity with an identity based on place. Who has rights to the site that produced a wheel of cheese or a bottle of wine?

David Pearson was appointed vice president and general manager of Vichon operations. Since the Mondavis did not yet own any vineyards in France, he initially worked with local wine cooperatives, purchasing their grapes and then producing the wine in nearby aging and bottling facilities. Many thought that the Mondavis would immediately purchase a domaine, but instead they took time to study the region closely. They needed to find the very best site, since not all parcels of land will produce great wine. Pearson spent two and a half years exploring the region: "We looked at the possibility of buying [an already existing] domaine, but none of them had the right qualities [of] total natural environment of soil, topography, and climate. Our project was as French and terroir-driven as any other. [I see] terroir as a unique site; it provides products of originality. The object was to determine the site."[21] Thus, from the first, terroir was part of the Mondavis' French strategy. They settled on the village of Aniane in the Languedoc, where they wanted to produce a syrah-based wine in the style of the Rhône, a wine region bordering Languedoc-Roussillon to the northeast. However, the Mondavis were unable to find a preexisting domaine, or even vineyards available for sale that had the necessary attributes for making a premium terroir-based wine.

Tim Mondavi and David Pearson felt that the village of Aniane, particularly the area north of the village in the hills, had the potential to create marvelous wines. At the same time, Mondavi felt that the cooperative system of making blended wines from many small growers, long the tradition in southwest France, had "prevented the stars from shining. We thought we could use techniques and investments and break an economic [barrier] that people had not been able to cross."[22] Pearson began to work closely with the mayor of Aniane to see if Mondavi could purchase communally owned lands located near the domaine La Grange des Pères, identified as possessing the ideal terroir to create "products of originality." Initially told they could purchase the lands, the Mondavi family was instead offered a one-hundred-year lease. Despite misgivings, they decided to proceed, proposing to invest at least eight million dollars to develop the vineyards, the aging cellars, and the bottling facilities.

So what went wrong? For one thing, there was no consensus among local citizens, wine growers, and politicians about whether this venture was good for the community. Pearson had worked carefully and closely with all parties involved to get initial approval, as is clearly indicated in the official Robert Mondavi press release from July 26, 2000: "Earlier this month, the local winemaking collective, representing 80% of all growers, voted favorably on working in partnership with Robert Mondavi to produce a separate, premium wine. This vote, and the recent positive vote by the Cave Coopérative of Aniane, sends a clear signal that the community of Aniane supports our plan to create a domaine wine that honors the tradition and terroir of the region." The initial approval, however, did not last. The socialist mayor of Aniane, André Ruiz, a key figure in getting support for the project, argued that the Mondavi winery would bring much-needed economic development. The region was struggling with an oversupply of grapes, as well as changes in farming practices and price supports resulting from the increasing importance of the European Union in determining agricultural policy in France. Ruiz successfully negotiated the long-term lease allowing Mondavi to develop a 108-hectare vineyard on communal lands. But by the following spring Ruiz had been voted out of office, as had town officials who supported the project. The new mayor, communist Manuel Diaz, was against the project.

By May 2001 the Robert Mondavi Winery had pulled out of Aniane and abandoned any attempts to create an ultrapremium wine on French soil. The company's press release said, "While we continue to believe in the value and integrity of our proposal, it is our deeply-held conviction that we

FIGURE 4. Vineyards and Arboussas Forest, Aniane, France. PHOTO BY AMY B. TRUBEK.

can only be successful in cross-cultural business endeavors when we work in complete partnership with members of the local community. The lack of support from the newly elected Municipal Council of Aniane as well as the administrative, legal, and political obstacles that have resulted from this change in local government, reflect the difficulty of forming a partnership and raise such uncertainty about the future of the project that it is no longer feasible to continue." In the summer of 2001, Mondavi sold all their holdings in France at a loss, for eighteen million francs, to Sieur d'Arques, a major cooperative of grape growers in the region. (In fact, this cooperative was one of the major suppliers to Mondavi's Vichon Mediterranean label.)

Ruiz, the former mayor of Aniane, claimed that the new city council was opposed to globalization and the incursion of the Americans, and that the Mondavi project was the primary reason he was defeated. But do anti-Americanism and antiglobalization really explain what happened? Is there perhaps another way to tell the tale of l'affaire Mondavi? I believe that this story is more about the power of terroir than about political vendettas.

THE PLACE

Aniane, population 2,125, is located forty-five minutes west and slightly north of Montpellier, a lovely university town near the Mediterranean. The village lies in a valley, bordered on one side by rocky rolling hills overgrown with pine and oak forests, wild lavender, and rosemary. This wild area is called *les garrigues*. Surrounding Aniane on all other sides, especially to the west, is flatter agricultural land, primarily planted with vineyards. Understanding the landscape around Aniane is vital to an understanding of l'affaire Mondavi. Nestled between flat plains and rolling hills, the town straddles diverse topography with historically divergent functions. The hills above the town, called the Massif de l'Arboussas, have been used primarily for hunting and foraging, while the flat plains have been used almost exclusively for agricultural production.

The majority of vineyards in the Aniane area are located in the flatter parts. Vineyards can be found throughout the region, however, even up in the hills close to l'Arboussas. Many people grow grapes on small, narrow plots that fan out from the center of town, and then sell their harvest to the local cave cooperative. The majority of wine grapes in the Aniane region are grown in these small plots. Only a few large domaines make their own wine. Unlike in Bordeaux, famous for its many privately owned châteaus with large vineyards, in Languedoc-Rousillon the bulk of the wine is produced by small growers. From the center of town, the road to l'Arboussas winds through a landscape that is partly wild, partly cultivated with vineyards. When standing at the beginning of the garrigues, to the left are the scrubby but magnificent shrubs and trees of the region. To the right the hills descend into the valley where Aniane, Gignac, and other wine-growing towns lie. The terrain becomes ever steeper and more remote. After winding through several small, narrow valleys, the road enters into the heart of l'Arboussas, with its rocky, ochre-colored soil. Much of l'Arboussas is owned by the town of Aniane. People come from the town, the region, and even Montpellier to hike, take a Sunday promenade, and picnic. A welcoming sign proclaims, "The commune of Aniane wishes you 'Bon appétit,' " and, below, "The commune entrusts you with this site—protect it!" This soil has a place in the memories and traditions of people from the region. As they make sense of all the assaults on their rural and agrarian way of life, they don't want any disruption to l'Arboussas. The sign in the picnic area, simultaneously welcoming and warning the visitor, hints at the deep, and perhaps deeply conflicted, feelings of the people of Aniane toward l'Arboussas.

THE FRENCH WINEMAKER

A central character in the Aniane drama is Aimé Guibert, proprietor of Mas de Daumas Gassac. Many who have commented on Mondavi's initial decision to focus on this area of Languedoc-Rousillon point to the presence of this esteemed vineyard. The entire *département* of Languedoc-Rousillon, bordering the Mediterranean west of Avignon, has become the new frontier for winemaking in France. Up until recently the region was considered the source of much of Europe's "plonk" (cheap) wines. Now, new companies are setting up shop and attempting to shed the plonk image with decidedly more upscale and expensive wines. Guibert's Mas de Daumas Gassac is a pioneer in the movement to make high-end wines in the southwest of France. The *Little Red Wine Guide,* published in 2000, argues that the wines of the region merit consideration similar to that given wines in the groundbreaking 1855 classifications of the Bordeaux region.[23] In fact, the guide endeavors to create similar classifications for Languedoc-Roussillon. The guide uses the term *catégorie* instead of *cru*, stating that *catégorie A* parallels Bordeaux's *premier cru* down to *catégorie E*, understood to be the same *cru*.[24] Mas de Daumas Gassac is the only domaine awarded a *catégorie A* or *premier cru*. Similarly, wine critic Hugh Johnson declares that Mas de Daumas Gassac is "the only grand cru of the Midi."[25]

Mas de Daumas Gassac is a relatively young vineyard, with vines planted only since the 1970s. Guibert entered the region as an outsider from Aveyron and did not follow many of the traditional practices of *vignerons* in the area as he developed a plan for planting and cultivating vines. The *vignerons* of the Aniane region had long planted primarily syrah, mourvèdre, and carignan grapes in the flatter plains south of Aniane, although some were grown in the hills leading to l'Arboussas. By contrast, Guibert's first plantings were almost exclusively cabernet sauvignon grapes, historically grown in Bordeaux. Furthermore, Guibert planted only forty hectares at Mas de Daumas Gassac in vines, leaving the remaining forty in garrigue, which is purported to impart flavors of thyme, rosemary, and lavender to the wine. Most of the domaine's plots are nestled near the garrigue in a series of small hills leading up to l'Arboussas. Guibert made these radical choices because of his sense of "plant growing or nutriment terroir," that is, the natural environment and the influence on the grapevines and the fruit of the vine.[26] He consulted with two renowned experts from Université Bordeaux, Henri Enjalbert, a professor of geography, and Emile Peynaud, a professor of oenology, both of whom visited the site. Enjalbert thought the domaine had tremendous potential, with the right characteristics for making exceptional wines: "This terroir of glacial deposit formed by the Riss, Mindel, and Guntz glaciation periods provide the essential elements necessary for a grand cru: deep soil for the roots of the vines to seek nourishment deep down; perfectly drained soil so that the roots of the vines are not permanently moist; soil so poor that the vine suffers, thus creating unique aromas of exceptional quality."[27] Once this unique terroir was identified,

Guibert set out to use grape varietals and adopt vinification practices that would take full advantage of it. He ignored traditional local practices, especially in his choice of grapes and his decision to intersperse vineyard with garrigues.

According to the winery's brochure, "If the discovery of the terroir owes everything to Henri Enjalbert, the codification of vinification and maturing owes everything to Emile Peynaud." Scientific analysis trumped local knowledge. For many years the *vignerons* of Aniane called Guibert *fada,* or crazy, for following the advice of Enjalbert and Peynaud.[28] Furthermore, since Guibert did not plant the grape varietals required to obtain AOC status for his wine, he had to label it as *vin du pays,* even though he intended to sell it at grand cru prices.

In many ways Guibert and Mondavi have much in common: both are outsiders committed to using scientific definitions of terroir to create unusual grand cru wines. At first Aimé Guibert, David Pearson, and Tim Mondavi had cordial conversations. "Mondavi came to visit me several times. . . . I encouraged him to establish here," says Guibert.[29] In fact, Mondavi was initially interested in developing a joint venture or possibly purchasing Guibert's vineyard, though the negotiations never came to anything.[30] As Guibert points out, Mondavi would have had to sing the praises of Mas de Daumas Gassac to strengthen the case for his own wines, since he intended to follow Guibert's practices of interspersing vineyard plots and forest. Guibert continues, however: "The day I learned that the politicians of Languedoc promised him part of a 2,000-acre protected forest to plant [grapevines] on the hillsides, I was ready to fight."[31]

INTERPRETIVE BATTLES

Guibert's vociferous response to Mondavi's choice of this particular terroir reveals the complexities and contradictions in the meaning of terroir for the citizens of Aniane, as well as for the French overall. The wine world's scientific definition based on "agronomic properties" is generally accepted as a type of best practice for anyone involved in the wine business in France. But as soon as this definition of terroir becomes the rationale for practices that trespass on understandings linked to a community's sense of tradition and identity, collective goodwill disappears. Thus Mondavi turned from friend into foe. Over and over, people in Aniane emphasized that the problem was not that an American wine corporation wanted a vineyard in the Aniane region; at issue was the particular piece of terroir it chose and the methods it used to obtain it. Chantal Borrida, for example, welcomed Mondavi's presence until she heard the news of the deal to lease portions of l'Arboussas. She referred to the "rootlessness" of Americans, noting that she herself is a tenth-generation citizen of Aniane, and said that in her town, "nous avons vraiment des racines" (we really have roots).[32] L'Arboussas is a part of Aniane's heritage, vital to its identity: "If it had been a private matter [between a landholder and Mondavi], there would not have been such an uproar," Borrida explained.[33]

Alain Carbonneau, a professor of viticulture at the Ecole Nationale Supérieure Agronomique in Montpellier, believes that the meaning and uses of terroir exist on four levels: cultural, scientific, viticultural, and *paysages*, best translated as "landscape." He argues that the interpretations of terroir from the perspective of culture and landscape arise from indigenous beliefs and practices that historically have been important to the French and that revolve around their relationship to rural agrarian life. The scientific and viticultural levels are more recent additions to the understanding of terroir, analytic endeavors that emerged in the early twentieth century to help explain and promote the qualities found in French wines, cheeses, and eventually other products.[34]

The Appellation d'Origine Contrôlée system, which designates certain places where wine, cheese, or other products have distinct characteristics and thus higher quality, uses a hybrid definition of terroir. Geography and traditional practices are used as initial gatekeepers for attaining AOC status, but the regulatory agency, the Institut National des Appellations d'Origine, also insists on scientific justifications to bolster and objectively document these claims, which must establish a link between environmental conditions and a unique terroir. Petitioners are asked to document the region's soil structure, microclimate, and so on in the dossiers they submit to obtain AOC status.

Aimé Guibert relies on scientific and viticultural expressions of terroir every day; they are part of his best practices as a businessman who makes wine for a living. But as a citizen of Aniane and France, he also has recourse to the other levels of terroir to preserve the integrity of the landscape, heritage, and identity of l'Arboussas. As Carbonneau explained, even in France terroir is most often understood as culture and landscape. These broader understandings mobilized the Association de Défense du Massif de l'Arboussas in its battle against Mayor Ruiz and le groupe Mondavi. In interviews and discussions citizens of Aniane repeatedly pointed to the potential destruction of the landscape and the loss of traditional practices—hunting, foraging, hiking—as the source of their discontent.[35] However, politics also played a role. For Aniane residents Mondavi's arrival offered a taste of the exotic, but it also brought a genuine fear of the unknown. Much of the displeasure focused on the methods used by Mayor Ruiz and other local politicians in their negotiations with Mondavi: the locals felt they had been left out of the process. The association, for example, posted an open letter to André Vézinhet, the president of the Conseil Général de l'Hérault, on their website: "We do not understand why elected officials could conduct transactions with the Mondavi group using such secrecy so that the population of Aniane found itself presented with a fait accompli, without any power to express their agreement or disagreement."[36] The negotiations were not publicized; neither were public forums held. According to David Pearson, Ruiz had a secretive management style and counseled him to keep quiet about the proposal until after the upcoming municipal elections. This secretive approach created an environment ripe for rumors, many of which tapped into fears of American imperialism. Local growers stopped Pearson on the street one day and said, "We hear you are going to build a Disney World up there."[37] The political and economic implications of what were perceived to be backroom deals add another important dimension to the story, one that was often overlooked by the press.

CULTURAL PATRIMONY AND GLOBALIZATION

Many journalists interpreted the citizens' response as another example of French resistance to globalization; whether this signified courage or stupidity depended on the author's leanings. Businessmen and politicians implicated by the Association du Défense de l'Arboussas regarded the group's actions as bad business practice. The events at Aniane transpired soon after the attack on a McDonald's in nearby Millau, led by José Bové and members of the Confédération Paysanne, a farmers' advocacy group opposed to globalization. The newly opened restaurant was pummeled with rotten tomatoes. Following this attack a tremendous outpouring of support for Bové ensued, both in France and around the globe, and Bové's trial became a cause célèbre of the antiglobalization movement. Critics alleged that the Association de Défense du Massif de l'Arboussas was antiglobalization, ignored new economic realities, and sabotaged real opportunities for economic development. In response the group claimed that they were "not opposed to globalization when situations are characterized by fairness and open discussion."[38] In *The French Challenge: Adapting to Globalization*, Sophie Meunier and Philip H. Gordon discuss what they see as the paradoxical relationship of the French to globalization: they simultaneously resist it and adapt to it. They argue that, in the end, for most French citizens the primary threat of globalization is cultural, not economic: the possible loss of the nation's dearly and long-held sense of *l'exception culturelle*.[39] Certainly, food and wine have historically been identified as valuable elements of France's cultural uniqueness, and thus the loss of control of its production, accelerated by the push toward open trade, not just within the European Union but globally as well, is a major concern. The increased industrialization of agriculture is also an issue.[40] Furthermore, the wine business has seen a tremendous rise in foreign corporations and individuals buying French vineyards and setting up shop. The cultural ramifications are many.

No one disputes the fact that Mondavi's proposal would have destroyed communally owned forest and wild lands to create new vineyards. What *is* up for debate are the consequences of such a proposal. In his support for the project, Mayor Ruiz highlighted the proposal to intersperse five hectares of vineyard with five hectares of forest and wild lands as an environmentally sound approach to the creation of new vineyards. Local environmental groups had, in fact, vetted the proposal, which could possibly have brought tremendous economic benefits, especially since the region has recently seen a drop in the price of grapes and wine due to overproduction. Many believed that the presence of a major transnational winery like Mondavi would have improved the reputation of all wines from the area.

The new mayor, Manuel Diaz, however, pointed out that the proposal did not guarantee that the vineyard would not eventually be expanded to cover the entire 108 hectares Mondavi intended to lease from Aniane. He believed that such expansion would create an "environmental catastrophe" and compromise residents' quality of life.[41] Arguments such as these are often simply explained as evidence of anti-Americanism and antiglobalization, and in general these and similar protests concern threats to culturally unique handiwork—not just food and wine, but film and literature as well. Some analysts consider these demonstrations an example of French intransigence, an unwillingness to accept the changes necessary to compete successfully in a global economy. But a closer look at events in Aniane reveals that the Mondavi affair involved more than naïve, knee-jerk anti-Americanism and antiglobalization. Rather, the citizens were staking claim to the process of economic transformation. Globalization does not have to be a timeless, placeless juggernaut, erasing all differences in values and practices along the way; part of having control over the process lies in being able to retain locally important traditions and practices. In the case of Aniane, l'Arboussas represents this local knowledge, the terroir of a people, their traditions and identity. Mondavi represented an approach to winemaking and terroir that concerned the soil but—crucially, as it turned out—ignored the place.

When it comes to food and wine in France, many people are involved in a fight to both preserve and promote a certain style of rural agrarian life. Aimé Guibert sees a direct connection between the declining understanding of terroir representing traditional agrarian values and the increasing economic incentives for adopting industrial-style agricultural practices. Guibert's concerns do not stop with his backyard: he feels that the opportunities for small farmers everywhere are dwindling. For Guibert good winemaking and all good farming come from proper stewardship of the land. You can find absolutely perfect viticultural terroir—the most amazing microclimate and soil structure—but if you do not adopt the right practices, the land and the wine will suffer. In an interview he spoke of a nearby vineyard, located in the same microclimate and possessing a similar soil structure as Mas de Daumas Gassac, whose wine has a lesser reputation because the proprietor does not care about the vineyard's terroir. Thus, in Guibert's eyes, "la terre est morte" (the earth is dead).[42] Mondavi argues that the plans developed for the Aniane vineyard were "anything but McDonald's."[43] He says the intent was to adopt very traditional vinification practices—including the use of oak fermenters and wild yeasts—and to use the customary grape varietal, syrah. The only radical decision involved the vineyard site.

FIGURE 5. House and grounds, Mas de Daumas Gassac, Aniane. PHOTO BY AMY B. TRUBEK.

L'AFFAIRE GOES ON

Filmmaker Jonathan Nossiter, an American who lived in France for many years, identified the dramatic arc of l'affaire Mondavi and put it at the center of his documentary *Mondovino*, released early in 2004 and included in that year's Palme d'Or competition at the Cannes Film Festival. The film quickly garnered a number of reviews in major French, English, and American newspapers and went from being a low-budget documentary to the next big thing, running in major movie theaters throughout the world. *Mondovino* is the third film by Nossiter; he also made the feature films *Signs and Wonders* and *Sunday,* as well as several films for television. *Mondovino,* however, is his first documentary and was inspired by his personal experience. Nossiter, who has some training as a sommelier, attributes his decision to interview people involved in making wine to a trip he took through Burgundy with a friend. They were both impressed not only by the intense commitment of the winemakers they visited, but also by the intricate relationships among wine families. Nossiter was particularly interested in how values and practices are passed on from generation to generation: "what survives, what does not, what is lost, and what is consciously rejected." There is no clear overarching narrative to the film; rather the viewer is introduced to a series of people involved in the wine world—winemakers, wine importers, wine critics, wine consultants—as they are being interviewed by Nossiter. Eventually, however, a theme does emerge: the various assaults upon small-scale, family-based winemaking (especially in France) and the resulting encroachments on a certain order, or, as a winemaker in Sardinia put it, the decline of a certain *savoir vivre*. In the world of wine, he says, people have lost their identity. "They don't know where they come from or where they are going."

The film is concerned with change: changes in how people make wine, where the wine is made, and how people drink wine, as well as changes in the winemakers themselves. And although the film is ostensibly a form of cinema verité, its organization leads the viewer inevitably toward certain conclusions. Nossiter's favored subjects, the small, peasant-style winemakers, are always filmed in their homes or outside, in the fields, passionately defending their commitments. Hubert de Montille, the patriarch of a small Burgundian domaine, says, "Wine was an absence of barbarism." Another new French winemaker says she wants to celebrate love and pleasure through planting grapevines and making wine. Aimé Guibert of Mas de Daumas Gassac in the Languedoc strides through the vines asserting, "Wine is dead." He rails against the increased reliance on consumer preferences in selling wine and especially against the practice of changing one's winemaking to attain higher ratings by the powerful wine critic Robert Parker. "It takes a poet to make great wine," says Guibert. By contrast, when Nossiter visits the larger, more "corporate" wine establishments, such as

Château Mouton Rothschild in Bordeaux or Mondavi in the Napa Valley, the viewer is introduced first to the public relations people, who are shown trying to manage the interviews. Michel Rolland, a well-known "flying wine-maker" who consults all over the world, is shown being driven from vineyard to vineyard in a chauffeured car or sitting behind a massive glass desk in his wine laboratory. "Languedoc sure is hicksville," he says at one point, hands folded in front of him, before he breaks into a huge belly laugh. As the film unfolds, the most powerful underlying change is revealed: the loss of a localized peasant tradition of winemaking to a newer globalized corporate mentality.

For Nossiter, and for many of the people he interviewed, changes in winemaking have changed the very taste of wine, eliminating the vital importance of terroir. The influence of wine consultants like Rolland (who in the film is repeatedly shown telling his clients, "just micro-oxygenate the wine") and wine critic Parker (whose reviews are powerful enough to make winemakers change their practices to please his palate) has inspired a trend toward uniformity in taste. Winemakers all over the globe vie for wine consumers, now found as much in the United States and Japan as in France and Italy, and many, if not most, of these consumers have no idea about terroir or the taste of place.

L'affaire Mondavi lies at the center of Nossiter's film. He introduces the controversy between the Robert Mondavi Winery and the town of Aniane with a series of interviews in the town. In one of the first scenes a waitress in a local café says, "Here the vine is everything. Maybe in Paris it is factories and all that, but *chez nous* it is the vine and the wine."

Aimé Guibert claims in the film that the Mondavi family was planning on installing huge billboards on the top of the hills. Another Frenchman, Michel Rolland, accuses Guibert of "stirring up a lot of ignorant people" and asserts that "rejecting Mondavi was a historic mistake. . . . Mondavi is a PR powerhouse. They [the people in Aniane] are truly *paysans*."

After the visit to Aniane, the scene shifts to a car driving across the Golden Gate Bridge, heading north to the Napa Valley. The Kinks song "Apeman" plays in the background. The scenes at the Mondavi winery in Napa and the interviews with Robert, Tim, and Michael Mondavi reveal the most about the strengths and weaknesses of the film. The scene begins with Nossiter driving up the long driveway to the entrance of the winery. Nossiter speaks to Robert Mondavi's assistant, Mary, who is concerned that the film-maker not show the Band-Aid on Robert's face where he just had a mole removed. Then along comes Nancy Light, the press attaché, who says that Robert is more than just a winemaker or a businessman, but is a philoso-pher as well. Next the film jumps to a shot of John, a guide giving a tour of the winery. He points to the vineyards and the nearby Mayacamas Moun-tains and intones, "Look at this beautiful place. When you drink our wine it should remind you of this beautiful place, or maybe a château in Bordeaux." Next the filmmaker is introduced to Tim Mondavi while the press attaché scurries forward, pointing out that Tim has another appointment that can-not be missed. In the next shot Tim explains why Mondavi pulled out of the Languedoc region several years ago, but then his explanation is interrupted by the tour guide walking through with his group. "Hello, how are you?" says Tim. John replies as he walks by, tourists in tow, "Super, how are you? I know what you are saying is much more interesting."

The scene shifts inside with Robert Mondavi and his other son, Michael. Robert seems to be behind his son, not clearly visible, as Michael discusses l'affaire Mondavi. Robert does not say a word as Michael ex-plains, "[People in Aniane] said, 'We don't want any more globalization. No more Danone, no more Mondavi.' So we said fine." He also says, "There was a combination of jealousy and fear that we might make some great wine." At another point son and father discuss their decision to take the busi-ness public and involve shareholders beyond the family. This scene reveals a genuine pathos, the Mondavis' sadness that they could not successfully integrate the European familial model of running a winery with a more integrated corporate model. The subtlety of this scene, however, is lost amid the frenetic scenes that precede and follow it, making the whole encounter resemble a farce more than a tragedy. Perhaps the reason Robert and Michael Mondavi appear so circumspect in the interview was because at the time they were negotiating the sale of the entire Robert Mondavi Winery for $1.36 billion to Constellation Brands, now the largest wine company in the world. In 2004 Michael started Folio Wine Company with his wife and two children to import and export high-quality wines, and he also hopes to start a new vineyard.

CONCLUSION

Even for those with the greatest investment in the instrumental elements of terroir—a certain soil structure, a specific geologic history—the need to incorporate terroir's broader attributes is imperative. Culture, in the form of a group's identity, traditions, and heritage in relation to a place, must also be part of the equation. A French bottle of wine, though ultimately a commodity that is bought and sold in the global marketplace, is never far removed from home. The Mondavi group's focus on the narrower definition of viticultural terroir may have led to the demise of their project.

Could a similar drama unfold in the United States? Would hundreds of citizens of Northern California come together to block the transfer of wild tracts of land on the slopes of the Mayacamas Mountains, for example, to a large multinational wine corporation? Perhaps. And the answer would probably be yes if that area were used for recreational purposes and would be compromised in some manner. But the narrative would be quite different. People in Northern California are more accustomed to outsiders coming into the region to make boutique wines and build fantasy vineyards. And because the majority of the population are recent migrants to the area, and new to winemaking as well, their connection to the place is more tenuous than it is for French citizens. The arguments against allowing an intruder, then, would be based on the preservation of wilderness rather than on agrarian and peasant traditions.

Soon after the Mondavi winery decided to leave Aniane, the famous French actor Gérard Depardieu decided to make wine there. Depardieu had already invested in wineries in Bordeaux and Burgundy. He was lured to Aniane in part by stories in the press of the town's resistance to the Mondavi proposal. Six months later, as he closed a deal on an already-existing seven-hectare vineyard, growers and winemakers in Aniane were disgruntled because of the high price he paid for the land. Philippe Coston, a local winemaker, said, "It's a kick in the teeth for local growers—it's impossible to buy anything around here that will allow you to make good wine."[44] Apparently, when livelihoods and traditions are at stake, even an idolized French actor with the best of intentions is not spared criticism. When we began our conversation, David Pearson disagreed with my analysis of l'affaire Mondavi. He did not feel that the story was about terroir, but had rather to do with personal vendettas and political machinations. However, as we talked he concurred that cross-cultural misunderstandings did play a part: "We did not have a cultural broker. That had to do with the Languedoc. We felt that the two partners had to be equal, [but we] had no real partners with such stature. We thought we could do it ourselves. Perhaps it was hubris."[45]

L'affaire Mondavi was a classic clash of cultures, with battle lines drawn using disparate interpretations of terroir. Ultimately, the Americans lost out because they arrived with an incomplete map of the territory. Perhaps we have a lot to learn from the French about attitudes toward the soil, respecting the landscape, the best ways to make wine, and, especially, the many meanings of terroir.

THREE

CALIFORNIA DREAMING

PLACE MATTERS IN FRANCE. A STRONG AGRARIAN TRADITION, THE SYMBOLIC importance of the peasant, and nationalist pride in all things culinary allowed a set of values and practices to persist in the midst of numerous social and economic transformations. Such an emphasis on practice, place, and taste was embraced at all levels of French society, from the individual peasant to the highest-ranking official in the French Ministry of Agriculture. At the same time, however, the twentieth century was also witness to tremendous changes in all aspects of the French food system, from the decline in the number of peasants working the land to the increase in large one-stop supermarkets. But these trends, symptoms of the increasingly interdependent and globalized markets emerging all over the world, have occurred throughout the northern hemisphere. And so the story about the French foodview and *terroir,* I would argue, is about the persistence of a food culture *in spite of* its shift from the center of everyday life to the periphery; embracing the taste of place is increasingly the result of conscious effort.

Looking at the raw data in France and the United States—the number of small farms, the consolidation of retail food markets, the increase in commodity farming for global markets—could lead to the gloomy conclusion that the French foodview is part of a disappearing culture, but this interpretation is not the sole choice. The key to understanding taste of place in the twenty-first century, I would argue, is focusing on what has persisted. Why have wine-makers, cheese makers, chefs, and others been able to continue to make claims for the quality of their products based on how they were made and where they come from? And how has the new reality of interdependent global markets for food in fact created new possibilities for terroir, moving it far beyond the borders of France?

Perhaps ironically, given the story of its origin, but certainly inevitably, in light of our global food system, the taste of place has become a transnational mode of discernment. Increasingly, the taste of place is an intervention into the vast array of placeless and faceless foods and beverages now available to people everywhere. And this intervention, combining many values and practices that comprise the French foodview, happens in many locales, including here in the United States. The American story of taste of place invariably differs from the French version, for reasons of history, politics, and culture. In particular, in the United States people's values—about taste, about agriculture, about identity—*inspire* a certain relationship to place. The stories that follow reveal these differences but also some striking similarities, especially the intense commitment of many to building a bridge between taste, place, and practice. If goût du terroir is becoming a truly transnational phenomenon, it can both reveal a food culture and build one.

California, especially Northern California, is the region of the United States that most fully embraces the taste of place. First, California is one of the richest agricultural regions in the country, and agriculture figures prominently in the state's economy. More important from the point of view of terroir, however, is that California, unlike other regions such as the Midwest, supports many different types of farms, farming practices, and farmers. Every type of enterprise, from the largest dairy farms in the country to tiny specialty organic farms, from boutique wineries to farmstead cheese makers— the whole spectrum of possible practices—can be found within the state's borders. Although the region was one of the last settled in the United States, it has the longest continuous diversified agricultural tradition in the country. The state's large size, varied climate, and diverse growing regions mean that much is possible here, from the most industrial factory farms to the smallest artisanal producers. Second, California makes the most wine of any state in the United States, and it has done so throughout the twentieth century until today. California's Wine Country also most closely approximates European viticultural regions, with a set of winemaking traditions, including winemakers who articulate terroir as a mode of thinking and doing influencing their everyday practices. Third, significant tastemakers and taste producers are engaged in celebrating the bounty of the region, including its unique tastes. This includes a dynamic group of chefs who have received national acclaim for creating a unique regional cuisine.

WINE COMES TO CALIFORNIA

As is the case with France, understanding the role of wine, both viticulture and viniculture, is crucial to understanding California's version of terroir and goût du terroir. The differences between the Old World and New World when it comes to making, drinking, and discerning wine are primarily historical, the result of different agrarian traditions. Archaeologists conclude that winemaking in Europe began as early as 5000 B.C.[1] The Greeks thought wine vital, considering it a sign of civilization. The Greek symposia revolved around drinking wine, and let us not forget Dionysus, the god of wine. Classical Roman civilization brought wine cultivation and appreciation to a new level and to new areas, notably Gaul (southern France) and Spain. The Romans certainly developed a notion of discernment related to wine. Lucius Junius Moderatus Columella wrote a treatise on farming, *De re rustica,* which includes an extensive section on grape growing and winemaking. He says, "We consider the best wine is one that can be aged without any preservative; nothing must be mixed with it for which might obscure its natural taste. For the most excellent wine is one which has given pleasure by its own natural qualities."[2] From the earliest days of winemaking, then, it has been maintained that allowing the wine to be about grape flavor rather than simply a vehicle for alcohol or any other dominant flavor is a superior method.

Greek immigrants brought viticulture to southern France as early as 600 B.C.[3] There is evidence of winemaking in the Rhône Valley during the reign of Emperor Augustus (27 B.C.–A.D. 14), and over the course of the Roman colonization of France viticulture and viniculture moved farther north, eventually extending to Burgundy, Bordeaux, the Loire, and even Brittany.[4] By the fifteenth century wine was being made throughout France, and in fact it was the primary export of the region. During this period wine was sold to nearby nations, especially England, Flanders, and the Netherlands. These early markets for wine depended on proximity and ease of transport, especially navigable rivers that could transport the large wooden barrels.[5] Wine production continued to be a major agricultural activity without significant setbacks until the great phylloxera epidemic beginning in the 1860s, which compromised most of France's vineyards. By the 1880s the French wine business was in a serious crisis. There were problems at every stage of production, from the phylloxera infestation that required the import of American rootstock to combat it, to ongoing issues of wine adulteration and fraud. By the late nineteenth century viticulture and viniculture were considered so important to the French economy and culture that these problems constituted a national crisis.

Wine has a long history in French territory, but a much shorter history on American soil. There was no known tradition of making wine from fermented grapes in the New World before European colonization. The European colonists did find native American vine species, a few of which were suitable for making wine, primarily the Concord, the scuppernong, and the Norton. After colonization, farmers in a number of regions attempted to plant vines and make wine. In the south, especially Virginia, viticulture did become part of the regional agriculture, but ongoing attempts to bring French vines and expertise by many, including Thomas Jefferson, failed. The European grape species *Vitis vinifera* was always preferred for winemaking, but there were many difficulties in successfully importing the vines and getting them to thrive in what was often a much harsher climate. Meanwhile, by the early seventeenth century Spanish colonists along the Rio Grande were successfully planting *Vitis vinifera* grapes, and by the mid-nineteenth century winemaking was thriving in California, relying primarily on the Mission grape, "probably a New World seedling of an unknown European parent."[6]

George Husmann, a professor of horticulture at the University of Missouri in the late nineteenth century, continued to believe that viticulture and viniculture had great possibilities: "[I am] convinced, more than ever, that America is yet to be the Vineland of the future, and that each part of our country has its own mission to fulfill; its own varieties to cultivate; its peculiar class of wines to make, and that our task has just commenced."[7] Although optimistic enough to have his own vineyards, he also discusses the obstacles he encountered along the way:

> Our beloved calling, entered upon so enthusiastically, and promising so brightly, has since met with many reverses. Prices, in consequence of over production of inferior grapes and wines, came down to their lowest ebb, diseases, and other disasters have occurred, and for a time it seemed almost as if grape growing had become a failure. Many who entered the ranks with high hopes, saw them frustrated, and left in disgust; many thousands of acres, once covered with promising vineyards, have been abandoned and rooted up, and the grape supplanted by cereals.[8]

Later on, however, Husmann reveals other challenges, namely fully understanding the best natural environments for growing grapes that can make good wine:

When writing my first little book I was under the impression that the hillsides along our larger streams were best adapted to the growth and health of the vine. After six years' experience in Southwest Missouri, on the prairies and high uplands removed from all larger streams, I have changed my opinion entirely, and now believe that the dry atmosphere and cool breezes of those uplands are much more conducive to the health of the vine. . . . Keeping this fact in view, we may consider our high table lands and hillsides, where the vines are fully exposed to the prevailing winds in summer, our best locations. These are also generally free from frost late in spring and early in fall, which is another important consideration for the vineyardist.[9]

Farming in the New World, where there were few traditions established to guide or constrain practices and there was seemingly an infinite amount of arable land, meant that viniculture and viticulture were part of an array of possibilities, easily adopted but just as easily rejected. The idea of a wine-growing *region*, an agricultural area known for viticulture and viniculture, emerged only in the twentieth century, primarily on the West Coast.

The practice of making wine from grapes was brought to the New World by Europeans. Catholic missionaries brought vines to California in the late eighteenth century in order to produce sacramental wines. The levels of production remained low, however, until Europeans started to migrate to the West in larger numbers in the mid-nineteenth century. As people began to realize that the climate in California was perfectly suited to growing grapes for wine, and that a market for wine existed in the eastern United States and abroad, a booming business began. Some of the earliest wine entrepreneurs were Agoston Haraszthy de Mokcsa (often called the father of California wine), Charles Krug, and General Mariano de Vallejo. There was tremendous demand for California wines, and during the 1890s California was producing between nineteen and thirty-five million gallons a year on average.[10] By 1898 Sonoma County alone made five million gallons of wine. Interestingly, wine in California was originally labeled with French place names (Chablis, Burgundy, Bordeaux), since there was no understanding of what made California wines distinctive.

The first French law protecting wine practices based upon a wine's place of origin was passed in 1905. By 1927 the Appellation d'Origine Contrôlée system was legislated, with the final, most elaborated version passed in 1935, creating the INAO as a branch of the nation's Ministry of Agriculture. During the same period in the United States, the passage of the Volstead Act enabled the implementation of the Eighteenth Amendment. The Volstead Act, or National Prohibition Enforcement Act, prohibited all production, sale, and transportation of alcoholic beverages. Rather than protecting the rights of winemakers and championing the uniqueness of wines from various regions, as legislation in France did, American legislation during this period signaled the end of a young but vibrant era in American wine production. Thus the American wine industry, located primarily on the West Coast, and particularly in California, is both old and new, due to the peculiar history of alcohol production and consumption in the United States during the twentieth century.

Wine production changed dramatically after passage of the Volstead Act and Prohibition. The only legal methods for producing wine involved exceptions, one "allowing heads of families to make up to 200 gallons annually" for home use and another allowing sacramental wine to be made for church use.[11] There was no legal market for retail wine consumption. Because of this, most vineyards turned to producing grapes that would be hardy enough to be shipped all over the United States for home wine production. Many vines were removed and replaced with alicante bouschet, a tough-skinned, high-yielding grape variety that is much favored by Italian American home vintners. The Gallo Brothers winery was able to hold onto their winemaking business by developing exclusive contracts with the Catholic Church to make sacramental wine. The Volstead Act was disastrous for commercial wine production all over the United States; overall volume declined from 55 million gallons in 1919 to 3.5 million gallons in 1925.[12]

Most small vineyards went out of business during Prohibition, and in California, always the U.S. region with the largest wine production, it took a long time for the wine industry to be revived after its repeal. In fact, the real proliferation of wineries back to pre-Prohibition levels did not occur until the 1970s. California's contemporary wine industry, therefore, has not been blessed or cursed (depending on your perspective) with long-standing traditions of viticultural and oenological practice, or with governmental regulation, oversight, or subsidies. The New World approach to winemaking has been much more entrepreneurial, as interested in anticipating market trends and building brands as in maintaining a centuries-old tradition of grape trellising. As old vineyards were brought to life and new vineyards established after World War II, many winemakers forfeited Old World traditions and installed the newest technologies in grape growing and harvesting, fermentation, and wine storage. In the United States most contemporary winemakers utilize modern technology much more completely than do their counterparts in France or elsewhere in Europe.

In the United States, there have been efforts to create designated winegrowing regions. Called American Viticultural Areas and administered since 1978 by the Bureau of Alcohol, Tobacco, and Firearms, these are regions defined solely by a specific geography, and there are now more than 150 of these "delimited grape-growing areas." In the decision to designate an AVA, grape varietal, production style, quantity of production, and historical characteristics are not considered. Some designated viticultural areas are quite small, such as the 1,700-acre Santa Rita Hills AVA in California. Other designated viticultural areas are vast, such as the Ohio River Valley AVA, covering 16,640,000 acres.

For those powerfully invested in promoting the quality of wine from a certain vineyard or region, or promoting wine in general, how quality is achieved must be considered every day. And thus it should come as no surprise that the definition of quality itself is highly debatable. In a *Wine Business Monthly* article, author Cyril Penn asserts that if you "ask a dozen people what quality means as it relates to wine, you're likely to have that many different answers."[13] He goes on to say that there is no objective way to measure quality, and then provides other people's thoughts on the matter. Grower Andy Beckstoffer's definition combines agricultural practices with market realities: "Quality is determined by the soil, the climate and the activities of the vineyard manager in how he manipulates and carries this forward." The article continues, "It is also a matter of how one manipulates nature, under cropping, over cropping, and bringing forth the flavors from the soil and climate that brings forth a vintage year. That said, the only objective determination of quality is the retail price of the wine, concludes Beckstoffer. 'The consumer rules.' "[14]

Penn goes on to report about a symposium, "Grape Expectations," held in 2001 at the University of California, Davis. At this event, which was "largely dedicated to defining quality," James Wolpert, chair of the Department of Viticulture and Enology, said that the industry is moving in two directions: "One [is] to try to measure something that people can agree is an indicator of quality, for instance tannin concentration, or specific tannin components, color and all the components. . . . Or you say, let's just make wine and use our sensory methods to say this wine has more of this character. . . . You let the wine talk rather than let the data talk."[15] The difficulties in deciding whether scientific data, vineyard practices, or cultural values ultimately shape definitions of wine quality underscore the comments of all the panelists from the university. Christian Butzke, also in the Department of Viticulture and Enology, says a quality wine is "one that elegantly reflects the varietal character of the grapes and the typicity of the vineyards they were grown in; it is made with the lowest possible input by the wine grower and maker, and incites pleasure, excitement, and fond memories in the memory of the consumer."[16]

Wolpert and Butzke's colleague Linda Bisson makes a distinction between the French concept of terroir and her notion of regional typicity:
"Trueness to style is an indicator of quality, and what I call regional typicity,
which I separate from terroir." She goes on to say that a lot of what really defines quality in wines is "personality": "If you look at the definition of personality, it means excellence and distribution of in-born traits. I look at
California and New World wines, and say, 'That's what we've got.' And that's
what they call personality. I think you can have personality as your definition of quality. You can say, 'They don't have terroir, but they have personality.' Personality is not as vague and cute as terroir."[17]

The comparisons between Old World and New World methods for defining quality continue with Leo McClosky's comments. McClosky represents
Enologix, a consulting firm that works with winemakers to help them develop highly marketable wines. The company relies on scientific analyses of
wine and the market in its work: "Enologix sells software that turns 'quality
metrics' into forecasts of market position with a database of 35,000 wines,
providing the 'color-flavor-fragrance-chemistry' of competitors." McClosky
uses a flavor wheel to define quality. "The flavor wheel is focused on attributes, and attributes are not associated with the economic value of wine in
Europe." Like the French Institut National des Appellations d'Origine in its
quest to verify terroir, he asserts there are objective measures for explaining
taste and quality, but his measures are not environmental or contextual but
instead rely on the scientific analysis of what is found in the glass: "We define quality as the color-flavor-fragrance intensity of a given wine with respect to all the other wines in its appellation," says McClosky. "Quality is a
metric, a number, and it's not an attribute."[18] Enologix wants terroir to concern locale (the appellation or place where the grapes are grown), but it does
not consider terroir to be the ultimate marker of quality.

Domaine Tempier, a vineyard near Bandol, in the southern Rhône Valley, represents the Old World approach to winemaking embraced by some

California winemakers. The patriarchs of the winery, Lucien Peyraud and his sons Jean-Marie and François, consistently shy away from mechanical and scientific methods when making their wines, and their winery is renowned for its great, and sometimes quirky, wine. In Kermit Lynch's classic wine memoir, *Adventures on the Wine Route,* he extols the virtue and champions the eccentricities of this winery and the family that runs it: "It is my experience that when anybody makes the acquaintance of the Peyrauds and Domaine Tempier, he or she tends to mythologize them. Everything seems so down to earth and wonderful and perfect. . . . And the setting contributes, too: the rugged hillside, the sea, and the enormous blue sky create a landscape of divine dimension. . . . Then when you get to know the Peyrauds better and you see how human they are, 'mad and wonderful' according to their friend Richard Olney, you love them even more." As Lynch goes on to tell the story of these very traditional French winemakers, he describes their minimal use of chemicals and machines in their procedures for making wine, a reason he thinks their wine is among the best: "When they are satisfied with the maturity, the grapes are harvested by hand, beginning with the most forward parcels. There is no harvesting machine. Fanatical care is taken to preserve the grapes intact from the vineyard to the winery."[19]

I visited Domaine Tempier with my husband on a sunny and remarkably warm day in late March. A simple farmhouse serves as headquarters. Daniel Ravier, the vineyard manager, took us on a marvelous tour of the vineyards and winery, and was happy to respond to all my questions about the nature of terroir along the way. Ravier is a firm believer in the existence of terroir and its importance to the final quality of a wine. In fact, he asserted repeatedly that he thinks the terroir of a vineyard is much more important than the grape variety to a wine's taste: any differences you find among wines primarily result from the type of soil, the exposure of the grapes to sunlight, and so forth. Ravier also believes in the Appellation d'Origine Contrôlée system, stating that it was the job of Domaine Tempier to protect both the spirit and the letter of AOC regulations for Bandol, the "geographic area" where the vineyard is located.

When we were down in the damp cave among the grand oak barrels doing a tasting of Domaine Tempier vintages, we ended up talking to François Peyraud. He agreed that the French have a unique commitment to goût du terroir and artisanal practices, but he felt both were under assault. We discussed a marvelous artisan charcuterie in the nearby town of Cadière d'Azur. I pointed out that you would be hard-pressed to find a shop like it anywhere in the United States. He replied that the older gentleman who owned the shop was the last of a dying breed: "The old people are not being replaced." He then said, "But I do know that Americans do not even know what a chicken looks like."[20] Peyraud concluded by saying the goût du terroir must be *experienced;* children and adults need to go out into the countryside to see, smell, and taste, and then they will appreciate the taste of place.

Ravier led us through a tasting of five red wines from the 2001 vintage. He began with a blended wine from a number of their vineyard parcels spread out in the valley and on the hillsides. He then presented more place-specific wines, concluding with one wine made exclusively from a parcel named Tourtine and another from Cabasol, a parcel downhill from Tourtine. The Tourtine parcel contains more uniform soil and is in a sunnier and windier location. Both wines are made almost exclusively from mourvèdre grapes. The Tourtine wine had cocoa and prune flavors, even a bit of licorice, whereas the Cabasol was more tannic and possessed a flavor more purely of red fruit. The grapes were grown a mere hundred yards apart, with all other conditions being equal, yet the wines tasted markedly different.

When I asked Ravier if it was possible to have terroir anywhere, even the United States, he responded, "Definitely." Our problem, said Ravier, is that we are young; we do not have the long history of growing grapes and understanding the soils they have in France. Our winemaking is still in its adolescence. For Ravier, we are trapped by our history (or perhaps our lack thereof), rather than by any natural defects. In a sense, Ravier is saying scientific terroir is within our grasp, but we are too immature to possess cultural terroir.

Discerning quality is a preoccupation of winemakers in both the Old World and the New. Given the subjectivity of taste and widely varying winemaking practices and traditions, the diversity of opinions should come as no surprise. When the question of discernment involves the consumer, whose knowledge of winemaking may be zero, do these debates about terroir, personality, typicity, attributes, and color-flavor-fragrance intensity direct choices? Penn claims that "years ago, quality was determined at the highest level by the owners of a series of Chateaux, dictating what the world's wine taste should be like. Wine writers now serve this purpose. The media in large part determines 'quality' by emphasizing ratings."[21] He sees a historical shift away from the vineyard owners and wine *négociants* as the main tastemakers toward a wider array of wine experts, especially the wine critics published in newspapers and magazines and, increasingly, on the Internet.

In the early days of wine criticism, most writers worked in the wine profession, often as wine importers, and used their expertise to educate consumers. By the late 1960s, however, and especially in England and the United States, there started to emerge wine critics with no direct ties to the wine trade, such as Hugh Johnson and Robert Lawrence Balzer.[22] They were "passionate amateurs," men enthralled by the mystery and complexity of wine who wanted to share their understanding with consumers.[23] The postwar prosperity of the United States, England, and other nations enabled the middle class to travel and entertain more frequently, and being knowledgeable about wine and food was part of the mix. Interestingly, Johnson and

Balzer became popular wine critics at about the same time that Julia Child was establishing herself as the great culinary populist, demystifying French cuisine for the middle-class American housewife. And like Child, these wine writers were unabashed Francophiles, perceiving France as the epicenter of great winemaking.[24]

By the 1970s the market for wine began to shift. For centuries, the majority of wine consumed was produced within the same region. As a result, wine drinkers' modes of discernment were based on repeated exposure to a fairly small number of wines; wine connoisseurship was the provenance of the nobility and elites. By the 1970s, however, the wine market expanded to include dedicated drinkers all over the globe, including Japan, Australia, and, of course, the United States. Most of these consumers were living in urban areas and had no relationship to the practices of viticulture and viniculture, and few traveled to Europe to visit vineyards. These wine consumers needed guidance. The primarily descriptive writing of André Simon, Hugh Johnson, and others was enjoyable to read—it described their trips to Burgundy and lovely lunches at various châteaus—but the time was right for a more practical approach, a means for "guid[ing] confused consumers to the better bottles."[25]

As a result, a new group of tastemakers who saw themselves as advocates as much as educators emerged. Robert M. Parker Jr. has been by far the most powerful of these figures, so much so that he is now credited with influencing consumer choice enough to even change the way people make wine. His philosophy of wine criticism, as amply revealed in the title of his popular newsletter, *The Wine Advocate*, stems from his training as a lawyer and his work with Ralph Nader in the early 1970s to protect consumers from fraud. An extremely passionate amateur in his college days, Parker trained himself in wine evaluation by creating a wine-tasting club and making frequent trips to France through college, law school, and his years as a lawyer for a bank outside Washington, D.C.

Parker started publishing his subscription-only newsletter in 1979. From the very first issue Parker's goal was to make the world of wine more accessible to Americans, and to enable anyone to purchase and savor high-quality wines, no matter their background. He did not like the way wine criticism promoted exclusivity, linking the capacity for discernment with being a connoisseur. He has always striven to be, as he puts it, "more democratic."[26] In order to accomplish this goal, Parker focuses primarily on sensory evaluation of wines based on his own physiological responses—what happens when he sniffs, swirls, and sips the wine from the glass. When he started writing about wine, most other critics spent as much time writing about where the wine came from as describing how it tasted. Their approach was more descriptive than analytic. Parker, however, was not particularly interested in this method, especially since he felt that certain winemakers had taken advantage of the elite status of their wines and sold their wines for more then they were really worth (judged according to his own, ostensibly objective standards). His innovation that is largely responsible for both his success and much of the controversy about his role in winemaking today was the creation of a numerical rating system for evaluating wines, similar to the one used by *Consumer Reports.*

In an interview with Charlie Rose, Parker discussed the importance of terroir to making fine wines. Parker's comments reveal his belief that certain practices do create better wines, but at the same time they reveal his very American sensibility that combating elitism is a form of democracy. First he says that "no great wine can come from a place without a great terroir," so place does matter. However, he also feels that terroir can enforce stasis and taste hierarchies, and he declares, "I am much more democratic." He also chafes at the underlying assumption of the AOC system that centuries of trial and error are required to determine proper terroir and make high-quality wine: "Globalism exists, but better wines are being made now than twenty-five years ago. We don't have to wait fifty or a hundred years to make great wines."[27]

THE CALIFORNIA WINE COUNTRY

Today wine is big business in California. In fact, "wine is California's most valuable finished agricultural product."[28] The wine industry employs more than 200,000 people, and "if California were a nation it would be the fourth leading wine producing country in the world behind Italy, France and Spain."[29] In 2004 California wineries shipped 522 million gallons of wine, with 428 million gallons remaining in the United States.[30] In 2004 there were 1,294 commercial wineries in the state. There has been a steady increase in all wine sales in the United States over the past decade, from 458 million gallons in 1994 to 668 million gallons in 2004, as well as an increase in per capita wine consumption. We are slowly becoming a culture that appreciates good wine and embraces the complexity of choices, willing to go beyond Bud versus Michelob. A cultural fascination with the world of wine (at least among a certain strata of American society) is revealed in the success of the 2004 movie *Sideways,* in which the most appealing characters were grapes (especially the pinot noir variety), vineyards, and bottles of wine! The movie is set in a wine-growing region south of Santa Cruz, and even though the four characters are looking for love, in the end the vineyard landscape best represents romance, and a truly great bottle of wine evokes the most passion.

As part of my research on terroir and the taste of place, I spent time in Northern California, especially in Sonoma County. My family accompanied me for the first part of the trip. We arrived in San Francisco and did all the usual airport activities—luggage, car rental, car seat—and then packed ourselves into a shiny red car and made our way north. We took U.S. 101 north over the Golden Gate Bridge and into the rolling hills of Northern California. Vermont's hillsides are a deep, dark, overgrown green, but here lighter hues prevail, with hints of gray and brown joining the dominant sagebrush notes. Again, unlike my home state's predominantly rural landscape, the area north of San Francisco is characterized by tentacles of development—strip malls and suburban cul de sacs—that snake along the highway. We were heading to Healdsburg, in the middle of Sonoma County, one of the state's acclaimed wine and food regions. As we neared our destination, the landscape began to become a mixture of the wild (hills dotted with live oaks and grayish scrub grass) and the cultivated (rows and rows of grapevines turned a golden hue, often with splashes of scarlet).

We drove past Healdsburg and turned right on Alexander Valley Road. The Alexander Valley is one of three well-known appellations around the town; the Dry Creek Valley and Russian River Valley are two other riverside landscapes producing distinctive wines. We drove across a low bridge with long grayish-green metal girders, their triangular shapes quickly framing vineyard, brush, and then river. Up ahead was Jimtown, a tiny hamlet in the middle of flat bottomland planted with acre upon acre of vines. Closest to the river was a vineyard parcel that was up for sale. The vines had not been pruned recently, and so wayward shoots waved in the breeze, an eyesore perhaps for a good vineyard manager, but a gorgeous scene for a visitor.

I have visited wine regions throughout France, northern Italy, and now California. The orderliness of these agrarian landscapes always seduces me, but at the same time I often also feel a bit let down. I experience a vague disquiet as I gaze out at hills covered with rows of vines tightly trellised, as if on a march. I realize that my unease comes from the dissonance between my imagination and what I see in Alsace, Piedmont, and Sonoma. When I mentioned my discomfort to my husband, he said, "Well, all the mystery is gone." For me, like for most Americans, knowing wine and understanding its many flavors, histories, and complexities is a received rather than a lived experience. Wine culture was never part of my everyday life. My parents drank wine fairly regularly, but we never made a trip just to visit a winery, and dinner table discussions rarely revolved around wine. Wine, I think, primarily represented sophistication. When I was a child, those curvaceous bottles and delicate glasses were part of the adult world, especially at the lively dinner parties my parents would often host. My father used to have these wonderful Brooks Brothers date books; slim volumes with delicate blue paper, they contained in the back lists of French wines rated according to vintage. These grids, with names such as Château Margaux and Domaine de la Romanée-Conti on the sides and then the years across the top, were magical to me, and seemingly unknowable.

As I grew older and more involved in professional cooking and the culture of restaurants, understanding wine became a part of mastery; to be a knowledgeable chef necessitated an ability to navigate grape varietals, vintages, and taste profiles, and the skill to develop good wine and food pairings. Developing discernment—being able to swirl the glass, sniff, taste, and speak knowledgeably about the hint of grapefruit in the sauvignon blanc or the minerality of a good Chablis—was part of a chef's job description. My experience of wine was really all in my head, in part in my imagination and in part in my mouth. My understanding of how wine was *made* came much later.

The mystery of tasting and *knowing solely from your taste experience* changes dramatically after you go on your first vineyard tour. Even though taste never disappears in conversation, now you are tromping through a vineyard, being told the grape varietal, the pruning methods, and whether the grapes are hand-picked or harvested mechanically. You are in fact on a farm, learning about farming. The mysterious has become prosaic. The experience is not that different from my childhood visits to the dairy farm next to my grandparents' house in northern New Jersey. Are the tanks that store wine so different from those that store milk?

Many involved in the world of wine, however, invested in wine's symbolic importance, maintain the mystery as part of the winemaking story. While in Sonoma we visited the Ferrari-Carano Vineyards and Winery. We had drunk their wines in restaurants several times, and had heard that the winery grounds included beautiful gardens, so we decided to take a tour. We drove up to the grounds, in the middle of the Dry Creek Valley appellation, not too far from A. Rafanelli Winery, a renowned small vineyard run by the same family for three generations. The grounds at Ferrari-Carano are extensively landscaped, full of hedges of boxwood and begonia, with signs pointing you toward Villa Fiori, a large neo-Italianate building constructed in 1986. Just as you are about to turn toward the boxwood maze and the entry to the villa, you are faced with a massive statue of a boar, named Boardeaux, a present to the owner from his wife, a reproduction of one they saw in a market in Florence. Here making wine seems to be part of yet a larger fantasy about accessing the sophistication of Europe, and developing this vineyard fulfills their quest.

The fact that we are on a farm making an agricultural product does not figure largely on the tour. Jim, our tour guide, introduces himself as "part of the hospitality team here at the vineyard." He starts the tour by indicating that the year 1981 was "the beginning of the Ferrari-Carano concept." The story, he says, starts in Reno. Don Carano, founder of the vineyard, the man responsible for the grounds, the villa, and the fountains as well as all the wines, is a lawyer specializing in gaming regulation who invested in a Reno hotel and casino, the Eldorado. Buying trips to Sonoma for the hotel's eight restaurants led him to decide to buy the vineyard land and make wine; he and his wife loved the area and wanted to have a second home here. His work in Reno allowed him to create this imagined Europe, a place where winemaking embellishes an agricultural practice but adds corporate methods and elite status symbols. Doesn't this tale, of building a place that mimics an imagined past without following any specific tradition, fit perfectly into our own agrarian history?

What is so amazing about making wine in California is that any number of imagined places and varieties of practice can occur simultaneously and synchronically. At A. Rafanelli Winery just down the road, the family grew grapes for other winemakers beginning in the 1920s and started making wine under their own label only in 1974. They do not have regular tours or a tasting room, and they produce only 11,000 cases of wine a year. Dave Rafanelli recalls, "Unlike some of [his] more prominent neighbors, [my father's] ambitions never strayed far from home. Dad was a farmer. He liked selling wine, but his heart was in the vineyard. He used to say, 'Pigs get fat but hogs get slaughtered.' He never wanted to grow the business too big."[31]

A story of invention and reinvention can be told about another family with vineyards in the Dry Creek Valley, as well as in the nearby Alexander and Russian River valleys. Ernest and Julio Gallo were the founders of Gallo Vineyards, today the second largest wine company in the world behind Constellation Brands. The Gallo brothers started their winery in 1933; Julio was the winemaker and Ernest the businessman. For many years the Gallo winery bought huge lots of grapes from all over California and made wine in their central headquarters in Modesto, in the middle of the state's rich agricultural region, the Central Valley. For forty years the family made inexpensive blended jug wines, wines that introduced many Americans to casual consumption. Over time, the younger Gallo family members, particularly Gina and Matt Gallo, wanted to create single-varietal, vintage estate wines. These wines would be made from grapes that came from only one specific vineyard, and the winemaking would take place in the region as well.

Julio Gallo had been buying grapes in Sonoma for decades, purchasing them from the Frei Brothers in the Dry Creek Valley since 1944. By 1978 the children of the Frei family decided they did not want to be farmers, and they offered the land to the Gallo family. Ernest and Julio Gallo saw an overall shift in the market toward making and selling wines with the varietal, the location the grapes were grown, and the vintage on the label, and away from blending and using generic labels like "Hearty Burgundy" and "Chablis Blanc," which they had been using for years. The Gallo family bought thousands of acres of vineyards in Sonoma and created a premium brand, Gallo of Sonoma. They now operate Laguna Ranch Vineyard, Barelli Creek Vineyard, and Frei Ranch Vineyard in the Sonoma region.

The story told during a tour of Gallo's Barelli Creek Vineyard combines technical information about how the grapes are grown with an entrepreneurial narrative highlighting the savvy and commitment of the company. Their first viticultural decision was to remake the vineyard landscape: the former owners had long terraced the sloping hillsides, but Julio felt that this opened the door to soil erosion and a greater risk of damage to the vines from wild animals and soil-based diseases. The entire 580 acres were therefore relandscaped using earth-moving equipment bought by the Gallo family after the completion of the Alaskan pipeline. All the topsoil was moved, the contours of the earth changed, and the topsoil replaced. A number of red grape varietals were planted: cabernet sauvignon, zinfandel, barbera. All of this effort, the story goes, was to take best advantage of the site: the soil, the microclimate, the wild vegetation. At the same time, they use drip irrigation, for, as the tour guide put it, "Out here is all under control; they can control how much water the vines get and when."[32] On the drive back to the tasting room the tour guide pointed out that despite the efforts of the Gallos, including a program that requires that 50 percent of the land in any vineyard remain wild, they strive to make affordable wines: "Gallo wants to make wines that are accessible to all Americans."

AMERICAN TERROIR

Terroir is important to winemaking in the United States, but what the term means here is very different from what it means in Europe. Here, terroir represents a less mechanistic and less invasive philosophy of winemaking. Karen MacNeil, wine expert and author of *The Wine Bible*, compares the New World and Old World approaches to making wine in her article "Is Terroir Dead?" She writes, "[There is a deeply] ingrained European belief that wine is made by nature not by man. . . . [W]ine, at least fine wine, is at its core a reflection of place."[33] In this added twist to debates about the proper way to make wine, the addition of a geographical divide—New World versus Old World—means that some American winemakers are called "Old World–style winemakers." Why? Because they believe in terroir and choose to actively ignore available technology in order to embrace another goal, the nurture of nature.

There is no better person to consult when looking at the nurturing goal of some California winemakers than Randall Grahm, proprietor of Bonny Doon Vineyard. Born and raised in California, Grahm is a graduate of the Department of Viticulture and Enology at the University of California, Davis, a program that has had tremendous influence on winemaking and the wine industry in California and the United States as a whole. His initial winemaking venture was a quest to make, as he puts it, "the great American pinot noir." He was not able to make a pinot that matched his standard, but Grahm did end up being quite successful with the grape varieties traditionally grown in France's Rhône Valley: syrah, roussanne, marsanne, and viognier. Grahm is a true believer in terroir: "It's the question of the moment—the oenological equivalent of 'Is God dead?' . . . Is *terroir* dead? . . . Maybe we are experiencing the pain of its absence. We're sensing its loss. Without *terroir*, winemaking is a hollow game, a hall of mirrors."[34]

Grahm's Bonny Doon wines are known for their unusual labels and intense varietal blends that reproduce the robust flavors of French and Italian wines. Always innovative and always interested in skewering the pomp and circumstance surrounding the world of wine, Grahm has recently begun to use screw caps on his Big House red wines. He expands on this decision in a press release, "Are You Getting Screwed?" in which he says, "Extensive research shows that the Stelvin closure makes a nearly perfect airtight seal, actually more airtight than cork. . . . There is also the significant manner of convenience. One need possess neither a post-graduate degree in mechanical engineering nor superhuman strength and dexterity (or even a corkscrew for that matter) to open the Stelvin closure. Opposable thumbs will do." As his embrace of the Stelvin closure reveals, Grahm is not simply a narrow traditionalist following European methods exclusively, especially when it comes to practices he considers to be more concerned with mystification than quality.

A tradition that Grahm firmly believes in, however, is terroir. He considers terroir to be about more than just geography and climate; it is also about a sensibility, or even a spiritual quest. He also feels that Old World wines are made in an "I-Thou" manner, as he puts it, but that New World winemakers find this approach difficult. Grahm has long complained about the tendency of American winemakers to focus on making a personal statement with their wines and thereby ignore the natural conditions of their vineyards.

The journalist Paul Gilster describes Grahm as "mix[ing] an Old World devotion to soil and *terroir* with a New World spirit of absurdly fecund inventiveness."[35] Grahm considers the French the masters of capturing wine's "somewhereness" or, in other words, the taste of place. He has called this quest the desire to find "the soul of the wine."[36] Grahm makes and talks about wines as if he were on a mission, attempting to preserve the integrity of somewhereness in the midst of the dominant market goal: making a consistent, homogenous product. For him, terroir allows winemaking to be a soulful rather than a mechanical enterprise; wine is the ultimate antidote to Coca-Cola.

Grahm is easily the most passionate American proponent of the importance of terroir to making great wines. His entire winemaking career has been a search "not [to] create the *terroir* but to discover the *terroir*." "Really, you are learning to listen," he says.[37] Many in the wine world see him as an iconoclast, a hippie from Santa Cruz who consistently ignores the conventional wisdom. However, what if he is actually part of the countercuisine network in the United States, a network that is slowly transforming our approach to food and wine, and ultimately our foodview as well?

I was buying Bonny Doon Vineyard's very affordable and drinkable wines long before I knew anything about Grahm's devotion to terroir. Over the course of my research into winemaking in California I realized his ideas about wine and winemaking placed him squarely in the group of American innovators inspired by the French notion of soil and place. I began to collect all his writings (he produces a marvelously funny newsletter and writes occasionally for wine periodicals). Finally, in 2004 I spent time with him and others at the vineyard's Santa Cruz headquarters, where I conducted participant observations and interviews and participated in a site survey and tastings. Grahm is thinking clearly, imaginatively, and fruitfully about what terroir might mean in the United States.

To visit Bonny Doon Vineyards I drove south from San Francisco toward Santa Cruz. I had visited Palo Alto about fifteen years ago, and I was struck by how much the area had been developed since the computer technology boom of the 1990s. Office park after office park lined both sides of the highway. Since I had just escaped from the dreary weather of northern New England in November, I was happy to enjoy the stronger sunshine of the West Coast, but as I was driving I kept looking for a sign or two of plant life. A palm tree perhaps? A bougainvillea plant? No, there was nothing in sight but cement and concrete. Finally, as I entered the outskirts of Gilroy, my senses were rewarded: I could see green fields and smell the garlic for which this town is so famous. My first stop was actually south of Santa Cruz, in Soledad, famous for its prison and, increasingly, as the location of Bonny Doon's vineyards. I had been invited to participate in and observe the next new thing at this pioneering company: biodynamic wine growing.

Bonny Doon Vineyard purchased 130 acres in this hot, fairly dry region in 1990. They pursued conventional wine-growing practices for more than ten years, relying on drip irrigation and regular rotations of fertilizer. Over

time, however, Grahm started to question this approach, feeling it ultimately did not serve his purpose of creating terroir-based wines in California. Although this conventional approach gave the growers maximum control
over the plants, it did not force their roots to reach deep into the soil, which
Grahm feels helps promote terroir. By 2002 it was decided that the vineyards needed to be treated differently; nature was going to run the show.

Biodynamic practices are often described as "beyond organic." This agricultural philosophy was invented (or perhaps received) by Rudolph Steiner,
the philosopher, educator, and cultivator best known in the United States for
his role in the Waldorf School movement. He introduced his ideas in a series of lectures he gave at the end of his life, but he never fully elaborated on
them, which leads to great variation in biodynamic practices among its ad-
herents, and frequent speculation about what Steiner really intended.

The task was to help make the mixture "Preparation 501." I was driven
to a work site where the bed of a large pickup truck was piled high with
cow manure. Out of another truck came hundreds of longhorn cattle
horns, collected only from cows that were pregnant or lactating. Our job
was to pack the manure into the horns, which would then be buried in a
large pit, covered, and left for six months. The horns would then be taken
out of the ground and the manure would be shaken out and mixed with
water. The result, called Preparation 501, would then be sprayed at three
to five gallons an acre. Bonny Doon is presently investigating the use of
helicopters for more consistent spraying (a development that certainly
could not have been anticipated by Steiner when he gave his agricultural
lectures). Steiner felt that this preparation helps plants to root and aligns
terrestrial forces.

Grahm has become more and more interested in biodynamic approaches
to wine growing over the past decade. His greatest influences, he says, are
his French and Italian winemaker friends, or, to be more accurate, the wines
that they are now producing using biodynamic methods. Grahm really

FIGURE 6. Preparing for the burial of longhorn cattle horns, Bonny Doon Vineyard, Soledad, California. PHOTO BY AMY B. TRUBEK.

tasted a difference in their wines after they began to apply biodynamic practices, and he was convinced that this new approach to nurturing the soil and grapes made a big difference in overall quality.

For Grahm, bringing biodynamics into his portfolio of vineyard practices is part of his all-encompassing quest for terroir. When I spoke to him out in the vineyard on that sunny November day, after a group of us had snapped on our surgical gloves and spent an hour scooping manure from a large pile and pushing it into cow horns, he said, "Basically, I am interested in terroir, bringing out the minerality from the soil. There are two ways [to do this]: having lots of mineral and rock, or getting the soil to be able to express minerality. Biodynamics can help make that happen."[38]

The folks at Bonny Doon cheerfully admitted that they were more pragmatic than ideological when it came to their decision to embrace biodynamic practices. John Locke (called J Lo by his colleagues), Grahm's then director of marketing, is a skeptic by nature, but he is willing to consider biodynamics if it improves the quality of Bonny Doon wines. Locke says that "biodynamicists are generally disagreeable," and he doesn't like their insistence on maintaining ideological purity.[39] He told me stories of extremely rigid biodynamic practitioners who would brook no deviations from their methods. Grahm, by nature a philosopher but now also a businessman, is inclined to agree. For Bonny Doon, he says, "it is not a dogma but a method for improving the vineyard, and thus the wine to the consumer."[40]

When I first arrived at the Soledad vineyards that warm morning, I spoke with Nicole Walsh, Bonny Doon Vineyard's manager of grower relations. Trained at Michigan State University in horticulture, with a specialization in viniculture and oenology, Walsh shifted among the languages of science, terroir, and biodynamics when she discussed their growing practices. She said of Bonny Doon's recent embrace of biodynamic methods, "I will do it, but I don't understand it."[41] They have brought in consultants from France to help make the switch and also hired a management company to oversee the schedule and the preparations. Walsh, like Grahm, has become a proponent of these methods because of the taste difference. She believes in the importance of expressing minerality in wine and sees that the biodynamic approach forces grapevines to go down deep in the soil. She also talks of the "balancing effect" of biodynamics, especially the way in which it results in wines with lower alcohol levels despite the fact that sugars remain present.

Grahm and everyone else I spoke to at Bonny Doon were not wedded to any single method of growing grapes, and so at this early stage of embracing biodynamics (this was the first time they had tried to use Preparation 501), their stance was experimental rather than dogmatic. But for Grahm, the quest is always the same: "[Biodynamics for me] is a small vehicle or a big vehicle, who knows, as a way to express *terroir*."[42] Thus, Bonny Doon is an example of a New World vineyard where they are always interested in the latest innovations and gadgets to enhance wine quality, but, uniquely, these maneuvers are always performed in the service of an Old World idea, terroir.

Grahm began making wine in 1979, originally using other people's facilities and blending grapes from various California vineyards. By 1983 he had created Bonny Doon, his own facility in the hills near Santa Cruz. The company has enjoyed steady growth over the past twenty years, including 17 percent growth from 2004 to 2006.[43] In 2006 they sold 348,000 cases of wine, with almost 50 percent of sales coming from their blended Ca' del Solo red and white wines. In 1995 Bonny Doon Vineyard began seeking out European partners, not only to purchase grapes to bring back to California to make their own wines, but also to create European terroir-style wines. Presently they have partnerships in Italy, France, and Germany. Most of their wines are sold through wine distributors, but they also sponsor a very popular wine club, DEWN, consisting of 6,500 members who have access to twelve unique wines a year. Bonny Doon now employs sixty people.

A philosophy major at the University of California, Santa Cruz, in the early 1970s, Grahm wrote his senior thesis on Martin Heidegger. He went to Germany to study German so he could read Heidegger, Hegel, and Nietzsche in their original language, but ultimately he became enamored with German wines. When we spoke of his first visit to Germany, he talked passionately of the marvelous 1971 vintage German Auslesen he drank, a *lieu de mémoire* for a transformative time in his life. After graduating from college he went to work at the Wine Merchant in Beverly Hills, a wine shop where he was able to learn about and taste the greatest wines in the world. Grahm fell in love with wine, but realized that "I will never be able to drink these wines because I can't afford them, so I will need to make them myself."[44] As a result, he decided to study viticulture at the University of California, Davis, considered a premier program in the United States.

When discussing wine and winemaking Grahm always makes comparisons between the United States and Europe. He came to Davis with his "ideology worked out—Europeans knew what they were doing."[45] In those days at Davis, this meant he was a contrarian. The prevailing point of view was what he calls "typical American hubris": his professors characterized American wine practices as the result of enlightened reason and the European approach as bound by superstition and tradition. The use of science and technology to create wines with "an absence of defect" was the order of the day. For Grahm, this emphasis on standardization and conformity went against all his ideals for making great wines.

Grahm struggles with history in his attempts to create terroir-based wines in the United States. He often speaks wistfully of a storied past, particularly in Europe, when values shaping wine connected with a set of practices to create the wines of his dreams. At one point in our conversations he said, "People made wine to please themselves in the old days. Now people make wine to please the market." But then he stopped himself, asking, "Or is this my fantasy?" Later he said, "Terroir is archaeology. It has historically developed over many generations. The theory is that terroir transcends the winemaker; there is something immortal about terroir." The many generations of effort, experience, and dedication to making wines that express the idiosyncrasies of place in Europe mean that Old World wines, grown in "old soils," are always at an advantage. He compares the Italian wine Heart of Darkness, which he imports, to his California wines, saying, "What is so discouraging [and] inspiring is that I taste Heart of Darkness, and if I live to be 150, I will never be able to make this here."

Herein lies the great paradox of terroir for American winemakers. The French have invested a great deal of money and resources in identifying the uniqueness of tracts of land long used for producing wine according to a set of environmental conditions such as climate, insolation, geomorphology, geology, and hydrology. Here in the United States winemakers can try to search out or mimic these conditions, yet in the end our nation's past choices and values always leave us far behind. In California winemakers are always reinventing the wheel: there seems to be no gravitas to New World efforts to create great wines, no weight of tradition to guide decisions and practices. Does our past determine our future when it comes to terroir? According to Grahm, it does. At the same time, he does not give up, because the future remains ours to conquer. Maybe Grahm *will* be able to bring the Heart of Darkness to the sunny California coast.

CULINARY TERROIR:
THE FERRY BUILDING MARKETPLACE

On the day before Thanksgiving I once visited San Francisco's Ferry Building Marketplace, which opened in 2003, with friends and family. The market sits directly on the waterfront, with the Bay Bridge to the right and the Oakland and Berkeley hills straight across the dark blue waters. The day was sunny and warm, and lots of holiday shoppers wandered around, picking up the last items for their holiday meals. At one point I was drawn in by the colorful fruit display—the persimmons, apples, and oranges—at the Frog Hollow Farm store. I looked around, noticing the picture commemorating Prince Charles's recent visit to the store, and then picked up the Frog Hollow Farm brochure. Inside was a list of all their products. As I read, my cursory glance became a close read. The text under "Who We Are" went as follows: "In 1976 Al Courchesne planted his first peach trees on 13 acres near Brentwood, California, next to Smith Ranch, owned by the relatives of

Sarah Coddington, his future business partner. The 'terroir' of this rich land always lent itself to growing first-class stone fruit. Even in those early days, Bay Area chefs and markets avidly sought the farms' exceptional apricots, cherries, nectarines, peaches, pears and plums." This was the first time I had seen the term *terroir* connected to fruit growing in the United States, and I was immediately intrigued. I looked up from the brochure, and to my surprise I saw Farmer Al sitting next to a table stacked high with apple and pecan pies (his picture was in the brochure). I walked right over and conducted an impromptu interview about his definition of terroir. A big, burly man dressed in a white shirt and overalls, he replied, "Well, it is 40 percent climate, 40 percent soil, and 20 percent cultural." I asked him to expand on the link between terroir and culture. For him the cultural dimension involves all his farmer neighbors who can tell him about the traditional fruits grown in the region and what farming methods have been shown to work. They are able to provide him with know-how born of tradition and experience. "I have spent thirty years farming this land," he said, and experience has made him a believer in all three aspects of his definition of terroir.

Why has this farmer adopted this term to explain the quality of his fruits? If he were in Michigan or Georgia, other rich fruit-growing regions, could he use such language to explain why his fruit is so good? Probably not. But Al Courchesne farms in Brentwood, a mere forty-five miles from Berkeley, fifty-five miles from San Francisco, and fifty-three miles from Napa. He grows peaches, nectarines, apricots, Meyer lemons, and more next to the largest wine-growing region in the United States. The temperate climate, ready access to sophisticated consumers, and proximity to major wine-growing regions make Northern California a perfect locale for building an American version of the taste of place. The foodview in this region embraces, even celebrates, a philosophy of discernment based on terroir. Farmer Al says 20 percent of terroir is cultural. Maybe that appears to be a small amount, but it is not if it is compared to the level of awareness of the cultural component of terroir in other parts of the United States. In the context of other regions of the country, California has fully embraced cultural terroir.

The Ferry Building Marketplace, an urban location for the dissemination of Northern California's version of the taste of place, is the serendipitous result of taking lemons (the 1989 Loma Prieta earthquake) and making lemonade (out of Meyer lemons, of course). Designed by A. Page Brown and completed in 1898, the Ferry Building immediately became a city landmark because of its strategic location on the waterfront and the 240-foot clock tower that was inspired by a twelfth-century bell tower in Spain's Cathedral of Seville. By the 1950s increased automobile traffic on the Bay Bridge and Golden Gate Bridge had led to a decline in the use of ferries and thus the building as well, which fell into disrepair. Furthermore, the Embarcadero Freeway, constructed in 1957, was built directly in front of the Ferry Building. By the 1970s automobile traffic overwhelmed thoroughfares in and out of the city, and ferry service to Marin County, north of San Francisco, resumed to provide a transportation alternative. In 1989, the Loma Prieta earthquake caused extensive damage to the Embarcadero Freeway, providing the impetus to tear it down in 1991. The Ferry Building and the central waterfront were once again visible and ready to embrace a bright future. Years of planning came next, as those involved tried to figure out the best use of the building and raised the money for the ninety-million-dollar renovation.[46]

After the Embarcadero Freeway was condemned, a group of farmers organized a farmers' market in the middle of the highway in front of the Ferry Building. Soon afterward, in 1993, a weekly farmers' market emerged in the plaza across the street from the terminal. Run by the nonprofit organization Center for Urban Education about Sustainable Agriculture (CUESA), it went on to become a successful weekly institution. The decision to tear down the Embarcadero Freeway created an opportunity to return the Ferry

Building to its former glory. From the beginning, the redevelopment plans involved celebrating San Francisco's strong food culture. The mission for the Ferry Building Marketplace, which involves the outdoor farmers' market and the shops and restaurants indoors, reflects such a commitment: according to its website, "The Ferry Building Marketplace is dedicated to the celebration of San Francisco's artisan food culture and cuisine and is supported by Equity Office, a company committed to fostering the values of this community." CUESA oversees the outdoor farmers' markets, and Equity Office manages all the shops and restaurants inside the building. To do business either inside or outside, applicants must meet certain criteria based on agricultural and business practices. CUESA uses a set of criteria including environmental sustainability, but also incorporates location and practices. Not only do the producers and vendors have to support CUESA's objectives of supporting small farms and connecting farmers with urban dwellers, but the producers must grow all their products in California, and preference is given to those grown organically. For vendors, CUESA prefers those who use organic, regionally grown produce and who have at least two years of experience in the restaurant or prepared food business.

CUESA has offices in the Ferry Building, where it employs ten people who work on market logistics and develop education and outreach projects. Seventy-five percent of the organization's almost one-million-dollar operating budget comes from the fees they charge for market stalls. CUESA uses a sliding scale to determine fees, which range from nothing for a small farmer just starting out to a hundred dollars a week for a premium corner space. Farmers simply pay the flat fee; restaurants that sell food at the market are also asked to pay CUESA a small surcharge based on weekly sales. The organization is responsible for negotiating all the agreements with the involved parties, including Equity Office, the San Francisco Port Authority, and Bay Area Rapid Transit (BART). Saturday is by far their busiest market, with more than fifteen thousand people streaming down to the waterfront to buy all manner of fruit, vegetables, and meats; numerous prepared items; coffee; and goodies such as fish tacos. On a recent visit I purchased sun-dried nectarines, organic roasted almonds, a farmstead goat cheese, and two kinds of heirloom dried beans. All of these foods were grown or produced within seventy-five miles of the market.

Given the way that Americans organize their lives, it may come as no surprise that Dave Stockdale, CUESA's executive director, says, "Parking is our biggest barrier." People complain regularly that it is too hard to find parking nearby, or say that they would come more often if it were easier to park. Certainly, it is challenging to carry home bags of groceries up and down San Francisco's steep hills using the city's buses, subway, or light rail vehicles, but in previous times carrying your food was a daily reality, and in some places it still is. Americans, however, have become accustomed to us-ing their cars as packhorses and are only so willing to sacrifice this conve-nience for the opportunity to meet the people who make their food or to gain access to the freshest ingredients.

Inside the Ferry Building is a mixture of shops selling artisan products—cheese, chocolate, olive oil, wine—restaurants, a coffee shop, bakeries, and fish and meat shops, as well as a kitchenware store and a bookstore. The list of purveyors is a veritable who's who of gastronomic luminaries from the Bay Area: Acme Bread Company, Cowgirl Creamery, Hog Island Oyster Com-pany, McEvoy Ranch Olive Oil, Scharffen Berger Chocolate Maker, and the Slanted Door restaurant. Outside the building, at the farmers' market, the décor is democratic. Everyone works inside a square canvas tent, and almost all use folding tables to hawk their wares. Inside, however, everyone attempts to create a distinctive mark. At Slanted Door, with its sleek wooden tables and chairs, large floor-to-ceiling windows look out over the bay. At the Cowgirl Creamery shop the counters are stacked high with dozens of farmstead cheeses from around the world. A door in the sleek white wall in the back leads to their refrigerated storage room. In the Ferry Building, a certain vocabulary of taste underlies many of the merchants' efforts. At the McEvoy Ranch store, a display describes their marmalade thus: "Meyer Lemon Marmalade is made from our estate-grown Meyer lemons, cane sugar, and pure water cooked only long enough to draw the natural protein from the fruit. The resulting marmalade is light in texture, has sprightly lemon flavor, and is well-balanced with sweetness." Just below the marmalade display, the brochure for Stonehouse California Olive Oil echoes the descriptions often written about wineries up north in Sonoma and Napa: "Our organically farmed grove, Silver Ridge, is located in Oroville, California, in the beautiful foothills east of Chico. Our century-old trees are comprised of Mission, Manzanillo, and Barouni olive varietals. Annual harvest begins in October, when the fruit is still green, and (weather permitting) continues through January, when the olives ripen to black, in order to obtain oil that reflects the full spectrum of flavors—from the fresh, grassy, early oil to the soft, buttery, late-harvest oil." Locating the process involved in making the products and describing the resulting flavor characteristics are primary sales tactics inside the market, confirming a foodview based on the taste of place.

This mode of discernment is defined by the new agrarian tradition emerging in the United States based on principles of sustainability. Inside and outside the Ferry Building these principles and values are constantly being articulated to the consumers that come to shop and eat. CUESA was funded by the San Francisco Foundation to create a photographic mural called *Sustainability A–Z*. Twenty-four large, moveable panels are located along the arched open-air passageway on the ground floor. Each panel, which serves as a door to an area that vendors use to prepare for the farmers' market, consists of a huge color photograph and accompanying text describing a principle of sustainability. Farmers' market vendors hang banners declaring whether they are "organic," "local," or "sustainable" operations, revealing to shoppers the values being promoted. Inside the building, the Stonehouse California Olive Oil brochure mentioned above claims,

"When you purchase a bottle of Stonehouse California Olive Oil, you are buying one of the freshest possible oils, supporting local agriculture, and using fewer resources than if you purchased imported oil." In France, the goût du terroir uses tradition as a guide; in California, we use printed guides to inform consumers of the taste of place.

For many, the jury is still out on the Ferry Building Marketplace. The dilemma, as aptly put by Karola Saekel, a journalist for the *San Francisco Chronicle,* was whether "San Francisco would finally have a world-class downtown food market on a par with historic European markets, Seattle's Pike Place, or New York's Grand Central Terminal? Or would this stay simply a spot for tourists, something like a Fisherman's-Wharf-cum-arugula?" Ultimately Saekel decides that the food is affordable and is accessible to a busy person on the way home for dinner, and thus is more like Pike's Place than Fisherman's Wharf.[47] Residents of San Francisco and nearby towns with whom I spoke generally agreed with Saekel, although some were uncomfortable with the glamorous scene at the Ferry Building and preferred the homier weekly markets in Marin and Berkeley. Also, many think this farmers' market is more expensive than others. I spoke to one woman who comes every week to the Saturday farmers' market. She said, "I think it is expensive, but it is a real draw for me. I really appreciate all the meat. I trust them [the vendors]. I do think some people consider it too hoity-toity."[48]

In the course of my research all over the United States and my day-to-day work in Vermont, people repeatedly pointed out to me what they identified as the *elitism* of the food and drink that I was considering. In California, Wisconsin, Vermont, and other places I would travel, this was a universal cultural critique. For most, this elitism revolved around cost: the grass-fed beef, heirloom tomatoes, and hand-rolled tortillas available for purchase at the farmers' market or for sale to a restaurant were elite products because they were more expensive. But expensive relative to what? In comparison, it seemed, to the cost of beef, tomatoes, and tortillas available at your local supermarket. Few people made the connection that the higher cost at the farmers' market increased the level of return to individual farmers and was in fact an exercise in food democracy. If the farmers at the Saturday farmers' market take advantage of the cachet of the market's location and the large number of customers with disposable income to charge slightly higher prices, aren't they following our culture's classic assumption about the capitalist economy, that if demand outstrips supply, one should adjust prices accordingly? Also, few people consider that much of the food and drink purchased at the grocery store is priced much higher than the costs of production. In 1993, for example, a box of cereal contained 14 cents worth of raw ingredients, while the consumer was charged $2.20. Today the market price for a box of cereal is between $4 and $5, and who gets to pocket the difference between the cost of production and cost to the consumer? Not the farmer.

The struggle to develop a foodview based on the taste of place in the United States requires reforming the common-sense assumption that the price at the consumer marketplace begins and ends any discussion of the status of a food or drink. The *cultural* assumptions—the values and beliefs about what is important and meaningful about food—continue to rely on a notion of food democracy based on the individual choice of commodities and the lowest cost to consumers.

CALIFORNIA CUISINE

Tastemakers and *taste producers*—winemakers, cheese makers, farmers, chefs, cookbook authors, and journalists—with the same investments and backgrounds as their French counterparts are the ones responsible for the goût du terroir emerging in California. When these individuals and their experiences are considered together, a certain pattern emerges. All the people I spoke to referred to a seminal experience in their youth that turned them away from the dominant American foodview. For the gastronomically inclined, a European sojourn was often credited with revealing an alternative sensibility. For those with a more agrarian background, the ideals of the back-to-the-land movement spurred them to action. In the late 1960s and early 1970s, the San Francisco Bay Area, with its political and cultural activism related to the antiwar and antiestablishment movements, provided fertile ground for all these people. As important, however, were the possibilities created by the physical environment—a temperate climate, a winemaking tradition, and ready access to good soil.

Alice Waters, owner of Chez Panisse restaurant in Berkeley, has led the effort to create a regional California cuisine by relying on a sophisticated use of the rich array of local ingredients. Waters, her restaurant, and the hundreds of people who have worked at the restaurant or provided food for it have been instrumental in developing a set of relationships between ingredients and method now called *California cuisine,* the standard now not only for most high-end restaurants in Northern California, but also many bakeries and other food shops as well. The national media often credit Waters with "inventing" California cuisine, often to the chagrin of others who also labor in fields, cheese plants, or kitchens in the region.[49] Everyone I spoke to agreed, however, that Waters has always been obsessed by obtaining the highest-quality ingredients possible. Not trained professionally as a chef, she has never focused too much on technical complexity when developing her dishes. An obsession with ingredients combined with simplicity of preparation was how one long-time employee at her restaurant defined the "Chez Panisse way."[50]

Waters always credits the time she spent in France during her junior year in college with defining her sensibility toward food. She lived with a family in Brittany and was amazed by how central food, drink, and the dinner table were to their lives. She also spent time in the outdoor markets, cafés, and restaurants, where she realized the care that went into growing, cooking, and eating food in France. Eventually, back in Berkeley, she met Paul Aratow, at the time a professor of comparative literature at the University of California, Berkeley. Aratow had just returned from a sabbatical year in France, where he had also fallen in love with the French foodview. They started Chez Panisse together in 1970 with no restaurant experience, but only a commitment to finding fresh local ingredients and a copy of the classic cookbook *La bonne cuisine,* by Madame Saint-Ange, to guide them. (This cookbook also influenced Julia Child as she, Simone Beck, and Louise Bertholle worked on *Mastering the Art of French Cooking.*)

Waters's primary concern has always been, as she puts it, "deliciousness." Her quest for great ingredients is primarily *aesthetic,* both sensory and visual in nature. In the early days she shopped in San Francisco's Chinatown, the only place she could find meat and vegetables that came close to her expectations. Although she eventually did begin buying from the back-to-the-land-style farmers now settling in Northern California and setting up shop in places like the Berkeley Farmers' Market, "there was a long training period" until solid relationships between the farmer and the chef could be created.[51] Over time, certain farmers embraced the restaurant's emphasis on great-tasting and great-looking vegetables and became important forces in the design of the menu. Recently at Chez Panisse, a farmer's arugula had begun to get too bitter, and so those at the restaurant were discussing purchasing a different green from him, or possibly having him grow a different variety.

Fran Gage, who has lived in San Francisco for almost forty years, is both a taste producer and a tastemaker. She ran a pastry shop for ten years, and after the shop was closed because of a fire she became a food writer, publishing three cookbooks, including *Bread and Chocolate,* a food memoir with recipes. She remembers that during her first few years in the city she found a brochure from the California Department of Agriculture for "you pick" farms. She organized several trips to different parts of Northern California to get fresh produce. A trip to France with her husband in 1970 was a real turning point: "The way the French people thought about food was mind-blowing to me."[52] She became obsessed with French pastry. Eventually she went on to open Fran Gage's Pâtisserie Française at Eighteenth and Market Streets. Sourcing high-quality ingredients was a priority while she owned the bakery; she primarily used distributors to purchase her ingredients, although her attempts to find a butter with a high butterfat content led her to work with a nearby creamery. Overall, Gage feels that the quality of ingredients available in the San Francisco area has improved tremendously since she started her bakery twenty years ago. She is especially impressed with the increase in the types and grades of chocolate now available. She also agrees that "Alice Waters did start a whole movement about paying attention to ingredients. [The movement] has gone way beyond vegetables. It has also become more realistic. The preciousness is gone and it has gotten more practical."[53] An aesthetic and gastronomic sensibility inspired by travel in France led a group of young, idealistic people to focus on food in the Bay Area, and their search for good-tasting and good-looking ingredients led them to the many small, diversified farmers and food artisans such as Al Courchesne of Frog Hollow Farm and Laura Chenel of Cowgirl Creamery and the many farmers' markets opening up in the area. The French foodview came to an American region with a rich agrarian tradition (including growing grapes and making wine) and a marvelous climate for all types of farming. All these people's efforts enabled the taste of place to make sense to an increasingly engaged group of consumers.

The emergence of a mode of discernment that relies on the taste of place to evaluate the quality of individual items—food, wine, cheese, meat—has become integral to this region's food culture. Does this translate, however, into a full-fledged "cuisine régionale" or "cuisine du terroir"? Is it possible to assert that there is a "California cuisine," one that rivals the cuisine of Provence or Tuscany? Sylvan Brackett, who works for Alice Waters and thought about such questions often as he worked with two collaborators on

The Slow Food Guide to San Francisco, is not sure. He acknowledges that farmers' markets now can be found all over the Bay Area, and thus fresh ingredients are widely available. He also notes that increasing numbers of young farmers committed to small-scale agriculture are showing up at the Berkeley farmers' markets. But he feels that in order to have a regional cuisine there needs to be a shared body of recipes, and "the only thing I can think of is cioppino."[54] Like Grahm, he worries about time: "Most of the regional cuisines have been worked out in places such as France and Japan. It takes a long time to make a regional cuisine." Brackett believes that regional cuisines emerge from places that adhere to "a traditional way of doing things." He wonders whether recipes using Northern California ingredients are transmitted through generations of a family. The array of possible food-views shaping people's everyday choices about what to buy and what to cook makes him question the feasibility of regional cuisine here in Northern California and, by extension, in the entire United States. One could say he struggles with the apparent lack of an overarching culinary narrative, a story of "how things should be done" that orders present practice with recourse to the past.

But does Northern California food fail to fit into a paradigmatic definition of regional cuisine, or does the prevailing definition of a regional cuisine fail to account for what really happens every day as dishes are created and meals are eaten in homes and restaurants all over the region? Ultimately, Brackett concludes that in Northern California there is a split between locality and ethnicity in the shaping of cuisine.[55] According to him, the focus on fresh, local, and increasingly organic ingredients is a *sensibility,* an informing of cooking practices that in the act of going from raw ingredient to finished dish is mediated as well by ethnic affiliations (be they professional or personal): French, Mexican, Thai, Chinese.

San Francisco's Zuni Café illustrates this version of a regional cuisine. Zuni Café, a nationally acclaimed restaurant co-owned by Judy Rodgers, has long been a proponent of using local ingredients. Rodgers, like Alice Waters and Fran Gage, had a profound epiphany about the importance of good food, and especially high-quality ingredients, on a youthful trip to France. She had the good fortune to end up as a high school exchange student in Roanne, France, where she was placed in the home of the owners of Les Frères Troisgros, a world-renowned restaurant. Then, as an art history major at Stanford, Rodgers spent her junior year in Paris. On her return she went to eat at Chez Panisse and "fell in love at first bite," for she found a version of the French food she so loved and admired.[56] After graduation she went to work for Alice Waters at Chez Panisse for two years and eventually took over Zuni Café.

The restaurant is located in an old triangular building at the corner of Market and Gough Streets. Huge banks of windows line the apex of the triangle, and diners are seated both downstairs, in a big open room by the kitchen, and upstairs, in a series of small, intimate spaces. The large open kitchen occupies the back of the building. The menu, a simple piece of cream-colored paper printed on both sides, describes the proffered dishes by naming the dish, the main ingredients, and where they come from. The main culinary influence is Mediterranean, but Rodgers celebrates the local sensibility and the city's ethnic diversity, too.

In her *Zuni Café Cookbook,* Rodgers combines autobiography, education, and recipes. She encourages readers to avoid slavishly following recipes and urges them to go outside:

> Cookbooks will give you ideas, but the market will give you dinner—study your market at least as avidly as your library. Look for a market that takes pride in featuring local, seasonal produce, however modest it may be in variety, and pay attention to that produce most of all. Clamor for organic and sustainably farmed foods. If there is a farmers' market in your area, shop there. Talk and listen to the growers. You can learn from the people who raise the food; they probably have more insight into the corn and lettuce that you are about to buy

than any cookbook. Fewer handlers and handlings mean that the grower can dare to pick ripe, and that more flavorful but fragile fruit and vegetable varieties become a viable option. By contrast, large-scale-for-long-distance packing practices demand hardy varieties and uniformity. They favor shelf life and looks, not flavor and fragrance. I'd rather pay the premium for a low-yield but delicious variety of melon or berry in peak season than swallow the cost of waxing apples or gassing strawberries just so they conform to an ideal market standard at any time of year, and any distance from the garden. Raw ingredients trump recipes every time; farmers and ranchers who coax the best from the earth can make any of us appear to be a good cook.[57]

Her philosophy of cooking makes Rodgers into an educator. She wants those reading her cookbook to *move*, to embrace a more responsive way of cooking based on an array of agricultural possibilities.

Going beyond Rodgers's culinary philosophy and looking more closely at the work that is done every day at Zuni Café reveal the many dimensions of place in a multicultural, cosmopolitan city. Down in the basement of the restaurant three prep cooks have worked together for more than a decade, chopping the onions, braising the beef, and doing the many other tasks necessary to get the ingredients ready for service every evening. All three cooks are immigrants: Quang Nguyen from Vietnam, Carlos Garcia from Mexico, and Mario Gonzalez from Nicaragua. Each one of them came to California with very little and now supports his family, both in the United States and in his home country. The three men took entry-level jobs at the restaurant with no previous training, capitalizing on the availability of restaurant jobs to people with minimal English skills. These men have no cultural or agrarian connection to Northern California, or to the food prepared each day at Zuni Café. Over time, however, they have developed irreplaceable skills, allowing Rodgers's values to be translated into practice every day.

A *San Francisco Chronicle* article highlights the importance of these three cooks to the success of Zuni Café. Rodgers describes how Gonzalez can brown meat for stew like no one else, and how Garcia can look at a case of romaine and estimate yield perfectly. "They're the first line of defense with products. They can warn us about yields and taste," the article explains, and "you can't learn that in school," says Rodgers. Kitchen manager Rymee Trobaugh is quoted in the article, saying, "I treasure their consistency." He also treasures their comfortable, low-testosterone camaraderie. "We're not this extreme-macho, in-your-face, French-led young guys out of the CIA." Making Rodgers's style of food requires the delicate treatment of ingredients and real attention to detail. These three immigrants have become the artisans who make that happen.[58]

During our conversation about regional cuisine, Sylvan Brackett mentioned an editorial by a San Francisco chef recently published in the *New York Times* Sunday magazine titled "To the Moon, Alice?" In the piece the author, Daniel Patterson, acknowledges the existence of a "California cuisine" and the importance of Chez Panisse and the restaurant's owner, Alice Waters. Patterson then goes on to critique the "tyranny of Chez Panisse." He feels that the restaurant's cuisine "has become not just one voice but the only voice speaking out on the values and the mission of that cuisine. . . . Alice Waters, the restaurant's founder and a tireless promoter of fresh and local food, has become to us what Beatrice was to Dante: a model of righteousness and purity, reminding us of our past sins while offering encouragement and inspiration on the path to heaven. The *only* path to heaven."[59] He continues by arguing that although these principles are noble and important, too many chefs have become slaves to the "fresh ingredients simply prepared" mantra. Along the way creativity and innovation have been lost. Brackett wondered out loud if the very fact that this editorial was written and given such play in the national media in fact confirms the emergence of a taste of place and a regional cuisine. I agreed that it did. And Patterson's critique, that the values of authenticity and purity have superseded other possible and equally valid culinary values—individual artistic expression, multicultural ethnicity, technical complexity—are similar to those leveled at the French terroir purists such as Aimé Guibert and José Bové.

A food culture relying on the language of discernment first articulated by the wine world and now embraced by olive oil merchants, coffee dealers, tea shops, and more has emerged in California. The cultural work has started, but is it finished? Those involved in building California's taste of place are fueled by their idealism, but is that enough to sustain such a foodview? During my stay in Northern California I spoke to a woman who runs a lovely general store in Sonoma County that features fresh local food. After fourteen years, she is burned out. She wants to sell the business, but that means selling the entire property as well. "This is my home. I look out the window and see the vineyards. All my friends are here, and my loyal customers." She cannot imagine not living in the region, and yet she also cannot quite imagine being wedded to the ups and downs of running the store, from the constant challenge of attracting and retaining good staff to developing new marketing strategies for more profitable food items. Sustaining the taste of place every day is not simple, or easy.

At the same time, since the ability to discern taste through place is being invented in the United States every day, the people involved do not in fact focus simply on *their* place; they feel comfortable roaming the globe for the *best* examples of the taste of place. While I was touring Chez Panisse, we went into the wine cellar. Racks of wines stretched from the floor to ceiling in the small, square room. I noted the small quantity of California wine. Their white and red house wines are produced in Napa, only fifty miles away, but the majority of their wines come from Europe, particularly France. Sylvan Brackett replied, "Well, we are anti–Robert Parker here, so we do not have many California wines. Our wine list has been heavily influenced by the sensibility of Kermit Lynch." Lynch, a Berkeley wine importer, is a longtime promoter of French wines. Place matters, but for those at Chez Panisse, the place must meet their definition of deliciousness, too.

So how, exactly, can we describe the quest for terroir and the taste of place in the New World? The main characters in *Sideways* identify with well-made wines, and they respect those whose efforts have allowed them their hedonistic pleasures. Perhaps this is the cultural terroir we need to embrace, the definition of the taste of place Daniel Ravier at Domaine Tempier feels we lack here. And since our agrarian histories are so different, it makes sense not to slavishly embrace European sensibilities. At the end of our discussion about the possibility of an American terroir, Randall Grahm finally concluded, "We [Americans] could theoretically be great synthesizers." Not inheritors, not inventors, but (to use another French term) *bricoleurs,* tinkering with what we have, imagining what is possible, and borrowing from our many ancestral pasts. Grahm continues such a quest for American terroir; he recently sold his larger, more commercial vineyards and wines to focus solely on creating terroir wines from smaller vineyards using biodynamic practices.

FOUR

TASTING WISCONSIN
A CHEF'S STORY

PERHAPS I AM A NAÏVE CULINARY OPTIMIST. I KNOW THAT WAL-MART, McDON-ald's, Olive Garden, and Sysco dominate our culinary landscape. I know that many Americans, when confronted with an office party in New Mexico, Illinois, or Kentucky, will as often as not buy a box of frozen prepared appetizers from Costco. How can I possibly believe that in the era of global convenience cuisine there is also emerging a modern *cuisine du terroir*, with fidelity to place and season?

Appropriately enough, I can believe it because of something I ate in a restaurant. Although we tend to assume that cooking and eating take place primarily in homes, restaurants are a part of our everyday lives: we spend 50 percent of every food dollar on food that has been prepared outside the home.[1] Restaurants no longer represent just a traveler's necessity or an anniversary event; now they are the answer to that oft-asked question "What's for dinner?" (or for lunch, or for breakfast). Scholars have linked cafés and restaurants to the increased importance since the eighteenth century of the public sphere in the West, as a new space for promoting dialogue and marking distinction.[2] However, restaurants, and the people who labor behind the scenes to transform the raw into the cooked, have also created new ways to experience and think about food.[3] It is often assumed that the food prepared in restaurants *reflects* a culinary tradition, but what if, instead, this food *creates* one?

Do Americans know how to cook using raw, unprocessed ingredients (the leek yet to be cleaned, the whole chicken that needs to be split) and work with them to create a finished dish? In almost every region of the country cooking from the bounty of the surrounding landscape is difficult and not a cultural priority, and this is most apparent when considering regional cuisines, where the use of locally and seasonally available ingredients is a central assumption. Between 1940 and 1998 the size of the average farm jumped from 135 to 469 acres, while the number of farms decreased nationally, from 6.1 million to 2 million.[4] Less than 2 percent of the population is involved in farming, there is a demographic shift away from rural to suburban and urban residence patterns, and our imports of food now exceed our exports. In this context it makes sense that chefs in restaurants are not just cooking but are shaping American cuisine as well.

In well-known restaurants around the United States chefs are selling their use of regional and seasonal ingredients in their dishes. Peter Hoffman at Savoy and Dan Barber at Blue Hill in New York City, Rick Bayless at Topolobampo and Frontera Grill in Chicago, Greg Higgins at Higgins in Portland, Ana Sortun at Oleana in Cambridge, Alice Waters at Chez Panisse in Berkeley, and Judy Rodgers at Zuni Café in San Francisco are a few examples, but the list goes on. And the restaurants involved are not just those that *Gourmet* and the *New York Times* celebrate, but they are also small, individually owned restaurants in suburban Cleveland and rural Vermont. Chefs know that distinguishing themselves in the business of cooking now requires knowing where their ingredients come from and how they are grown or raised, as well as identifying those ingredients and their origins for their diners.

At the same time, large-scale supermarkets remain the location of choice for individual American home cooks shopping for ingredients. Five supermarket chains now account for more than 48 percent of all retail food sales in the United States, compared to 1997, when they accounted for just 24 percent of all sales. Wal-Mart is now the number-one food retailer in the United States.[5] The vast distribution systems needed for these large retailers demand high-volume, homogenous food. Knowing and naming are not part of their business of selling food.[6]

In the United States, fewer and fewer of us do much cooking from scratch, and most of what we eat has little to do with where we live. When we decide what to eat for dinner, we surf the options: Thai, Mexican, Emeril, Julia. The food at chain supermarkets has traveled more than 1,500 miles on average. We eat strawberries and raspberries in the dead of winter; our fish come from distant oceans. Contemporary agriculture employs the same tactics of consolidation and mechanization as industrial manufacturing, and the food it creates has a uniform taste and can be sold anywhere.

Why are some chefs championing their knowledge of ingredients at the same time that almost all consumers know so little about where their food comes from and have less and less direct access to local food? A connection exists between the consolidation of choices available to Americans shopping for food and the turn toward local ingredients by these chefs. This connection is related to the way Americans think about food, or the way perceptions frame choices. Two models for understanding and acting dominate in our attempts to procure ingredients and cook: the inevitability of modernization and the quest for an agrarian utopia.[7] The first model rests on the assumption that an industrialized, globalized, and consolidated food supply is the unavoidable consequence of our modern ways, and the second depends upon the assumption that in our past the food supply was knowable, based in communities, and in some sense purer.[8]

Most often these two models are seen as incompatible: you must reject one to embrace the other. The story of chefs building regional cuisines in restaurants, however, suggests that we examine a third way, or perhaps a middle way, one that exemplifies what Gustavo Esteva and Madhu Suri

Prakash call "grassroots postmodernism," a response to modern conditions focused on "rooted local thinking which inspire[s] local actions."[9] The results are an emerging model of food that combines social values with entrepreneurial activities.

According to this alternative model, the central perception of how food is sourced and made shifts from either a monolithic (autocratic) capitalist system or the invention of a (nostalgic) precapitalist tradition.[10] Networks of people—farmers, chefs, and others—combine a quest for economic livelihood with the goal of a sustainable food system. But for these people the quest is also sensory: they want to create food of high quality. They are pursuing a business, a mission, *and* a craft.

I came to understand the importance of restaurants and chefs to contemporary American regional cuisines through an engagement with my own senses. This occurred several years ago while eating dinner at Odessa Piper's restaurant, L'Etoile, in Madison, Wisconsin. I still remember the surprise I experienced during dessert as I cut through the layers of baked filo to find only small nuts nestled in a simple brown-sugar penuche. I was expecting more—maybe fruit or chocolate. I took a bite and was stunned. The nuts were hickory nuts, and they tasted like an intense cross between a pecan and a walnut. Combined with the penuche, they reminded me of maple-walnut ice cream, but the flavor was more complex, with something of a smoky campfire. The texture of the nuts was more delicate than that of either pecans or walnuts; they were almost flaky.

"What are these? Hickory nuts? Where did they come from?" I asked the waiter.

"Oh, they are a local tradition, from here, Wisconsin." Now I was amazed.

I grew up in Madison. The foods I remember from my childhood came from the state's ethnic groups: German bratwursts, Cornish pasties, Norwegian lutefisk. My family ate at L'Etoile on special occasions, but I hadn't been there in years. After I was seduced by the hickory nuts, I realized L'Etoile combined local thinking and local action. In my hometown, of all places. Hickory nuts were just part of a full range of regional ingredients being used by the restaurant's sophisticated chef, Odessa Piper.

Regional cuisines around the world have emerged from attempts to take best advantage of the foods produced locally, typically the only foods available. Regional cuisines are the result of agricultural practices responding to the local environment, and they have arisen from the need to feed surrounding communities rather than distant cities.[11] Northern and southern India, for example, have historically incorporated different staples in their diet, the north using wheat and the south rice. The north has a temperate climate, while the south (and northeast) has a more tropical climate. Rice plays a role in cuisines throughout India, but the proximity of southern India to rice-producing areas means that rice dishes tend to dominate the regional cuisine. Staple cooking oils made from plants suited to the different climates (mustard in the north and coconut in the south) also came to define the cuisines.[12]

When pressed, most Americans can name several regional American cuisines, a combination of ingredients, flavors, and dishes distinctive to a certain geographical region and climate. Southern and Southwestern cuisine immediately come to mind. Iconic ingredients and dishes shape these cuisines: grits, chiles, barbecue, salsa verde. Since we are a nation of immigrants, the inspiration for these dishes usually came from somewhere else, the places left behind. Many of our regional cuisines, however, now consist of only a few ingredients or dishes, often produced any way, anywhere.

Historian Warren Belasco sees American regional cuisine over the past fifty years developing in two directions: the elitist and the populist. Belasco writes, "While elitists craved the perfect smoked wild turkey with fiddlehead ferns, populists pursued the perfect sub with fries."[13] He argues that the more populist fare—Cajun popcorn shrimp and Buffalo chicken wings, for example—became part of the mass consumer food system.[14] Many regional foods were co-opted into mass-market food production. Belasco cogently describes what happened when the counterculture first created healthy foods and then battled with the mass market over who could claim that their products were "healthy," "natural," or "organic." He values the efforts of those involved in building, as he puts it, a countercuisine, rejecting the industrial and capitalist methods favored by the logic of the modernization model. Nevertheless, he wonders if, in the end, their efforts to change the way Americans think about food resulted in American regional foods becoming either part of a "museum" or part of a "multicourse postmodern menu."[15] Piper's story reveals the perils he outlines, but also the possibility for another ending to the story.

Piper is one of an increasing number of American chefs who defy the inevitability of modernization when they cook. She thinks first about where she lives. She takes her inspiration from Wisconsin's bounty, and her cooking is firmly located there. Her dishes, however, are not inherited from the past. Hers is not your mother's cooking.

In 2004 I spent time back home in Madison, talking with Piper, working as a prep cook in her kitchen, and visiting the farmers who supply her restaurant. I wanted to understand how her cooking—what she calls a "regionally reliant cuisine inspired by the creativity of necessity"—came about.[16] I wanted to participate in the everyday rhythms of the restaurant. Priscilla Parkhurst Ferguson has said that "cuisine is not food, it is food transcended, nature transformed into a social product."[17] Witnessing such transformations every day at L'Etoile and learning the dreams, tastes, and realities of Piper, her kitchen crew, and all her food purveyors, I gained a working view of a new culinary model, one that acknowledges both "traditional" and "modern" ways of creating a cuisine.

A CHEF'S STORY

Piper, born in 1952, owned and operated L'Etoile for twenty-eight years, a rare feat of longevity in the restaurant business. Little about her story is usual. Unlike many chefs who draw on their culinary pedigrees for their cooking philosophy, she draws on hardscrabble, back-to-the-land, and political origins. Before she began her restaurant career she lived for two years on a self-sufficient commune in New Hampshire. She then lived for two more years on an organic farm in Rolling Ground, Wisconsin. With her delicate features, long strawberry-blond hair, and bright blue eyes, Piper is still easily imagined as a hippie. She hitchhiked from the East Coast in 1969, arriving in Wisconsin wearing a woven poncho and an Indian-print skirt. "I was very much a '60s activist," she told me.

Piper is intense and at times remote. During conversations she often stops speaking and stares off, searching for words to express her thoughts— except when the subject of Wisconsin foodstuffs comes up. Then she is immediately engaged and animated. JoAnna Guthrie, owner of the organic farm in Rolling Ground where Piper lived, was Piper's mentor. Guthrie was a world traveler, a member of the Theosophical Society, the esoteric, eclectic religious group founded in 1875, and a woman intent on cultural change. Guthrie believed the way to transform American culture was through farming organically and the "little arts" of cooking, serving, and dining. "She didn't treat me seriously; she treated me like a wild child," Piper says. "Her influence caused me to clean it up. JoAnna Guthrie was a cultured lady."

Chefs often create professional lineages for themselves, most frequently tracing their roots back to European ancestors (the French chef who trained them, for example, or the American chef who was trained in Europe or by a European). Piper, who has been profiled in numerous local, regional, and national publications, always mentions Guthrie as her sole culinary mentor. Guthrie, however, was not a trained chef. In fact, she never worked on a farm or in a restaurant before she started one of each in Wisconsin in the early 1970s. Instead she was a social visionary, an early exponent of new age spirituality. This very different genealogy helps explain Piper's intense focus on creating a regionally reliant cuisine. Her foodview was shaped by her revolutionary apprenticeship under Guthrie.

Piper first encountered Guthrie at the latter's home in Chicago, where she and her husband at the time, Dennis Smith, were holding salons promoting theosophy and social change. Guthrie, Piper says, was upset by the purposelessness of the young people she was meeting: "She looked at this generation of seekers and said, 'You need to clean up your act.' " She did not believe that "dropping out" was the proper response to the problems of the day. Guthrie believed that "if we were going to transform society, we had to do it within society using their rules."[18] To that end, Guthrie decided to start a working farm that would become a bucolic retreat for people to come together and work out solutions. She bought a farm, initially called Phoenix Farm, in Rolling Ground, west of Madison. Piper went up to Rolling Ground and ended up staying for two years.

Guthrie also decided Americans needed to be educated about the "art of living," which included making and eating good food. Thirty years ago, fresh ingredients and French food were practically unknown in the nation's heartland. In 1973, Andrea Craig opened Andrea's Restaurant on the Capital Square, just as the Dane County Farmers' Market was beginning to take hold there (she later sold the restaurant to Piper, who changed the name to L'Etoile). Craig recalls trying to make coq au vin, or chicken stew, in the early 1970s and having great difficulty finding fresh mushrooms anywhere in town; only canned button mushrooms were available. She ended up begging her food purveyor to hunt down fresh button mushrooms, an ironic turn of events since Wisconsin is well known (by foragers at least) for its abundance of wild mushrooms.

In 1972 Piper helped Guthrie open the Ovens of Brittany, the first bakery in Madison to produce French-style pastries and breads from scratch. The early workers were all Guthrie disciples, committed to her new age philosophies: "We cooked for her. She was our palate and tasted everything we made," Piper says. "There was a huge amount of personal investment. We were so identified with what we were cooking." No one really thought of it as a business, and they never concerned themselves with costs, but only with obtaining fresh, high-quality ingredients. At first it was difficult to get unsalted butter from the local distributor, for example, so Piper and her colleagues went to nearby supermarkets and bought all the unsalted butter they could find.

According to Guthrie, restaurants and bakeries committed to these principles would introduce people to the true art of living. Guthrie wasn't interested in either managing people or making a profit. Her goals were saving the land, making great food, civilizing Americans, and creating peace. Her vision still propels Odessa Piper and L'Etoile.

FORAGING A LOCAL CUISINE

Piper's cooking is not typical of the Midwestern cuisine that I knew. Rather, it reminds me of French *cuisine du terroir,* or "cooking from the land," meaning with ingredients cultivated in the surrounding region. The phrase also embraces wild foods, and those, too, are found at L'Etoile: plums, crabapples, black walnuts, ramps, purslane, watercress, clover flowers, mushrooms, and, of course, shagbark hickory nuts.

Piper grew up near Hanover, New Hampshire, where her thrifty Yankee parents foraged for mushrooms and other wild foods. As Piper puts it, "I was blessed with life choices knowing what was happening in the wild." Her grassroots approach to ingredients was further solidified when just after high school she joined the Wooden Shoe commune in Canaan, New Hampshire. The goal at Wooden Shoe was to raise and grow all their own food, and she recounts that "an image from the time at the commune is of us trying to grind the wheat to make our own flour." There were times when they did not have enough food, and thus foraging was not just a nostalgic endeavor but a necessity.

Helen and Scott Nearing's classic account of self-sufficient living, *The Good Life,* and their subsequent book *Continuing the Good Life* were important to Piper both philosophically and practically during her time at Wooden Shoe, and then at Phoenix Farm in Wisconsin. *The Good Life* documents a twentieth-century attempt to re-create the past, or, as the Nearings put it, it is "a book about a twentieth-century pioneering venture in a New England community."[19] The Nearings decided to leave New York City in 1932 to live a life based on a "use economy" rather than on the "price-profit economy" they saw dominating American society. Rather than moving out West, however, as pioneers did in the previous century, they chose to move to a remote valley in Vermont. The book is part social treatise and part cooking and gardening manual. JoAnna Guthrie was very influenced by the Nearings, and when Guthrie, Piper, and others were trying to set up Phoenix Farm, "we turned to Rodale Press and the Nearings for instruction."[20]

Since self-sufficiency through farming and foraging were pivotal tasks at both Wooden Shoe and Phoenix Farm, Piper's cooking apprenticeship truly focused on the ingredients first, and only later on techniques and traditions. A passage in *The Good Life* eloquently describes the fundamental assumptions of Piper's approach to cuisine: "These food habits of ours we found simple, economical, and practicable, though they were perhaps not usual for twentieth-century Americans. With advancing civilization, the American diet pattern, like everything else, has undergone a thoroughgoing change. The business of procuring the necessities of life has been shifted from the wood lot, the garden, the kitchen and the family to the factory and the large-scale enterprise. In our case we moved our center back to the land."[21]

When she opened L'Etoile in 1976, Piper heard about shagbark hickory nuts and began to ask where she could buy them. Eventually, a vendor at the Madison farmers' market brought her some. Now L'Etoile purchases two hundred pounds of them a year, and they are a central feature on the menu.

"They are the nobility of nuts," Piper says, "what the black truffle is to mushrooms." Shagbark hickory nuts have "more flavor . . . more snap, more toothfeel than either pecans or walnuts." Unlike most nuts, hickory nuts require toasting to intensify their flavor and create the shattering texture that makes them unique. Each meal at L'Etoile begins with a hickory-nut shaman, a crisp, light cracker made of chopped hickory nuts, flour, and butter. The cracker is garnished with fresh goat's milk cheese, a seasonally changing selection of chopped herbs, and half a hickory nut. Piper says, "I really want to get the miracle of this place into everybody's mouth right at the start."

Shagbark hickory *(Carya ovata)*, a North American native, is a relative of the pecan that's widely found in Ohio, Indiana, Illinois, Wisconsin, and Iowa. It's hard to miss because the unique bark peels away from the tree in thin strips from six inches to four feet long. The trees are often found along roadsides. On the small dairy farms that still dominate the rolling hills of southern Wisconsin, the cornfields and cow pastures are interspersed with stands of oak and hickory.

Gathering hickory nuts has long been a part of rural Wisconsin family life. I went looking for hickory nuts during the late fall, when the leaves had turned a vibrant mustard yellow. The nuts had dropped to the ground, and their husks, formerly moist and green, were now hard and black, having split open along four ribs to expose thin but strong inner shells. Several people have told me that when they were young, their families would take a drive in the country and pull over when someone spotted a tree. The kids piled out of the car and raced to see who could pick up the most nuts the fastest. These people recalled with pleasure the nut's luscious combination of sweet and smoky flavors. But when the subject of shelling came up, their eyes tended to glaze over.

Shelling the nuts is drudgery. Once the hard shell is broken, typically with a hammer, the meats have to be pried out. One serious harvester I met uses a dental pick. A pound of nutmeats requires a lot of cracking and picking and scraping—up to four hours' worth—which explains why hickory nuts are rarely found in supermarkets or restaurants. Conventional wisdom in Wisconsin holds that this activity is "one for the old-timers."

The main place one can find shelled shagbark hickory nuts for sale today is at farmers' markets. At the Madison farmers' market longtime farmers or retirees run the stands that sell the nuts. Harvey Ruehlow of the Nut Factory says, "The old guys are dying off, and the young people don't have time." He and his wife, Beverly, learned to forage and pick from Harvey's dad, who loved to eat cinnamon rolls topped with chopped hickory nuts (old-timers use hickory nuts only for baking). Most of the nuts are bought by chefs and gourmet home cooks.

Shagbark hickory nuts are central to Piper's regionally reliant cuisine. This cuisine, like France's regional cuisines, develops in relationship to the surrounding geography. In France, specific places are known for their distinctive foods that serve as a building block for the regional cuisine. In *The Food of France* Waverly Root famously divides the entire country into the domains of butter, lard, and oil, and then describes seventeen different culinary regions. He says there is an "ecological relationship, I suppose you might call it, between geography and cuisine."[22]

The building blocks of a regional cuisine are foods that prosper in a particular environment, such as olives, rosemary, and truffles in Provence and apples in Normandy. During the twentieth century the French worked hard to preserve and promote the geographical identity of food and wines. The *produits du terroir* awarded Appellation d'Origine Contrôlée status (and others that were not) concern the past, the heritage of a place. These are ingredients and dishes with a history.

These efforts have always been conservative, in the literal sense. In Bordeaux, cabernet sauvignon grapes are the traditional varietal, and Bordeaux wines must be made from cabernet sauvignon grapes in order to be awarded AOC status. In Provence, olive oil, goat cheese, and olives are long-standing and celebrated ingredients. The downside of protecting traditional foods and practices in France has been to turn *produits du terroir* into arti-facts in a living history museum. Innovation and change are frowned upon. Such conservatism can also be seen in the often-timeless quality of the food served in restaurants there.

A modern American *cuisine du terroir* has to be more orchestrated. Most of Wisconsin's citizens do not interact with the land on a daily basis. Our re-cent history revolves around trampling on rather than preserving the agrar-ian landscape. Thus many are skeptical about the existence of terroir here, for we have lost our culinary lineages to a place, if they even existed in the first place. If nurturing and responding to the bounty of a region define a *cuisine du terroir,* ours must be intentional. Ingredients, recipes, and dishes that reflect Wisconsin are not the lucky accidents of times past.

To find local foods anywhere in the United States takes concerted effort. France, in comparison, has been able to retain greater connections among land, ingredients, and regional cooking and eating habits. The French can thus choose between the small cheese and pastry shops, butchers, and farmers' markets that populate towns big and small and the massive Car-refour supermarkets found at the edge of every town. In the United States, however, we have moved toward mass-produced, mechanized, and homoge-nous food in the last century. Most Americans can only choose between big and bigger supermarkets. And these days it is a strange combination of rural folks and urban foodies who are knowledgeable about taste and place.

With the ever-increasing consolidation of agriculture, Americans have also become accustomed to a decline in varieties of ingredients. Confronted with fingerling and Red Finn potatoes, most are flummoxed. Their culinary reper-toire extends only to russets, reds, and possibly Yukon Golds. We find it much more difficult to trace our foods back through time, identifying the same grape or the same style of goat cheese that was consumed in the past, whether it was ten or one hundred years ago. Here, *cuisine du terroir* has to be invented as much as preserved. At L'Etoile, you can see this dual sensibility at work.

The French foodview was part of Piper's unorthodox training in the restaurant business. When JoAnna Guthrie started the Ovens of Brittany, she decided to adhere to two operating principles: one, to look to France for ideas about cooking techniques and dishes to prepare, and two, to always cook from scratch. Piper says that in the early days, "we were literally cooking out of *Mastering the Art of French Cooking*."[23] Their countercuisine was inspired by both the forests and farms of Wisconsin and the regional French dishes they used as guides.

The regional foods that make up a *cuisine du terroir* taste of the land from which they come. Certain plants and animals are adapted to a particular spot—its soil, rocks, and climate—and draw out a distinct flavor. Among foods from a single locality, strong harmonies can occur. Historically, such foods developed slowly, and generations living in one place tended to favor what worked well and tasted best, other things being equal.[24] In many ways Piper is inventing a Wisconsin *cuisine du terroir* from scratch. Her ingredients reflect the triumvirate of values long promoted by Europeans: geographic specificity, artisanal methods, and locally adapted varieties and breeds. But equally important for her are "communities and cultures. Terroir is something that arises out of the relationships between artisans and the land," she says. She doesn't work alone. She also says she is committed to the "love that brings something out between people and agriculture." And doesn't bringing the pioneer spirit into the *business* of making food suit us in the United States, where we are more often spurred on by passion and enterprise than inspired by customs and tradition?

TASTING WISCONSIN

Directly across the street from L'Etoile is the Dane County Farmers' Market. Since it opened in 1972, it has become the largest farmers' market in the United States, and it is one of only a few that require vendors to produce everything they sell. Each week more than three hundred farmers, cheese

FIGURE 7. Harmony Valley Farm Stand, Dane County Farmers' Market, Madison, Wisconsin. PHOTO COURTESY OF RICHARD DEWILDE, HARMONY VALLEY FARM.

makers, bakers, and other food producers from all over the state set up stands and thousands of customers stroll the market, always (in a practice without clear origin) in a counterclockwise direction. During an early lean period for L'Etoile, Piper herself made croissants and sold them at the market, using the proceeds to buy produce at other stands. That's when she first made friends among the vendors.

The market is Piper's muse. Every Saturday she is there by 8 A.M., wearing a hefty butcher's apron and carrying a wicker basket. Either she or the restaurant's "market forager," who when I visited was Julie Wuesthoff, pulls a child's red wagon. The women spend the entire morning traveling back and forth between the market and the restaurant and talking to vendors about what is new or special. L'Etoile has fifty-five seats and occupies a long, narrow rectangle. The kitchen is at the back, a small bar with a shiny copper counter is in the middle, and a brick-walled dining room looks out onto the street. Decoration in the dining room is minimal, save for a five-foot-high map of Wisconsin that covers a wall between the windows and a stairwell. More than sixty red pushpins dot the map. From each, a red string leads to a small card, one for each of the Wisconsin farmers, artisans, and foragers who provide the restaurant's ingredients.[25]

A map connecting the lamb chops with Crawford Farm in New Glarus, the apples with Weston's Antique Apple Orchard in New Berlin, and the hickory nuts with Ray Pamperin's Green Market in Juneau creates compass points for the diner navigating the menu. With the farmers' market and L'Etoile (and now several other restaurants) at the center, there has emerged a new tradition of farmers and chefs working together, developing a cuisine based on taste and place.

The creation of this year-round supply of high-quality Wisconsin ingredients requires the hard work and good will of many people. L'Etoile makes a popular salad of roasted mushrooms, either wild or cultivated exotic ones. When I ate the salad, it contained maitake, chicken of the woods, and honeycups, all wild and from Wisconsin. The foragers rarely call in advance, and the varieties they offer change from week to week. "Sometimes they show up at seven at night during service," Wuesthoff said resignedly, "but we're always happy to see them."

The mushroom salad also includes sprouted peanuts, almonds, lentils, and blanched carrots. I complimented Piper on the contrast between the crisp, sweet carrots, the various fresh sprouts, and the rich, earthy mushrooms. "I wish I could take credit for that idea," she replied. It came from the Sprout People, a farm in the small town of Gays Mills. Otherwise she probably would have continued with a more traditional accompaniment to the mushrooms, such as cooked green lentils from France. But the unorthodox mix is perfect, and it comes from Wisconsin.

The carrots in the salad come from Harmony Valley Farm in Viroqua, ninety miles northwest of Madison. Piper began to buy from the farm, one of her most important suppliers, in the late 1980s. When you drive from Madison to Viroqua, you arrive at a high plateau, and then, following the twists of a country road, you descend into a valley with a small river. Harmony Valley's long and narrow fields are almost all on bottomland. When I visited the farm, many of the leaves were already gone from the trees. Brown fronds of asparagus waved in the breeze, and the year's first frost had turned the strawberry leaves a purple that contrasted with the light brown millet planted between the rows.

Richard DeWilde has farmed organically for twenty years; Linda Halley had been helping her parents on their farm in Rock County, south of Madison, when she joined him at Harmony Valley in 1992. The two now grow more than sixty kinds of vegetables in addition to maintaining a small herd of Black Angus cattle; their community-supported agriculture program has more than 450 member families, and, in addition to selling to restaurants and at the Dane County Farmers' Market, they sell to Whole Foods. Linda Halley describes their relationship with Piper, saying, "We have a dialogue."

Sometimes Halley and DeWilde experiment with new crops that might appeal to chefs like Piper. One year they tried cardoons. Halley and DeWilde helped Piper tackle the greatest challenge of cooking with regional ingredients—finding regionally grown produce in winter. (Alice Waters, America's grand dame of using regional ingredients in a restaurant, has visited Piper and L'Etoile three times to see how much is possible in a snowbelt. Critics continually point out to Waters that local, seasonal cooking is easy in her California climate.) Piper had wanted to extend her use of Wisconsin produce to the winter, but she had no space at the restaurant for a root cellar in which to store the fall harvest. Almost no restaurant keeps food for a long period of time. Few can afford to tie up cash buying ingredients far in advance, and in the typical restaurant kitchen there is not a lot of space. Piper wanted to extend her local buying into the winter season, but she had diffi-culty figuring out how to make it happen. She approached them and asked if Halley and DeWilde could store crops and deliver them to her every two weeks. "It was a learning experience for her and us," says DeWilde. Piper had to estimate in advance the varieties and amounts of vegetables she would need during the coming winter and early spring. Harmony Valley Farm had to pro-vide long-term storage space. This extended conversation between farmers and chef has shaped their farming and cooking, transforming both the agrar-ian landscape and, as Piper puts it, "the landscape of the palate," too.

Often when people come by the Harmony Valley stand at the farmers' market they will say, "We ate this at L'Etoile. How can I cook it?" The farm now sells to other restaurants, including Harvest in Madison and North Pond in Chicago. The two items they grow exclusively for Piper are Cape gooseberries and crosnes, a root vegetable that is a cross between a parsnip and a Jerusalem artichoke. A particular twist to their farming practices in-spired by chefs is a focus on visual aesthetics: red savoy cabbages and beauty heart radishes taste great *and* look beautiful. At the farmers' market, these beauty pageant vegetables are piled high: chioggia beets; dark green lacinato kale; kuri, butternut, and delicata squashes; garlic and chili wreaths; and more. Harmony Valley's farm stand is gorgeous.

On L'Etoile's cold-weather menu are Harmony Valley parsnips, parsley root, beets, winter radishes, sweet potatoes, horseradish, carrots (red, yel-low, and orange), red cipollinis (small, flat Italian onions), gold ball (heir-loom) and sweet scarlet (Japanese hybrid) turnips, red Savoy cabbages, and Jerusalem artichokes. The last is one of Piper's "totem" winter ingredients. She roasts the tubers until they are soft and uses the puree to boost the fla-vor of soups, including classic vichyssoise and sweet pea, and to form a base for sauces like the one she calls "a winter beurre blanc." She uses the puree in place of mustard to bind vinaigrette, the Jerusalem artichokes' sweetness subtly balancing the vinegar's sharp acidity.

FIGURE 8. Harmony Valley Farm, Viroqua, Wisconsin.
PHOTO BY AMY B. TRUBEK.

The amount of fresh regional produce does decline to 30 percent of all the produce L'Etoile serves from January to March, but the use of preserved Wisconsin fruits and vegetables brings the total amount of Wisconsin produce to 60 percent even in the dead of winter. Although Piper can't consistently create winter menus that use regional ingredients exclusively, each year she devises one "Menu for Impossible Months" that uses only three ingredients not originating in the Midwest (salt, pepper, and chocolate).

Chefs' quest for flavor has also benefited longtime farmers who have ignored the push toward growing fewer varieties. One of Piper's favorite market stands is Weston's Antique Apple Orchard. In his late seventies, Ken Weston, whose parents started the orchard in 1934, is a former professor of mathematics who is articulate and fit. He is often at the stand, and he is the only full-time employee of the orchard, which has more than 700 trees and 101 varieties. Some, such as Avocado and Old Church, are wild crosses of the antique varieties first planted by Weston's mother. Many of the varieties are difficult to find elsewhere in the United States: Ashmead's Kernel, Cox's Orange Pippin, Pink Pearl, Hidden Rose, Caville Blanc d'Hiver, Black Gilliflower, King David.

When I visited the stand with Piper one October morning, a volunteer offered me a Montgomery Ward McIntosh, describing it as "the original varietal before all the oomph was taken out." The flavor was sweet and smooth, with a finish like rosewater. Although Piper already knew the taste of all the varieties on display, she examined each one with the intensity of a sommelier at a wine tasting. She would pick up an apple, sniff it, turn it around in her hand, and mention possible uses for it that night at the restaurant.

Throughout the year L'Etoile's menus offer variations on a theme: a few ingredients dominate from appetizers through desserts. During the fall, Piper and her staff expand and deepen their use of apples, which come from Weston and from Future Fruit Farm, an organic producer of apples, pears, and other tree fruits. Last October, at the peak of apple season, the restaurant's amuse-bouche combined a pickled wild crabapple with toasted walnuts, Roth Kase buttermilk blue cheese from nearby Monroe, and toasted walnut bread. The combination was at once creamy, tart, and earthy. Next, seared foie gras was set against Pink Pearl apples and a cider glaze. Among main courses, Wisconsin rainbow trout came with more Pink Pearl apples, whose pink blush echoed the colorful skin of the fish.

Apples also showed up with cheeses and then dessert. Both at L'Etoile and at the farmers' market, I was surprised at the modest quality and limited number of farm-made Wisconsin cheeses, but Dairy State cheese making remains heavily dominated by industrial producers. Piper had nevertheless found more than fifteen Wisconsin artisan cheese makers. My plate held Hook's cheddar, Carr Valley fontina, and Pleasant Ridge Reserve cow's milk cheese, which is made in the style of a Beaufort. The cheeses were accompanied by thinly sliced apples, all russet varieties chosen for their crunch and honeyed flavors. Hook's ten-year-old cheddar made an especially neat contrast of soft and rich with the tart and crisp. The restaurant's tarte tatin was made with Spitzenbergs, which keep their shape when cooked and combine tartness with sweetness. Piper calls Spitzenberg "the apple equivalent of the Riesling grape," aromatic and melding sweet with dry.

On Sunday the restaurant was closed, and much of the kitchen crew drove to Weston's Antique Apple Orchard to pick windfalls and press cider. They brought back to the restaurant more than sixty gallons of cider, and the next day it was put to simmer on the stove. Three days later it had been reduced to about ten gallons of viscous syrup they call "cider redux," a signature ingredient of the restaurant. It serves as a base for both sweet and savory sauces, it glazes meat and fish, and it is dribbled on plates as a garnish.

Piper's culinary vision always remains earthbound. During the weekly menu meeting that Tuesday her goal was to bring out the unique flavor of each apple variety—its particular appleness. Many ideas were proposed, but at the heart of each that was chosen were the distinctive tastes of the apples. No dish merely displayed the technical virtuosity of the chef and kitchen staff. For dessert, Piper wanted "an apple implosion, caramelized and soft

FIGURE 9. Tractor and trees, Weston's Antique Apple Orchard, Wisconsin. PHOTO BY AMY B. TRUBEK.

but still with a shape." Chef de cuisine Tory Miller wondered, "Could we garnish with a caramelized or brûlée apple?" The conversation turned to cider ganache, a Piper creation in which cider redux is reduced still further with heavy cream to become something like Latin American *dulce de leche*. Pastry chef Alisha Bartholomew went to work. On Friday night, an apple charlotte was on the menu, and the deep, velvety ganache served with the light maple-flavored genoise was sublime.

BUT IS IT JUST A RESTAURANT CUISINE?

Does it reduce the significance of modern Wisconsin *cuisine du terroir* that it depends so much on one professional chef cooking in one restaurant? No, not if we consider the importance of restaurants to our everyday decisions about where and what to eat. Today information about ingredients, techniques, and dishes is more likely to be passed from chef to customer than from mother to daughter. Most people first taste and learn about hickory nuts, pasture-raised beef, radicchio, or cloth-bound cheddar in restaurants. A regional cuisine in our postmodern era must involve both the domestic and public spheres, for we cook and eat in both arenas.

When chefs serve local food, they educate diners by exposing them to unexpected flavors and preparations. "The taste of place is very much an acclimatization of the palate. That recognition does not occur naturally," Piper comments. When chefs feature local foods, they become teachers, introducing their customers to the importance of freshness and season. Each L'Etoile menu begins with a short paragraph detailing the Wisconsin ingredients used that week, ending with these lines: "Some of the finest foods produced anywhere in the world are available here in the Midwest. We thank you for supporting the farmers who supply L'Etoile and valuing their commitment to these patient arts."

Chefs constantly seek variety—they want distinctive ingredients to create unusual dishes—and they have the purchasing power to influence the market. Small farmers respond to their demands by diversifying what they grow and how they grow it. But challenges arise when an entrepreneur is guided by a social mission rather than economic concerns. Piper readily admits that she has never used a traditional restaurant business plan:

"[Running the restaurant] always felt like a highly personal mission or obligation. It was my turn to carry the torch for a while."[26] This sense of mission kept her going, even during difficult financial periods. Eventually she was able to make L'Etoile a viable business, paying her workers good wages and taking a salary for herself, as well as paying dozens of farmers, foragers, and others for their products. She did not take iconic regional dishes and place them on a menu full of standard restaurant fare (prime rib and mashed potatoes, lasagna). Instead, she developed her menus using her *vision:* Piper was an agrarian utopian when she *thought* about her food, but along the way her taste of Wisconsin became part of a modern, market-driven business.

The "middle way" of American regional cuisine is certainly fraught with contradictions. In a cold climate like Wisconsin's, this means buying locally in the winter is difficult. Putting large amounts of food by in the harvest months is not always feasible. More and more restaurants across the United States are buying locally and regionally, but their use of these ingredients drops off sharply in winter, and higher costs often limit the amount of local produce that a restaurant can buy at a given time. A pound of hickory nuts costs around $17, while a pound of pecans is only $8. No matter how much chefs in Wisconsin might love hickory nuts, most rarely use them. Piper's idealism and imagination mean that she makes unusually large and consistent purchases of regional ingredients, but even she tends to reserve Harmony Valley Farm's carrots as showpieces on the plate; when she's making stock, carrots from California will do. Still, she does distinguish herself from other chefs also committed to purchasing local food in several ways: the extensiveness of her direct buying; the starring role these ingredients play in her menus; and her responsiveness to their characteristic flavors in the creation of each dish.

Meanwhile, regional ingredients and foods don't make it into the average home because they are not widely available, they are frequently more expensive than other foods, and they are sometimes unfamiliar or intimidating.

Shoppers might look at a display of frisée or Jerusalem artichokes, wonder what exactly one does with them, and then move on. But the same home cooks might take on the challenge if the raw materials are put into a context: perhaps they have eaten them in a dish at L'Etoile, heard a story about them shared by the grower, or received a recipe from a friend who shops regularly at the farmers' market. At Madison's year-round farmers' market, each purchase, each personal exchange affirms the connections necessary to sustain a *cuisine du terroir* in the years to come.

And Piper's cooking has a widening influence. Harmony Valley Farm also sells to other restaurants that stress regional ingredients, including Harvest in Madison and North Pond in Chicago. Harvest's two owners worked at L'Etoile before opening their own restaurant two doors down and right across the street from the farmers' market. Piper believes many people have already begun to recognize a Wisconsin taste in the ingredients from the region. She speaks of "a newly arrived polyglot cuisine starting as people settle in and familiarize themselves and cook." She says, "We're patterning and imprinting."

MOVING ON

In May 2005 Piper sold L'Etoile to chef de cuisine Tory Miller and his sister, Traci Miller. Piper had long wanted to shift away from the day-to-day work of running the restaurant and spend more time with her husband. This took a long time, but Miller was interested in owning the restaurant and wanted to preserve the restaurant's philosophy of regionally reliant cuisine.

I visited Miller at the restaurant six months later and had dinner there with my father. We made our way slowly up the stairs. We got to the top of the stairs and stopped briefly on the landing, looking out over the triangular bar just to the right. Who was sitting at the bar eating dinner but Odessa Piper. She had just flown in from Maryland to spend a few days transcribing recipes and had decided to stop by the restaurant. Piper and I exchanged hugs, chatted a bit, and then each sat down to taste the food prepared by the next generation of L'Etoile.

The menu looked much the same, with the same paper, font, and lovely L'Etoile design, a cross between a burst of shooting stars and a delicate wildflower. When Piper owned the restaurant, the menu always began with a paragraph praising the farmers and the others who provide the ingredients. The new menu has a similar narrative, now on the reverse, with a list of the farms and ingredients that are featured on this season's menu right below. Though the menu was missing Piper's lofty and lyrical voice, the Millers gracefully related their cooking philosophy: "We've observed that this cooperation with people and their environment is at the heart of all great cultures, and we strive to cultivate artisan traditions for our own."[27]

When we sat down, we were offered the now-classic hickory nut shaman, a buttery cracker with a goat cheese star and a toasted hickory nut on top. After we placed our order we were given an amuse-bouche of apple soup with very finely chopped bacon and a bit of cream. The soup, which was a nice balance of tart and creamy, seemed to use apple cider as its base. For an appetizer I had salad of Shooting Star Farm sylvetta and frisée, Willow Creek Farm lardons, croutons, and a New Century Farm poached egg with a Dijon mustard and red wine vinaigrette. Miller definitely goes in for a less rustic presentation style than his predecessor, even though his underlying assumptions about ingredients and combinations remain in the Piper tradition. The croutons are perfect little quarter-inch squares, the lardons lovely two-inch bâtonnets. Miller was trained at the French Culinary Institute, and mastery of the classic cuts is a must there. His style adds a new level of precision to the look and taste of the food. The egg is nicely poached and tastes lovely mixed into the slightly sharp greens. Next we were presented with an intermezzo of seaberry sorbet. The seaberries are an unusual berry variety grown at Karendale Farm in the nearby town of Oregon. The flavor was just lovely, combining tangerine, raspberry, and grapefruit notes in a sorbet with a lovely light orange color.

For a main course I chose Wild Lake Superior walleye with Snug Haven spinach, steamed Manila clams, crisp potato ribbons, lemon aïoli, and shallot broth. The walleye was perfectly prepared, the skin crispy and the flesh moist. The shallot broth was delicate and contrasted well with the creamy and citrusy aïoli. The clams were a bit extraneous but well prepared. Miller sees this dish as a variation of the classic Great Lakes fish fry, with the potato ribbons a welcome substitute for the typical greasy French fries.

Earlier in the day I had taken a tour around the Dane County Farmers' Market and then talked to Tory Miller. When he came out to greet me, he was harried but welcoming. He and Traci had been working hard over the past few months to renovate and revamp the café downstairs, which they had renamed Café Soleil. In the past the café had focused primarily on baked goods and coffee and drew in the largest crowds on market Saturdays. Miller was working on expanding the menu options to include a number of sandwiches and other items. His sandwiches were inspired by his relationships with the farms: warm roast Willow Creek Farm pork shoulder and Artesian Farm trout salad, for example. The café menu was taking up a lot of his time, often because of the new problems posed by, say, transforming a lovely free-range turkey coming in the back door into a brined and roasted slice of turkey breast that could be served in a sandwich. Most cafés or delis in town would be happy with the preboned, brined, roasted, and generally processed turkey breasts that they can buy from their distributors. The difference between Miller's approach and that of a nearby deli was an investment in time, which always translates into increased cost, although for Miller the ultimate reward was a much higher-quality sandwich and a continued relationship with the farm Blue Valley Gardens, which provided the turkeys.

I asked Miller about his feelings about continuing the many working relationships Piper had formed with farmers, cheese makers, and others over the years. "I believe in them as well," he replied. "Over the two years I was chef de cuisine I had formed strong relationships with them, too." In fact, Miller did most of the day-to-day ordering while working under Piper. When I asked Miller how he thought the farmers were responding to the new regime at L'Etoile, his response surprised me. He said, "I think the farmers are taking care of me a lot more. At first everyone wondered if I was going to continue to buy locally as extensively as Odessa." When they realized that Miller was as committed to them as Piper was, and that he was going to come to the market every Saturday (he now has a blue wooden wagon he brings with him each week), they began to help him out. He would stop by a stand and discover that special items had been set aside for him. And, "If I forgot to place a midweek order, the farmers would bring along what they thought I need." L'Etoile is truly a collaborative effort.

Miller's background is remarkably unlike that of Piper, but he, too, combines agrarian idealism and market realism when he speaks of the restaurant's future. Miller, who is in his early thirties, hails from a restaurant family in Racine, Wisconsin. His family owned a diner named the Park Inn, and he and Traci grew up working there. He attended college for several years before he attended the French Culinary Institute in New York City. He ended up living in the city for five years, working in a number of restaurants. His major culinary influence during that time was Bill Telepan, until 2004 the chef at the Judson Grill and now the owner of the newly opened Telepan. Telepan also relies on farmers and markets for his culinary inspiration; he just published the cookbook *Inspired by Ingredients*. Miller's culinary apprenticeship occurred in the nation's biggest city, but amidst the concrete he sought out chefs celebrating the soil in their restaurants.

Eventually, Miller decided to come back to Wisconsin, where he wanted to work at L'Etoile. His lifelong experience in small restaurants means he understands the importance of cultivating relationships to success: "My goal is delicious food and happy customers." His quest for deliciousness starts from the soil: "You get all these ideas from the great ingredients, and you want to be able to use them." He also needs to consider food costs, for "it is a constant battle, especially when I see waste with expensive ingredients."[28] And so the dance between idealism and realism continues.

I was impressed that Miller's aspirations extend beyond the walls of L'Etoile to include other nearby restaurants. He spoke of the new brewpub coming in next door, between L'Etoile and Harvest, another restaurant that uses local ingredients extensively. "I want to establish this corner of the [Capital] Square that is local and sustainable. I want us to all work together for better returns for our farmers." Surprisingly, Miller does not display the hyperindividualism that characterizes many young and talented chefs: "A lot of people want to hold on to their power—but to me, if everyone is chipping in, it *will* be better in the long run. This is how I want L'Etoile to affect the community. I like the feeling of community I get."[29]

In southern Wisconsin, where there are passionate believers like Odessa Piper and Tory Miller and the thriving Dane County Farmers' Market, I see hope for a countercuisine built as much on the relationships of people with one another as on the land around them. Unlike Old World cuisines, the emerging regional cuisine in southern Wisconsin isn't based on allegiance to the past but on nurturing each and every ally. One of L'Etoile's hickory nut suppliers told me, "Odessa has been a big influence on us keeping at this." According to Piper, "All we did is pay attention to the relationship between artisans and the land, and now we have a beautiful cuisine."

More than forty years ago Elizabeth David, in her book *French Provincial Cooking,* commented on France's *cuisines du terroir,* which she saw even then as threatened: "Recipes alone are not enough. A flourishing tradition of local cookery implies also genuine products; the cooks and the housewives must be backed up by the dairy farmers, the pig breeders and pork butchers, the market gardeners and the fruit growers, otherwise regional cookery simply retreats into the realms of folklore."[30] She realized then the necessity of a network of people working in concert to any vibrant regional cuisine.

And for David, chefs and restaurants play a crucial role in promoting "dishes derive[d] from peasant and farmhouse cookery."[31] Like Piper, however, she does not think the chef's job is to invent a culinary heritage museum; rather, "the professional cooks and housewives adapt the old methods to changing tastes . . . [and] chefs develop new dishes based on the old ones but still using the essential ingredients."[32] Restaurants have long created vital spaces for a *cuisine du terroir:* spaces of collaboration, of imagination, of commensality. As cooking occurs more and more outside the home, those chefs, restaurants, cookbook authors, and others are more important than ever to any cuisine. For better or for worse, the *business* of food may be where our culinary futures lie.

In Madison, bratwursts and Cornish pasties are still standard fare, especially on football Saturdays, when seventy thousand people have tailgate parties before they head to the football stadium to watch the University of Wisconsin Badgers play. But now there is another version of regional cuisine in the making. Piper, her more than eighty purveyors, L'Etoile's customers, and shoppers at the farmers' markets all look to the land for their livelihood and as their inspiration. As Esteva and Prakash put it, "Without the tending of human hands, top soil is being blown away, along with the stories, rituals and practices that make 'cultural soil.' "[33] Like Elizabeth David, Piper and all her allies take to heart the importance of regional ingredients as they create a thoroughly modern taste of Wisconsin, combining the rationales of the market with utopian ideals. And so a contemporary American *cuisine du terroir* is created.

FIVE

CONNECTING FARMERS AND CHEFS IN VERMONT

JUNE 1994 WAS THE FIRST TIME I EVER ENTERED THE STATE OF VERMONT. THIS was not a vacation. Since I was a child, my lodestar for New England respites had always been the seashore. This time, however, I was driving up Interstate 89 and over the Connecticut River separating New Hampshire and Vermont for a job interview at the New England Culinary Institute (NECI). Finishing my dissertation, broke, and thinking about gainful employment, I decided to look for a job at a culinary school. A former cooking colleague and graduate of NECI recommended I give them a call. A month later here I was, driving into the Green Mountains.

I had spent a lot of time in France in the past years doing research. During my most recent trip I had spent a week in Alsace, a rural, hilly, and agricultural province in northeast France bordering Germany. Driving into Vermont, looking at the hills rising on either side of the highway, mostly forested but also covered by pasture and farms, my first thought was "Oh, this looks a lot like France, especially Alsace." I was pleasantly surprised and a little awestruck by the beauty and remoteness of the landscape. Little did I know as I drove north and worried about interview questions that Vermont's landscape would come to be a big part of my life.

In due time I moved to Montpelier, Vermont, to start a job at the New England Culinary Institute. Fresh from eight years of living in center city Philadelphia, with some trips to India, England, and France thrown into the mix, moving to north-central Vermont was truly like moving to a foreign country. Every decision was different: how to drive, where to shop, what to wear. I remember being amazed at how much time people spent talking about their gardens and their woodstoves. And I will never forget going to my first party that first winter. I watched as more than half the guests took off their big, clunky boots and then proceeded to replace them with wool or fleece slippers! I was in foreign territory.

Since I was working at a culinary school, my initial introduction to Vermont was very much through food. The chefs I worked with every day were passionate about all aspects of food and cooking, from the ingredients to cooking methods, creating menus, and satisfying customers. Early on I realized that although most had been trained in French techniques, when it came to thinking about ingredients, they tended to look to the surrounding region. I was amazed to hear stories of chefs going out into the woods to forage for mushrooms, ramps, and other wild foods to bring into their kitchens. And then there was the cheese. Everyone loved to talk about the small cheese makers in our midst, from larger concerns such as Cabot Creamery Cooperative to the hands-down favorite among chefs who shopped at the local farmers' market, Lazy Lady Farm, run by Laini Fondiller. Over time, I became more and more interested in Vermont's world of food, and that interest informed not only how I taught, but also how I made daily decisions about what food to buy and where to buy it.

I was not alone in my desire to combine my fascination with Vermont farms and farm products and my pedagogy. During the mid-1990s there were a number of chefs and administrators thinking about the importance of the farm-to-table connection for the school and our students. Chefs David Miles, Jamie Eisenberg, Lyndon Virkler, Brad Koehler, and others were all combining practical skills and information about the food system in their courses. We were all taking our students on field trips to visit local farmers, cheese makers, farmers' markets, and even local slaughterhouses. Working at NECI and living in Vermont, I came to see an intersection of culinary and agrarian values and also witnessed these values becoming a part of everyday practices throughout the state. Such an intersection may not have been as clearly marked had I ended up at a culinary school in another region or in a major metropolitan center. Here in Vermont a happy confluence occurred between a growing number of small, diversified farmers and a constant flow of chefs and culinary students. Farming, cooking, and eating became fruitfully connected.

An example of such new connections was the decision by Pam Knights, at the time head of public relations and outreach, to bring Michael Ableman to speak at NECI. Knights's initial interest was in supporting the organic agriculture movement. She dates her decision to become active in promoting organic agriculture to the spring of 1994, when she first heard Ableman speak at the annual conference of the International Association of Culinary Professionals. She was inspired, and "his talk changed my life," says Knights. Ableman farmed organically in suburban Santa Barbara, California, for twenty years (he now farms in British Columbia), and he was interested in the growth of organic farming worldwide. Ableman is also a photographer and activist.

When she heard him, Ableman had recently published *From the Good Earth*. In 1984 Ableman traveled to mainland China and realized that traditional farming practices were under threat around the world. He ended up traveling internationally and creating a gorgeous photo essay documenting both what remained and what was being lost in food and agriculture around the world. Ableman had developed a multimedia presentation to promote his new book. This sophisticated and compelling presentation, during which slides of small farmers from around the globe showed behind him on three different screens as he spoke about the plight of farming today, captivated Pam Knights.

Knights invited the author and farmer to Vermont as part of the New England Culinary Institute's guest lecture series in January 1995. I remember going to Ableman's presentation on a bitterly cold January day, sitting in a crowded room of students, faculty, and others watching slide after slide of gorgeous small farms and beautiful food. After his talk we were motivated to do even more with our students. I went on to create an "agriculture" portion of my food history class, eventually getting local organic farmer Joey Klein involved (he ended up continuing to teach at the school for many years). Jamie Eisenberg started to bring her students to Intervale, an urban farming project in Burlington, and she also developed a purchasing program with a small farmer there. Pam Knights continued her outreach efforts and began to develop relationships with individual farmers and the Vermont Department of Agriculture as well. Ableman's passionate advocacy for small-scale organic farms echoed the calls of many sustainable agriculture advocates in Vermont.

By bringing together the voices of farmers with the voices of those who work with food primarily *after* it leaves the fields and farms, Knights and others have helped usher in a new chapter in the long history of Vermont's working landscape. This new chapter, I argue, involves building a network of taste producers and tastemakers, including farmers, cheese makers, chefs, and other food artisans as well as government officials and consumers. All of these people are allied by their desire to maintain Vermont's working landscape and preserve family farms by focusing on the unique taste of place found in the Green Mountain State.

FARMING VERMONT STYLE

Before the arrival of Europeans, and, in fact, for more than a century after the colonists had begun to settle in coastal New England, Vermont was sparsely settled. It is estimated that in 1600 the total Native American population in the region was around 7,500, consisting chiefly of two Abenaki settlements, one in the Champlain Valley and one in the Upper Connecticut River Valley.[1] Even though the first European explorer thought to have contact with the Abenaki, Samuel de Champlain, arrived in 1609, permanent settlements of Europeans were few and far between until the late eighteenth century.

As environmental historian William Cronon points out, initially the early colonists were focused on re-creating their primarily agrarian worldview based on fixed property and domesticated agriculture. Even though the Abenaki did cultivate corn, beans, and a few other crops, their mode of subsistence relied primarily on hunting and gathering. Early conflicts involved a culture clash between the Native Americans' "mutable and mobile" notion of land and the Europeans' much more settled "world of fields and fences."[2]

The European worldview came to dominate throughout New England, reaching Vermont along with the wave of settlers who came in the late seventeenth century. The earliest group of settlers was primarily involved with subsistence farming, but by the 1820s most Vermont farms were commercial enterprises or attempting to become so, with proprietors who were looking to do more than simply feed their families. In Vermont there was a fairly quick "transition from extensive farming geared to subsistence to intensive farming geared towards markets."[3] Thus, most of Vermont's agricultural history revolves around different phases of commercial agriculture.

Wheat and other grains intended for consumption in Northeast towns and cities were important early commercial crops in Vermont. In 1849 Vermont produced 535,955 bushels of wheat, more than Maine and New Hampshire combined.[4] Potatoes were another important crop during the nineteenth century; in 1899, 3.5 million potatoes were produced in the state.[5] Vermont became known for producing excellent seed stock and breeding hardy varieties, notably the Green Mountain potato, which was sold nationally.[6]

For much of the nineteenth century Vermont was also famous for breeding high-quality merino sheep; "as late as 1863 Vermont Merinos took first prize in a competition in Germany, beating out 1,761 sheep from all over Europe."[7] By 1880 Vermont's landscape was filled with the state's highest ever number of farms: 35,522.[8] From this moment on, the story of Vermont farming goes from more to less: fewer farms, less acreage, less diversity.

By the late nineteenth century, farms producing wheat, potatoes, and merino sheep (for wool) were all in decline. The main factor was the expansion of agriculture to the west and the advance of the railroads. Another important factor, however, was the depletion of the already predominantly poor soils in the state. The initial rush by farmers to capture lucrative commercial markets led to rapid deforestation and nutrient depletion. The number of sheep in the state declined from 580,000 to 270,000 between 1870 and 1900.[9] By 1929 only 13,248 bushels of wheat were produced, a miniscule amount compared to the half a million bushels produced only eighty years earlier. Today Vermont has few working wheat farms.

While wheat and sheep farming were going into decline, by 1870 dairy farming was enjoying some success. As Northeastern cities began to see an influx of industrial workers and new immigrants, the demand for milk and cheese became greater than the nearby farms could supply. The advent of refrigerated train cars allowed even farms in the Northeast Kingdom, the remote highlands in the northeast corner of the state near Canada, to sell milk to Boston and points beyond. Making cheese, particularly hard English-style cheeses such as cheddar, became a major operation, shifting from farmsteads to a network of cheese plants up and down the east coast. By 1900 Vermont dairy farms were shipping millions of pounds of butter, cheese, and milk to urban markets throughout the Northeast. Dairy farming remains the dominant agricultural enterprise in the state today. Today Vermont's human population is 624,000, and the population of cattle and calves is 300,000.[10]

As historian Kevin Graffagnino points out, however, farming in Vermont has rarely been a consistently prosperous activity. As farmers have striven to meet the demands of distant markets for more than two centuries, "even in the best of years Vermont farming often consisted of a great deal of hard work for very little return."[11] Vermont farmers have always tended to diversify by combining the commercial farming of one major crop with the supply of other items, producing "maple sugar, apples, firewood, potatoes, corn, wheat, Morgan horses, and a variety of other crops and livestock just to make a living."[12]

During the twentieth century land dedicated to agriculture in Vermont went into a steady decline, as it did in most of the Northeast: the number of acres devoted to farming decreased from 4,724,440 in 1900 to 3,527,381 in 1950.[13] By 1997 only 1,262,155 acres were dedicated to farm production.[14] Dairy farming remains the dominant type of farming in the state, but the last fifty years have witnessed a shift toward fewer larger farms. In 1953 herd size averaged 25 cows, whereas today the average is more than 115 cows, and there are approximately 100 dairy farms counting more than 300 cows. Dairy products account for 70 percent of the state's receipts from agriculture, and cattle comes in a distant second, with 8.9 percent of total receipts.[15]

In various pockets of Vermont, other approaches to farming emerged at the same time that larger-scale dairy farming came to occupy center stage in the state. These farmers focused on using organic practices to grow crops and raise animals. These farmers were often smaller than neighboring dairy farms, both in overall acreage and levels of productivity. Many of these farmers were new to both farming and Vermont, part of the back-to-the-land movement initially inspired by the agrarian idealism of Thoreau, John Burroughs, Helen and Scott Nearing, and others.[16] In fact, Helen and Scott Nearing, called the great-grandparents of the back-to-the-land movement, started their efforts in self-sufficient organic living at Forest Farm in southern Vermont, where they moved in 1932. By the time the Nearings moved to

Vermont, the state's commercial agriculture, except for dairy, was in decline due to competition from the Midwest and West.[17] Even before the Great Depression many farms in Vermont were aspiring commercial enterprises that often ended up being mostly self-sufficient.

For the Nearings, self-sufficient farming was the ideal rather than a disappointing reality, as it was considered by many of their neighbors. They convinced many of the hundreds, if not thousands, of people who came to visit them at their farm near Stratton, in southern Vermont, to embrace a rural lifestyle based on principles of simplicity. Like the colonists, they came to Vermont to create a farm of fields and fences. However, the early settlers "dreamed of a world in which the returns to human labor were far greater than in England."[18] As Cronon points out, "Hopes for great windfall profits had fueled New World enterprises ever since the triumph of Cortes, and were reinforced by traditions as old as the Garden of Eden."[19] The agrarian utopia envisioned by the Nearings, on the other hand, represented a rejection of the commercial, profit-based economic system.

Their example inspired a wave of rural settlement throughout the Northeast. Often these settlements were also experiments in communal living, based upon the principle of providing for all the needs of its residents from labor on the land. Rebecca Kneale Gould, in her book *At Home in Nature,* explores the modern homesteading movement as a spiritual response to dominant forces in American society. Homesteading, according to Gould, is a response to modernity, one that enacts a certain relationship to nature and rejects a certain set of powerful cultural values, namely consumerism and industrialization. Gould argues that "making meaning through settlement, the conquering of nature, through technological prowess and unrestrained consumption has been the dominant strand in the American story. Homesteading has been another, less popular one. As an ongoing practice, homesteading holds promise for our uncertain ecological future while also having certain limits we ought to consider."[20] Gould focuses on spiritual practices, using a broad interpretation of spirituality that goes beyond organized religion. Gould concentrates on the story of Helen and Scott Nearing, pointing out their almost monastic austerity and their discomfort with any practices that appear too hedonistic: she notes that the Nearings' sense of their own exceptionalism profoundly influenced their everyday life, leading them, for example, to exclusively eat seasonally and locally, but also leading them to direct "disdain . . . toward their unenlightened neighbors in Vermont." Such exceptionalism contained a spiritual dimension, too: "The Nearings saw themselves as somehow 'saved' from the beliefs and practices of the dominant culture from which they had fled, a culture that respected neither personal health, nor social justice, nor the value of the natural world."[21]

Many of the back-to-the-landers of the 1960s shared that same sense of cultural exceptionalism. Many involved with the social change movement of the 1960s embraced the subsistence style of agriculture inspired by the Nearings, but over time the Nearings call that "back to the land" meant being involved only in a "use economy" became too limiting a goal, socially and economically. Another shift in small farming, one still inspired by an agrarian ideal, occurred. This approach to farming was based on small farms using an alternative set of farm practices to those promoted by the increasingly dominant paradigm based on industrial, commodity production. This shift is reflected in the increase in farms between one and forty-nine acres between 1964 (1,043) and 1997 (1,457).[22] Meanwhile, larger farms went into a steep decline during the same period.[23] Small-scale diversified organic farms in Vermont actually saw growth over the period that could otherwise be considered a long period of decline.

A loose group of farmers from the back-to-the-land movement began to meet in the early 1970s to discuss methods of growing wholesome and organic food. These farmers became allied in their commitment to diversified farming techniques, or organic practices, or both. "Food for the people and not for profit" was the rallying cry for what eventually became the Northeast Organic Farming Association (NOFA). One of the founders was Samuel Kayman, who went on to create Stonyfield Yogurt. Initially the group drove their farm products down to New York and Boston, but soon they realized that they should try to sell closer to home. NOFA, which at the time included farms in New Hampshire, decided to work on creating farmers' markets throughout the region. By 1977 NOFA had created a certification process that enabled farms to guarantee to customers that their products were organic. Initially the vast majority of certified organic farms were owned by people who had come to Vermont as part of the back-to-the-land movement. More recently, however, as the market for organic foods has become more stable and in fact is witnessing tremendous growth, some native Vermont dairy farmers are also switching to organic practices.[24]

Presently there are 355 certified organic farms in Vermont. Jack Lazor in Westfield, who has a small dairy herd and makes yogurt from the milk of his Jersey cows, came to Vermont in 1975 and has been actively involved in NOFA-VT for years. There are also a number of small, diverse farms in the state that generally follow the principles of organic farming but, due to a dislike of regulations or philosophical differences with the certification process, have chosen not to pursue certification. Hank Bissell, a vegetable farmer in Starksboro, for example, came to Vermont in 1980 to "change the world" and has developed a "generally organic" approach.

By the 1990s the organic farming movement had moved beyond local control and become a national phenomenon increasingly on the radar of the federal government and the large-scale food industry. Many of the farmers and advocates involved with building the organic farming movement in Vermont felt that the creation of the National Organic Board and the system of oversight it organized shifted the principles of organic farming far away from the intent of the founders of the movement. The federal standards regulated how farmers treated the soil, but they said nothing about the location of those soils or the size of the farms treating the soil organically. As NOFA-VT executive director Enid Wonnacott puts it, "The strength of this movement was its underground, non-bureaucratic approach, [an effort] not to repeat the mistakes of conventional agriculture. Now, we are [asking the question] 'How do you maintain local organic in the context of industrial organic?' "[25]

As organic farming became larger in scale and more industrial in nature, Vermont's small farmers needed a new method for finding markets for their varied goods. It became clear that they needed to find outlets outside the dominant commercial system. The Northeast Organic Farming Association had worked to help set up farmers' markets, cooperative retail stores, and other venues for selling the organic products. Since Vermont was such an attractive place for people whose farming practices were inspired at least in part by social and environmental ideals, by the 1990s, a critical mass of like-minded farmers existed. As well, because Vermont's topography is mountainous and the growing season is short, a fair number of small conventional farms remained diversified—producing eggs, maple sugar, cheese, and apples, for example—throughout the long period of agricultural consolidation after World War II. Maple syrup has remained a steady crop.

But in order for farmers to move beyond agrarian utopianism and successfully navigate the world of commercial agriculture, they had to find markets for their products. The story of Vermont's working landscape changes at this point. As always, the quest for markets continues, but now the search is local. And at the time there was not much to find. The centuries-old tradition of the general store in every town continued in many Vermont communities for years, but by the 1980s those in Vermont had come to rely on national distributors rather than local farms for their food purchases. The tradition of local farmers' markets had also begun to disappear; in 1980 only six regular markets were operating throughout the state. All these small-scale diversified farmers had to grapple with the perpetual dilemma of modern farmers—finding consistent and sustainable markets for their goods.

FROM FARM TO TABLE:
THE STORY OF VERMONT FRESH NETWORK

The New England Culinary Institute was founded in 1980, starting out with four students and one chef-instructor. A decade later the school had two campuses, hundreds of students, and as many or more employees in teaching, administration, and food operations in Montpelier and Burlington. The growing presence of the school helped create a critical mass of taste producers and tastemakers who increasingly interacted with Vermont farmers. The visit of Michael Ableman to NECI inspired Pam Knights to reach out to the Vermont Department of Agriculture. Now that she understood more about the challenges facing small organic farms, she wanted to involve the culinary school in efforts to promote Vermont farms, thus helping to create new markets for local and organic foods. Her collaborative efforts led to the launch of Vermont Fresh Network (VFN), an innovative attempt to provide such local markets for farmers. Vermont Fresh Network, like Odessa Piper's work in Wisconsin, represents another example of treading a middle ground between agrarian utopianism and commercial capitalism in an attempt to create the taste of place.

According to Knights, she began to meet with Roger Clapp, at the time the deputy commissioner of agricultural development, in the fall of 1994 in order to coordinate a larger, statewide effort in association with Ableman's upcoming visit. Working closely together, Knights and Clapp were able to get Sunday, January 22, 1995, declared Vermont's Organic Awareness Day (so proclaimed by then-governor Howard Dean). An event held at a local hotel, "Vermont's Organic Awareness Day: Today and into Tomorrow," was cosponsored by the Northeast Organic Farming Association of Vermont,

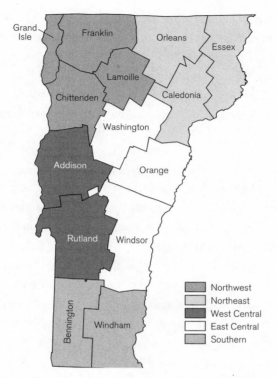

FIGURE 10. Regional map of Vermont Fresh Network.
COURTESY OF VERMONT FRESH NETWORK.

Gardener's Supply Company, the Vermont Department of Agriculture, Food, and Markets, and the New England Culinary Institute. Knights feels that this event created the initial momentum leading to the founding of Vermont Fresh Network. In particular, she sees the event as introducing two ideas that became central to VFN: the importance of eating the landscape, and the need to foster direct conversations between farmers and chefs. Vermont's Organic Awareness Day generated a lot of energy and the desire to pursue these issues.

Knights started working at the New England Culinary Institute in 1984 as a restaurant manager and front-of-the-house instructor. She was raised in Marshfield and attended the University of Vermont, where she was one of the first students to matriculate in the newly created major in environmental studies. After years away she returned to Vermont with her then-husband, Patrick Matecat, a French chef who became a teacher at NECI and ultimately opened his own restaurant. Eventually Knights took on responsibility for restaurant promotion at the school.

Clapp grew up in the Boston suburbs during the Vietnam era and was greatly influenced by the social protests of the time. As Clapp puts it, "The stark hypocrisy of our country napalming children in the name of freedom caused many of us to search for meaning in new directions. At Tufts University I joined a living/learning group called Roots and Growth. We studied Thoreau, the transcendental movement, and Brookside Farm of the 1800s and developed our own organic vegetable enterprise, as well as relations with the back-to-the-land movement in New England, with much of it happening in Vermont." He then went on to join the Peace Corps and did rural development work in central Africa. Eventually he ended up in Vermont because "it became very clear to me that Vermont was a place where agriculture was still taken seriously. It also became clear that most of the money was being made in agricultural processing and marketing."

Knights's and Clapp's efforts were inspired by the ideals and practices of the small-scale, diversified, and often organic farmers now a part of Vermont's working landscape. Their initiatives were also influenced by their day-to-day work marketing food and agriculture to consumers in Vermont and beyond.

One year later, in January 1996, NECI invited well-known chef Larry Forgione to be the keynote speaker at another cosponsored event, the Vermont Fresh Food Network Forum. This forum was more focused, and the organizers attempted to develop some practical initiatives: "The panelists will not only speak from experience, but will identify three to five controllable factors that impede the successful interaction between the different links in Vermont's fresh food chain."[26] The event had gone from showcasing small-scale organic agriculture to working on dismantling barriers in the Vermont food system by focusing on relationships between farmers, chefs, and consumers.

According to Knights, this forum launched Vermont Fresh Network. The more than one hundred participants, many of them local farmers and chefs, agreed on the need to develop direct markets and communication and to help preserve Vermont's working landscape. As a result, the Vermont Department of Agriculture and NECI began a formal collaboration. The first information sheet produced by Vermont Fresh Network about its goal described it thus: "Formally established, the goal of the VFN is to develop markets for Vermont dairy, livestock, produce, and horticultural products in Vermont's food service sector, while working to preserve the rural character of Vermont's landscape through the creation of partnerships between chefs and farmers." The initial slogan for VFN was "Eat the Vermont Landscape." Clapp came up with the slogan in response to an article he had read claiming that landscapes could not be eaten; yet, he wondered, wasn't that truly the source of Vermont's uniqueness? Clapp thought that the campaign could foster a sort of agricultural tourism.

By July of that year Vermont Fresh Network was officially launched, with the venue and victuals provided by the New England Culinary Institute. Roger Clapp gave the inaugural address. The newly developed logo, a dark green background with a white plate containing a farm scene and a knife and fork on each side, was unveiled. Knights then went on to organize the Vermont Fresh Network Marketplace, whose goal was to connect farmers and chefs with the help of Elisa Mitofsky Clancy, an employee of the Vermont Department of Agriculture. This event, which attracted ninety-six growers and sixty-four chefs, became the prototype for the organization's annual forum.

In the early 1990s, many people involved in promoting an alternative to our industrialized system began to explore ways of decreasing the number of steps between farmers and consumers. Farmers' markets began to increase, and some small farmers started to experiment with the notion of community-supported agriculture, initially started in Japan. At the time, some Vermont chefs and farmers were already involved in direct buying. Doug Mack of Mary's at Baldwin Creek, for example, had been working with local farmers for some time, such as Hank Bissell of Lewis Creek Farm in Starksboro, who had been selling directly to Mack for almost a decade.

Forgione, who gave the keynote at the January 1996 event, was cochair of the Chefs Collaborative, a subsidiary of Oldways Preservation Trust, a small nonprofit working to promote traditional foodways and healthy eating. Oldways organized a number of events and tours involving chefs, who in turn started to organize around similar concerns. The Chefs Collaborative was founded in 1993 by a group of chefs working together with Oldways: "In the early 1990s chefs around the country were recognizing that they could improve their cuisine and make a difference for local farmers. Chefs Collaborative was founded to promote the virtues of local, seasonal, and sustainable ingredients within the restaurant community and to the greater public."[27] Chefs were increasingly identifying their *style* of cooking with their *choices* as to where, what, and how they sourced their ingredients.

Why did Vermont's Department of Agriculture decide to devote time and resources to VFN? Roger Clapp says VFN was part of a larger strategy to build new markets for agricultural products in Vermont by getting producers closer to consumers. This would allow farmers to get a larger share of food dollars spent in the state. Clapp was especially interested in promoting the direct connections in restaurants, which he saw as having tremendous potential. The presence of a nationally known cooking school in this small state meant that over the past twenty years Vermont has collected many committed and educated chefs running all manner of restaurants.

Restaurants would be a wonderful place to tell consumers stories about where their food comes from and thus raise awareness. And, as Clapp puts it, formalizing the process and "putting some of the promotional power of the Department of Agriculture behind it helped take it [shortening the steps] to another level." Clapp sums up his philosophy of agricultural marketing this way:

> When I got into a position of leadership, I made it my business to leverage Vermont's marketing cachet to benefit those that were still making a living on the land. Along with the dairy farmers, there were a lot of back-to-the-landers growing organic vegetables; raising sheep, goats, and deer; tapping trees; and looking for ways to make it all work. With the support of the industry, Vermont legislature, and other partner organizations, we were able to attract several creative investments in farmstead cheese operations, specialty meats, community-supported agriculture, farmers' markets, and host of other initiatives that continue today. Vermont Fresh Network was just one of these ventures where the creative drive was already there, and once we got the movers and shakers together, I did my best to get out of their way.[28]

By 1997, Knights and Clapp wanted to develop mechanisms to ensure that farmers and chefs controlled the partnerships themselves. They appointed a board of directors. By 1998 VFN was incorporated as a 501(c)(3) nonprofit organization, and the organization began to exist independently of the Vermont Department of Agriculture and the New England Culinary Institute. The administration of the organization remained at the VDA until 2000, when VFN became a freestanding organization. Although Clapp and Knights moved on from their jobs at VDA and NECI, the involvement of these two institutions has continued, with present and past employees of each institution consistently sitting on the VFN board of directors.

The initial mission set out four main goals for the organization: to develop lasting relationships between Vermont chefs and farmers; to support

Vermont farmers; to build brand loyalty for Vermont-grown and -produced foods; and, finally, to educate this community of farmers and chefs with a yearly forum. The organization's seven guiding principles are unified by a focus on educational outreach and relationship building. Some examples are "Educate and create communication between chefs, farmers, producers, and distributors and devise strategies and systems to implement the farm-to-table program" and "Educate the public about the quality, pleasure, wholesomeness, nutritional value, freshness, and safety of Vermont-grown foods, as well as the economic impact of supporting local businesses." These are the foundations of Vermont Fresh Network.

Ten years later, the organization's goals remain much the same. VFN wants to build markets, and it uses all available avenues to achieve this. The group's promotional literature begins by expressing a desire to preserve the working landscape: "The quality and beauty of Vermont's landscape depends upon working farms and working farmers." The idea of "cuisine tourism" is introduced, too: "Our beautiful open fields and scenic landscape also attract tourists and improve our own quality of life." Finally, the importance of chefs to both the landscape and tourism is articulated: "The Vermont Fresh Network is dedicated to promoting and publicizing Vermont chefs and restaurants that use Vermont-grown and -produced foods. Chefs that purchase the products of our working landscape are helping to maintain this agricultural heritage and contribute to the future of Vermont's farm economy. For this reason, VFN connects farmers with chefs, and promotes these partnerships."

Vermont Fresh Network tries to nurture an alternative foodview, one that transforms the rural value of "knowing your neighbor" into a part of doing business. This is one way to build the taste of place. In order to accomplish such a task, the goals of Vermont Fresh Network must be broad and must be involved in a number of aspects of our contemporary food system: the state's agricultural economy and heritage; the rural landscape and tourism;

and local food businesses and the cuisine of the region. Vermont Fresh Network, the first statewide nonprofit promoting direct partnerships between farmers and chefs, has been an innovative organization, and many others in other agricultural regions have emulated VFN when looking to diversify markets and develop connections to restaurants. Perhaps as these organizations serve to inoculate such a foodview in regions all over the United States, values and practices will be transformed, and we, too, will embrace the taste of place.

MAKING IT HAPPEN

I went to the ceremony and luncheon that officially launched Vermont Fresh Network. It was an unusually hot July day for Vermont; the temperature was over 90 degrees, and the hillside where the ceremony took place offered no shade, although we were able to look out over Montpelier and down the spine of the Green Mountains as we ate and listened. Over the years I kept up with the organization, and eventually my husband became a member of the board of directors. During that same period I was awarded a fellowship that allowed me to do research and write on local food systems and sustainable agriculture. I immediately thought of VFN and decided to do a case study on it, for I thought it represented an innovative example of the taste of place in action. As part of my research I interviewed members and board members, I combed through old files, and I interviewed the staff members. As I was completing my research, the position of executive director became available. To make a long story short, I moved from being a mere observer of VFN to being a true participant-observer, as I held the part-time position of executive director for almost two years. To say that my day-to-day participation allowed me greater understanding and insight into the complexities of creating the taste of place in the United States is an understatement. I was pulled under by a tsunami of systemic issues, practical concerns, and competing visions. Safely back on shore, and having had some time to reflect, I think VFN's best efforts and greatest obstacles speak to all that is possible, but also all that is very fragile in the way we farm, cook, and eat today.

Vermont Fresh Network's mission is broader than that of many nonprofits involved in agriculture and food activism because it involves players in *all* aspects of the contemporary food system. The focus is not solely on farmers or consumers, but instead the organization identifies chefs as the vital pivot between farmers looking for viable markets for their products and consumers looking for a good meal. What happens when such a mission moves into action is a lot of cognitive dissonance. The farmer and chef members of VFN mostly agree on the ideals of preserving Vermont's working landscape and fostering local food connections, but when it comes to the day-to-day realities of making it happen, well, that can be an altogether different story.

Many chefs understand the benefits of buying directly from a local farmer. Local farmers can provide a fresh-tasting, high-quality product with a longer shelf life. A chef who develops an ongoing relationship with a farmer or artisan producer can also request produce, meats, or cheeses that are custom-produced for his or her operation. Relationships between local producers and local chefs support sustainable agricultural practices, provide fresh, healthy ingredients for restaurants, and support the local economy. Yet the relationship between a farmer and a chef poses unique challenges because farmers and chefs *think* differently about food. Farmers focus on the field, while chefs concern themselves with the plate. Learning to communicate effectively is a major step in the creation of a strong connection between farmer and chef.

Much of Vermont Fresh Network's daily work concerns bridging these differences. Chefs tend to relate to food on a day-to-day basis: the individual ingredients for all the items on the lunch and dinner menu need to be immediately at hand. Farmers, on the other hand, think about growing seasons, weekly orders, and packing methods. Consumers, finally, think about cost, convenience, and their latest dietary restrictions.

Harmonious relationships between farmers and chefs start with an understanding of each other's daily practices. Farmers often comment on chefs' emphasis on aesthetics: they do not want holes in their arugula leaves; they are always interested in a product with a new shape, size, or flavor. At the same time, as VFN points out in its "Tip Sheet for Farmers," "Chefs don't like surprises. Consistency is key and should be part of everything you do, from ground work like determining back-ups in case of product shortage all the way to regular customer service visits." Perhaps paradoxically for farmers, chefs like diversity *and* uniformity. A new purple-tinged variety of arugula sounds great, but ideally a chef likes all the arugula washed, bundled, and consistent in size and shape. Such expectations certainly emerge from a general cultural expectation for machinelike consistency for *all* goods, but uniformity also reduces the amount of work that has to be done in the kitchen.

Chefs, accustomed to a command-and-control method of ordering ingredients, have to be guided toward thinking like a farmer, toward considering growing seasons, payment methods, and distribution possibilities much more thoroughly than they are accustomed to doing. The geographic circumstances that enable Vermont to retain small, diversified farms—mountainous terrain, often steep valleys, and low population density—also mean that farmers must travel long distances on difficult roads to get their goods to market, and the situation is even worse when they're delivering to scattered restaurants. Vermont Fresh Network is asked repeatedly to help solve distribution problems. One possible solution that has been discussed is creating a regionally based distribution system for farm members. Purchasing trucks and getting involved in daily delivery is expensive and risky, so VFN has shifted to aiding and abetting farmers rather than actually performing deliveries. Chefs can often be quite inflexible about their delivery expectations, and the tip sheet for chefs tries to open up new avenues: "Consider if you or an employee drives by the farm on their way to work and can pick up the order. Helping with delivery will strengthen your relationship because it lightens some of the stress of the farmer."

So, how does Vermont Fresh Network try to accomplish its mission? What methods have been used to fulfill the organization's mission and adhere to their guiding principles? Six major initiatives have remained fairly constant since the earliest days: signing the handshake agreement that assures that the restaurant will have partnerships with at least three VFN farmers; organizing publicity with the VFN logo; printing a dining guide for consumers; creating an information brochure for partners (now on its website); distributing the "Fresh Sheet" to chefs; and organizing annual forums. Farm to Table tours and, more recently, Farmers Dinners, as well as other events linking farmers to restaurant meals have also remained fairly constant as VFN activities.

When VFN was launched, its main goal was to facilitate relationships between farmers and chefs, and the organization's founding principles reflected this core value. Advocacy was never explicitly on the agenda. In that vein, all farmers and chefs who signed a handshake agreement were considered VFN partners, and there was no distinction made according to the *level* of commitment, that is, according to the quantity of local goods purchased or sold or the number of partners. This remains the underlying principle of the handshake agreement. The only change that has been instituted is the addition of a membership fee: $30 for farmers, $50 for restaurants or chefs, and $100 for corporations, institutions, or organizations. Presently, farmers need to have a handshake agreement with one VFN restaurant member, restaurants or chefs need to have agreements with three farmer members, and food producers need agreements with three farmers and three restaurants or chefs. Breadth or depth of partnerships does not affect membership status. Anyone who fulfills the minimum requirements can

FIGURE 11. Vermont Fresh Network logo. COURTESY OF
VERMONT FRESH NETWORK.

receive the benefits of membership. Also, VFN does not regulate these relationships, and it assumes all its members will work with their partners directly. VFN served as an information clearinghouse whose primary function
was to generate information for all member partners, initially in the form of
a brochure listing members, contact information, and a short description of
each individual operation. The organization now uses its website to provide
information to farmers, chefs, and consumers.

It has been a decade since the seeds of VFN were first planted, and since
then it has accomplished many of its initial goals. Its greatest accomplish-
ment has been to raise awareness at every step in the state's food system,
from farmer to distributor to chef to consumer. Connections between farmers and chefs make sense, and partnerships between them no longer seem

unusual or radical, but instead just a part of doing business. VFN has also received a lot of media attention inside and outside the state, and it has helped inspire others to formalize and promote similar relationships.

Now that farmer-chef connections have been established throughout the state, and VFN has successfully helped shorten the number of steps between farmer and consumer, people involved with the organization are looking toward the future. At the same time, certain challenges to the mission, vision, and guiding principles of the organization have remained constant.

VFN has always faced two types of challenges: those related to the administration of the organization, and those related to the problems of our globalized and centralized food system. Roger Clapp says that from the earliest days of VFN he was concerned that there was no differentiation of membership in relation to their degree of participation. He also "pushed getting more involved in distribution. . . . Farmers spend an inordinate amount of time on delivery for the amount of goods that are sold."[29] The varying degrees of partner commitment and obstacles faced due to the food system infrastructure continue to be major concerns for those involved with VFN today. Another ongoing theme has been the difficulty in maintaining and nurturing farmer-chef relationships once they are established.

Once VFN was able to facilitate direct connections between farmers and chefs, larger issues began to arise. The present state of our food system, with the constant push towards centralization and consolidation, means that it is easier for a chef to work with a national distributor to source goods than to work with individual local farmers. At the same time, farmers find it difficult to transport their product and to meet the often-variable desires of chefs, especially their demand for a consistent appearance and supply of product. VFN was able to initiate relationships, but it was less equipped to overcome the challenges to maintaining these relationships that bypass the dominant delivery system. Such problems face *all* direct-market initiatives between farmers and chefs in the United States. Vermont has some unique issues due to its rural and mountainous geography, but otherwise, the problems are the same everywhere.

The organization has struggled for years to define its role in solving the food system infrastructure issues that plague all partner members. The "Fresh Sheet" is one way VFN has attempted to create an alternative to the traditional distribution system. The "Fresh Sheet" effectively pulls together in one document information about member farmers, and this mimics the ordering forms provided by larger regional and national distributors. The hope was that a familiar ordering style would translate into larger local purchases by chefs. *Time* became the major obstacle to the effectiveness of the "Fresh Sheet": the time it took to contact the farmers, who are often busy out in the fields; the time sensitivity of many of the available ingredients, which is much different than the constant availability provided by the national distributors; and the time it took to contact each farmer to individually place the order. In the end, technological advances have enabled the "Fresh Sheet" to be posted on the web, and farmers are now able to update and change their information themselves, and chefs are able to access it whenever it is convenient.

Meghan Sheradin, now the executive director of VFN, recently launched an exciting joint project enabling farmers and others to use specific broadband sites to place and take orders. This project is a logical extension of earlier efforts, such as creating a distribution map that tells farmers when other members are making deliveries, which could facilitate farmers working together to make distribution easier and more efficient. All these initiatives are natural extensions of the founding principles of the organization.

Convenience remains a powerful motivator for chefs in all types of restaurants, especially those with a high volume of daily sales. The ease of ordering from a distributor, who takes on the tasks of both ordering and delivery, is hard to pass up. If building a direct relationship with a farmer is not a priority, or it is difficult for a chef, there is little incentive for him or her to continue the effort.

Straddling the different needs of farmers and chefs preoccupies all organizations trying to create direct markets for farmers. In 2001, for example, the Portland chapter of the Chefs Collaborative first organized a daylong Farmer-Chef Connection conference. In 2002 they launched an additional Fisherman-Chef Connection event. More than 150 chefs and farmers participated in the 2003 conference, during which opportunities for linking the supply of fresh food and the demand for quality ingredients were explored. Following the conference, surveys were mailed to the participants. Among the various questions posed to farmers were how far they would be willing to travel to make deliveries and why their farm would be a great partner for a restaurant. Chefs answered questions such as which were the best times of the week to contact them and which products they would really like to buy. The conference also produced a popular guide to local and seasonal products. During the conference, one period was devoted to "speed dating," during which chefs would meet different farmers for twelve minutes each to discuss possible purchasing relationships.

The cliché "Where there is a will, there is a way" should apply, given the level of investment by farmers, chefs, nonprofits, and, increasingly, consumers in bypassing the dominant food delivery system. Our "habits of thought" in the United States, as anthropologist Susan Carol Rogers puts it, have not typically included thinking that cooking and eating food from our neighbors are important to the "well-being of society as a whole," whereas in France celebrating farming and farmers contributes to the "social good."[30] Even dedicated American chefs cannot ignore the assumptions of the American foodview as they try to build the taste of place, given that they must succeed economically or forgo making any difference. Unfortunately, those building the taste of place, even in an enclave such as Vermont, must contend with the reality that "conceptions of farming as a way of life crucial to the well-being of the American national psyche, spirit or social fabric . . . have neither the mainstream respectability nor broad influence" that they do in France.[31] The organization of daily life—how to grow foods, how to order them, how to build a menu, and how to decide which restaurant to visit—remains a process heavily influenced by convenience, consistency, and cost. Making a turn toward the local entails leaving behind familiar patterns and practices. For now, building local relationships and markets remains profoundly counterintuitive and countercultural.

MEMBER STORIES

The counterculture thrives in Vermont, however, and Vermont Fresh Network members are building an alternative day by day. Innovation and experimentation are the order of the day. In Vermont, the farming culture is as diverse as the topography, and older farmers mingle with new converts. And all manner of restaurants are involved in building local markets, from an expensive restaurant in a Relais & Châteaux property, to a family-owned diner, to the dining service of an elite liberal arts college.

Every Vermont Fresh Network farm and restaurant has a fascinating story to tell about the many ways the taste of place is being created, then sometimes imagined differently, and then created anew. Leslie Myers, owner of Smokejacks restaurant in Burlington, has developed a standard menu of appetizers, entrées, and desserts, but she has also long featured another menu consisting solely of farmstead cheeses, most from Vermont or elsewhere in New England, that can be served as an appetizer, entrée, *or* dessert. The Heleba family from outside Rutland have dedicated themselves solely to growing heirloom potatoes. Randy Ziter, proprietor of the Putney Inn, preserves the bounty of the harvest and serves it all year round. Steve and Lara Atkins at Kitchen Table Bistro in Richmond host farmer dinners modeled on popular wine dinners, including, for example, a five-course menu featuring heirloom apples in every dish. Lilac Ridge Farm grows an acre of mesclun greens just for Riverview Café in Brattleboro. The two longer stories below of Vermont Fresh Network members Laini Fondiller and Tod Murphy represent the wide array of possibilities for building the taste of place given our dominant foodview and the organization of our food system.

LAZY LADY FARM   Lazy Lady Farm rests in the heart of the Northeast Kingdom, a remote outpost of Vermont known for having independent-minded residents and tracts of unspoiled forests. Started in 1987, this fifty-acre farm was carved out of a larger dairy concern that long ago closed up shop. From the remains of a traditional farm, owner Laini Fondiller has created part of Vermont's agricultural future.

Despite the farm's name, Fondiller is anything but lazy. A small, compact woman, she is more of a whirling dervish, spinning here, there, and everywhere. Luckily, much of that energy is expended creating exceptional farmstead cheeses as well as kid and goat sausages. When you visit Fondiller at the farm, comprised of sloping hillside and forest not far from the ski resort of Jay Peak, she moves constantly. She darts from the cheese room, where she makes ten goat cheeses as well as blended cheeses, to the barn, which houses her herd of twenty-five French Alpine goats. She then takes a quick walk down to the cave, where she ages cheeses, and then up to the nearby field, where she climbs up on a tractor to finish haying the field before the sun sets.

Fondiller started making cheese fifteen years ago with milk from one goat. Soon she had a devoted, even cultlike, following. Initially she only sold her Pyramides, Capriola, and Petit Tomme at local farmers' markets, though now her business ships cheese all over New England, including to L'Espalier in Boston and Murray's Cheese Shop in New York City. Her business is now evenly divided between sales inside and outside the state.

The cheeses of Lazy Lady Farm are distinctive. As David Hale, executive chef of the New England Culinary Institute and a longtime fan of Fondiller's cheese, puts it, "There is a consistency; she has identified the flavors in her cheeses. Her cheese has *terroir,* and it reflects her personality, too."[32] Fondiller uses milk from a single herd of goats to make her cheeses, and they graze on open pasture that includes witchgrass and pinegrass. Her approach, however, brings an American touch to the French definition of terroir; she feels no compulsion to promote the *patrimoine* of Vermont cheeses. Interestingly, she preserves the traditional methods of cheese making she learned while living in France for two years, yet she has never been conservative in her approach. She makes numerous styles of cheeses, focusing on what is possible rather than pursuing authenticity. She attributes her inventive approach to the advice of her French mentor. He said to her, "These are not the methods of the past; this is how we do it right now." Fondiller says that these words "really set the stage for me being open to all that came along."[33]

Fondiller hails from Indiana but has lived in Vermont since 1979, always working in some aspect of dairy farming. In 1982 she went to France to learn about making cheese, where she became smitten with goats and sheep: "I had been working on dairy farms, but I knew they were in trouble."[34] She came back to Vermont much more knowledgeable about cheese making and imbued with her French teacher's pragmatic approach. "Il faut faire comme il faut," he told her. You do what you have to do.

Everyone who knows Fondiller has a story to tell about her unique approach to farming and cheese making. Several years ago the American Cheese Society held their annual meeting in Vermont. Friends urged her to submit cheeses for the society's prestigious competition, but Fondiller did not want to pay the $100 entry fee. A friend finally gave her the money as a present. She submitted her Pyramides and ended up winning first prize in the category of soft ripened goat's milk cheese.

FIGURE 12. Cheese in the cave, Lazy Lady Farm, Westfield, Vermont. PHOTO BY AMY B. TRUBEK.

Despite her nonchalant attitude, Fondiller is the very model of creative entrepreneurship. She presently makes eighteen different cheeses and claims, "The customer keeps pushing me into more stuff. 'Can you make this cheese larger? Can you make it smaller?'" She outgrew the small cheese room in her house and decided to construct a separate building for making, packaging, and shipping her cheese. "I decided to do the cheese room when a friend told me about a low-interest loan through Vermont Community Loan Fund . . . a 4 percent loan. I had totally grown out of the old cheese room and had to do something or I would die in there from stress overload."[35] Her partner, Barry, built her cave for aging cheese by hand, digging out the dirt shovelful by shovelful.

For years she struggled to find ways to sell the farm's kids and "retired" milking goats. Only a small market for goat meat exists, few slaughterhouses are willing to process an unfamiliar animal, and it is difficult to get the product to interested customers. Fondiller worked to move every single barrier. She founded a meat cooperative, Pride of Vermont Farms, to market and distribute her goat sausages and other products.

One day an article on an Italian goat prosciutto—*violini de capra*—captured her attention. "I got very excited. [I thought] this is what we should do."[36] She ended up applying for a United States Department of Agriculture grant to study in Italy. Awarded the grant, Fondiller traveled to Italy in the fall of 2001.

She spent two weeks learning to how to make *violini*, which is aged under the exact same conditions as her cheeses—at 55 degrees Fahrenheit and 90 percent humidity. "*Violini* is very subtle and has a sweetness to it," she says.[37] Fondiller wants to produce and sell the prosciutto soon, but she needs to find a meat-processing plant willing to embrace making such an unusual product. Right now she is involved in a project to purchase one in nearby Troy, to be run as a cooperative. Hopefully this will be the place where Vermont's own goat prosciutto will be made.

For now, Fondiller and her assistant, LaDonna Dunn, continue to work each morning in her new workspace. One day they focus on the nutty yet sweet Petit Tomme, which has a surprising heft for a small cheese. On another day they work on a new cheese, Lyle Lovesit, blended from cow's and goat's milk. As one avid cheese lover puts it, eating a piece of Lyle Lovesit is like eating one of Willy Wonka's experimental candies: first it has the classic buttery taste of a Camembert, but then you are surprised by the mouth-puckering sharpness typical of great goat cheese. Chef David Hale calls the cheeses of Lazy Lady Farm "little treasures."[38] Fondiller's quirky mix of low-tech farmstead cheese making and inventive problem solving has enabled her to build an utterly unique taste of place.

THE FARMERS DINER   The coffee mug at the Farmers Diner is decorated with the diner's logo, a farmer on a horse-drawn plow. On the other side of the mug is Wendell Berry's dictum "Eating is an agricultural act." Tod Murphy, owner of this restaurant, once located on the main street of Barre and now reopened in Quechee, has listened to Berry's call to arms. He also wants to bring farming and eating back together. He believes that when people know who grows and raises their food, individuals and the community become healthier. This idea is central to Murphy's entrepreneurial vision. The motto "Food from here" appears on the diner's placemats, menus, and table tents. Murphy is also fond of saying, "Think locally, act neighborly."

Many of our nation's founders, most notably Thomas Jefferson, imagined that agrarian values—the importance of small landholders, rural communities, and local governance—would always be the country's bedrock. These agrarian values are the inspiration for the Farmers Diner. The past 250 years, however, have dramatically transformed the structure of our agricultural system. Small, self-sustaining local communities and food systems are no longer part of the bedrock. Instead, some see them as an exercise in nostalgia, while others, like Murphy, consider them a noble aspiration. However they are perceived, as Murphy found out while developing his business, there is no question that our system of food production, distribution, and consumption does not support these values.

The Farmers Diner is one of more than 220 restaurants in Vermont Fresh Network. Murphy knew about VFN long before he opened the diner in 2002; he had been raising veal calves for several years previously and had approached a number of VFN chefs about selling them his product. Although many were interested in developing a relationship, few wanted to purchase a whole calf. Instead, they wanted premium cuts such as steaks and roasts. He became frustrated by this "pick-and-choose" approach and wanted to figure out a better way. Most chefs realize that other cuts—the rump, shank, and tail, for example—are more flavorful, but American consumers today do not desire such dishes. This leads to the strange market reality Murphy encountered: high demand for certain parts of an animal, low demand for others. The distance between market realities for farmers and chefs shaped Murphy's decision to create a vertically integrated food business. He hopes to open five diners and a central commissary in Vermont. The mission of the Farmers Diner is to spend seventy cents of every food dollar within 100 miles. This means a lot of work, because buying locally takes extra effort.

Take the hamburger, the quintessential American dish that's probably on the menu of every diner in the United States. An iconic hamburger usually consists of ground beef, lettuce, tomato, onions, pickles, and sometimes cheese, all served on a bun. For most Americans, it's the combination of these ingredients that makes a hamburger authentic, the real thing. A local hamburger, made entirely from ingredients that come from within 100 miles of Barre, would be a popular dish with customers and not a very difficult one for the cooks to prepare. Where is the problem? The ingredients. Vermont is a northern state with a cold climate. How do you provide fresh, flavorful tomatoes for your hamburger in January, when all of Vermont is blanketed with snow and the sun is low in the sky? Lettuce poses the same problem.

Most restaurants purchase tomatoes and lettuce grown in Mexico or California or Florida during the winter. The produce is shipped to Vermont in large tractor-trailers, traveling from 1,000 to 3,000 miles from farm to plate. To remain true to his vision, however, Murphy needs a different solution to the constraints that the long Vermont winter creates.

During a conversation in January about the difficulties of purchasing fresh local vegetables in the winter, he told me, "These days, I go into the diner kitchen, grab a California tomato from the box, and stand on a crate. I drop a tomato on the ground. Nothing happens. No splash. No splurt. The tomato just rolls away."[39] The cooks are surprised, but he makes his point that tomatoes purchased in January from distant regions bring no flavor to the meal, so why include them in the dish? Since Murphy is seeking to create the deluxe local hamburger, tomatoes from somewhere else do not make him happy

Eventually, Murphy hopes to contract with Vermont farmers to grow tomatoes and lettuce, along with other vegetables, in greenhouses. Currently there are several entrepreneurial farmers growing tomatoes in greenhouses year-round in Vermont and shipping them to markets throughout the East Coast. The juicy, red, ripe, and flavorful tomato grown in Vermont may be available to Murphy by next winter, but his pursuit of local flavor will require more effort and will cost him more money.

Obtaining a consistent supply of local ground beef is a lot of work for Murphy as well, since the industrial model of production has been successfully transferred to livestock. In fact, this sector of farming has seen the greatest transformation away from the small-scale local system. Farmers used to raise a few cattle, sheep, or pigs and bring them to the butcher a few times a year, but today a small group of powerful corporations dominates the livestock industry. Tyson Foods, which recently purchased Iowa Beef Processors, is the world's largest processor and marketer of beef, chicken, and pork products. Four meatpacking companies process more than 75 percent of all cattle slaughtered in the United States. More than 98 percent of all poultry in the United States today is produced by a handful of large corporations. The goal for most of these businesses, as it is for many large corporations, is vertical integration. Businesses strive to own all the components necessary for livestock production, from the grains used for feed, to the slaughterhouses and processing plants that turn the live animals into meat for the supermarket, to the facilities used to distribute the finished product.

A by-product of this approach is a push toward centralization in production. Vermont, traditionally a state with only a limited number of small farmers raising cattle, has not benefited from this shift in production strategies. In attempting to serve local beef in his restaurant, Murphy faced challenges at every level: finding farmers in the area who were still raising cattle and pigs; locating a small slaughterhouse that could accommodate occasional small numbers of animals; and finding a meat-processing plant still in operation. During the past twenty years, with the consolidation of the livestock industry, the number of slaughterhouses in Vermont has declined from twenty to twelve. Several meat-processing plants have closed as well.

As Murphy developed his business plan he realized he would need to address these obstacles or he would never be able to achieve his goal of using more than 50 percent local products. Murphy ended up purchasing a meat-processing plant in a nearby town, as well as a truck to pick up all the local ingredients and deliver them to the restaurant. He decided that in order to succeed in his quest to purchase from nearby farmers and support his community, he needed to adopt the business model of his behemoth competitors: vertical integration. In his vision, the "vertical" business is locally integrated and so remains in the community, with the Farmers Diner acting as the hub of a wheel, with all the farmers and allied producers and facilities extending outward into the region.

Vermont Smoke and Cure is the name of the processing plant Murphy purchased to help him supply his restaurant with local meat. When I visited the facility I was struck by the complex decisions Murphy is forced to make every day in order to preserve his ideals and achieve his goals. On our tour of the small plant we stopped at the smoke box, where bacon is prepared.

Larry Tempesta, the plant manager, explained the differences between smoking commercially grown pork belly and the local pork belly brought in by farmers: "Locally, every farmer has a different way of doing things."[40] Some keep their pigs in the barn; some fatten them up with grain right before slaughter; some let them roam freely. Unlike commercially produced swine, which are bred, raised, and slaughtered to be uniform, the local pigs are highly variable, so it takes Tempesta much longer to brine and smoke local batches of pork belly to make bacon. The machine that slices the bacon works best with long, even, rectangular pieces of pork, which means that the local batches require an extra step; after smoking the pork belly, workers need to trim the meat to fit the slicing machine. To make the business viable given such complexities, Murphy and Tempesta produce three lines of processed meats: commercial, private-label, and Farmers Diner brand. Their private-label business is doing very well, as the small farmers in New England are pleased that a small meat processor is available again nearby.

Murphy decided to develop the Farmers Diner business as a result of his own experiences in trying to raise and sell veal calves in Vermont. He saw how years of farming under the commodity model had transformed practices among farmers he knew in Vermont. "The art and science of farming has disappeared," he says.[41] Farmers have been forced to become technicians rather than stewards of the earth. Consumers have lost the connection between eating and farming. The Farmers Diner, Murphy hopes, will begin to change how we farm and how we eat.

Murphy is a true agrarian idealist: he talks with great pride of his visit to Wendell Berry's farm in Kentucky and the letters he gets from Berry exhorting him to do more and buy even more locally. In public gatherings he often quotes from Berry, Bill McKibben, Joan Dye Gussow, and other advocates of simple living, organic agriculture, and local food systems. In a conversation at a conference I have heard him say, "Wendell Berry says the Farmers Diner is democratically priced local food."

Murphy, however, is also a next-generation advocate of the taste of place, several steps removed from the "opt out" philosophy of those who participated in the back-to-the-land movement. When translated into a set of practices, his idealism is informed as much by the latest management theories and franchising models as by Berry's call that "the agrarian standard, inescapably, is local adaptation, which requires bringing local nature, local people, local economy and local culture into a practical and enduring harmony."[42] From the initial planning stages Murphy imagined a local food future modeled on the rise of Starbucks; he was always looking for potential investors, drumming up publicity to attract investors, searching out a good management team, and thinking about five restaurants, a commissary kitchen, and more.

Murphy's larger entrepreneurial vision set him apart from others in Vermont intent on building diversified farms that could sell their goods to interested individually owned restaurants. His ambition and willingness to promote his larger aims even when many of his plans had yet to be realized made him appealing to a national audience but often suspect back home. Local suspicions were in some ways confirmed in August 2005, when Murphy abruptly closed the Farmers Diner after two years in operation. Many in the community pointed to inconsistent service and food quality as a major issue. However, Murphy says he closed the restaurant because it was not able to successfully carry out the larger business model: "We needed to prove we could run the restaurant. [We] saw it as a test site or model and hoped in two years to open a larger restaurant in a more populous area."[43] His problem was that the "margins were razor thin. The diner was just too small, and we didn't have the throughput we needed."[44] He also points out that people who traditionally work in diners "were not used to using raw, local food," since most diners rely on purchasing ingredients that have already been processed (precut French fries, already portioned carrots, prepared coleslaw) from major distributors to save on food and labor costs. Compared to most diners, at the Farmers Diner there was "much more labor involved in prepping the food. We could spend fifteen hours a week just prepping potatoes."[45] He also talks of the higher costs involved in having a "good management team," especially the addition of a farm liaison in charge of creating a local supply chain for the restaurant.

This talk seems quite removed from Berry's call to abandon the market model for the agrarian standard. However, Murphy is trying to tackle an issue that is absolutely central to the goal of transforming the nation's food system into one based on local relationships, local flavors, and local economies: scale. In order for farmers to want to grow specifically for local markets, they must be assured that the market is viable. Murphy came to realize that *higher volumes locally guaranteed* could change the way farmers farm and possibly increase the number of farms in the state. At the same time, in order to make food considered affordable by average Vermonters— called "family-priced meals" in the restaurant business—he would have to increase volume in order to lower costs. The average price of an entrée at L'Etoile is $25, whereas at the Farmers Diner it was $10. If the price difference is not the result of the use of cheaper ingredients, then what can account for it?

Murphy has not packed up his idealism and given up on his vision of opening diners that spend seventy cents of every dollar on local purchases. Instead, he decided to create a bigger restaurant by purchasing an already-existing diner in Quechee, near major Vermont tourist destinations. This version of the Farmers Diner opened in the fall of 2006. "Our goal has always been to get to the next level," Murphy says. "We need a good management team in order to open a restaurant of 100 to 120 seats. It comes down to size."[46] If he is successful, Murphy could be a leader in the transformation of Vermont farms, farming, and food, building a version of the taste of place based on practices from both the land and the boardroom. If not,

Vermonters will have learned, yet again, that the market is a harsh master, and farming is hard.

One summer, when I was the executive director of Vermont Fresh Network, I was asked to have lunch with Patrick Mundler. The director of the Social Sciences and Management Department at the French Institute of Agriculture in the Rhône-Alps, Mundler had been funded by the U.S. State Department to explore local food initiatives all over the country. We chatted about his trip and his work in France, and then I provided an overview of Vermont Fresh Network and the organization's goal of creating direct partnerships between farmers and chefs, thereby building the taste of place. He was very engaged, and when I finished, he said, "Oh, we need a Vermont Fresh Network in France." I replied, "But I thought chefs did buy directly from farmers in France, especially in rural areas." He replied, "Well, yes, but increasingly the chefs would rather just buy from distributors." Perhaps the gap between French and American agrarian values is closing, despite all our past differences.

SIX

THE NEXT PHASE
TASTE OF PLACE OR BRAND?

TOD MURPHY OF THE FARMERS DINER ONCE SAID, "FOOD IS LOCAL AS LONG AS it is knowable."[1] Murphy spoke of knowing food in a discussion among advocates for sustainable agriculture and local foods about what defines local food. In the course of my research on taste of place and my work at Vermont Fresh Network, I attended numerous meetings at which people discussed the feasibility of using a fifty-, a seventy-five-, or a one-hundred-mile radius (from a restaurant or a supermarket, for example) as the criterion for determining whether a food was "local." Such discussions inevitably stalled in the face of all the impossibilities. In Ohio, for example, there could easily be no lettuce, no wheat, no cheese, and no wine available, and the list goes on. A restaurant serving only pork, sauerkraut, and Brussels sprouts in January would not do well in twenty-first-century central Ohio, although many of the citizens' ancestors may have been eating just that menu two hundred years ago. The allure of Murphy's definition lies in its valuation of place without focusing on a defined geographic radius. In his estimation, "local" foods encompass a much wider range of possibilities, including wines and cheeses that come from somewhere else. By expanding the repertoire of local foods to incorporate the use of locally based food and drink from around the globe, taste of place can account for but also transcend our contemporary reality, a world of consumer choice allowing the where, when, what, and how to be hidden from view. What is required to retain a local calculus while allowing such locales to exist in the national and global marketplace? Somehow cheeses, breads, wines, and other foods must become *known* rather than *unknown* commodities.

The taste of place is rooted in geography, but it is not confined solely to a specific region (contrary to the definitions favored by local foods activists). Using the taste of place to intervene into the web of global trade flows—not just for wine and cheese, but also for bananas, mangoes, chocolate, coffee, tea, salmon, cod, and more—offers greater possibilities for economic and cultural sustainability. At the same time it also bumps up against many competing and conflicting ideas about how to handle what is, in effect, a global market system. From the point of view of the consumer, not every person who drinks wine or eats cheese, bread, or, for that matter, maple syrup knows much about the origins of these foods or beverages. And, for the 98 percent of Americans who do not farm for a living, and especially the 55 percent who live in urban areas, how can they know much about our cheese, chocolate, coffee, and wine? We have plenty of *information*—we get it through advertising, word of mouth, custom, diet and health experts, cookbooks, and magazines—but almost all of our knowledge is abstract, a series of received recommendations, guidelines, or sales pitches. Our everyday lived experience, meanwhile, does not include farming, or having conversations with farmers, or, for many, even ever seeing a farm. Most of us are ignorant about the processes involved in getting food and wine from the farm to the table. And if Americans are going to stay off the farm, how can we gain experiential knowledge? This paradox—the chasm between what we know for ourselves about food and wine and what we must be told—lies at the core of any contemporary effort to build the taste of place.

At the same time, the link between taste and place is becoming *more* important as our entire globe becomes implicated in a set of agricultural and food practices driven by the rationales of a marketplace that, above all, provides an endless array of homogenous commodities: a strawberry is a strawberry is a strawberry, no matter if it comes from your backyard, California, or Chile. French farmers, growers, bureaucrats, and others were truly prescient when they championed the importance of an agrarian tradition and linked it to sensory experience and environmental conditions. Ultimately they were able to capitalize on the value of knowing food through place, process, and taste, thereby creating place-based commodities that took local knowledge and made it powerful around the world. The French foodview also allowed for such agrarian and culinary traditions to persist in France, even as Carrefour superstores sprouted up in suburbs and towns, and agricultural imports and exports expanded the boundaries of the nation's larder.

There is no question that the global food and wine landscape has changed dramatically in the century since the passage of the first French law supporting the Appellation d'Origine Contrôlée system and the founding of the Institut National des Appellations d'Origine. Global competition to capture agricultural markets has become increasingly intense, and the "taste of place" has become more an argument and less a part of a culture's common sense. A cacophony of voices now clamors for the attention of consumers, hoping to guide their everyday choices with compelling information. Our choices—at the supermarket, at the farmers' market, in the restaurant—now include the following options: organic, healthy, fair trade, authentic, wild, biodynamic, humane, and raw, in addition to local. All these descriptors for food and beverages theoretically help consumers *know* more, telling them as they navigate their way through the aisles of Whole Foods that the Styrofoam package of chicken breasts, the bag of coffee, the flat of strawberries are more than a placeless industrial commodity.

On one hand, knowledge is power. Shoppers at Whole Foods can imagine, and will possibly assume, that the free-range, cage-free, hormone-free chicken and the fair-trade and fair-wage-certified Nicaraguan coffee are higher-quality groceries, and that these choices are, as Murphy would describe them, "knowable" foods. On the other hand, there is little uniting all the various efforts to "know better food," to paraphrase the marketing tagline of Vermont's Strafford Organic Creamery. Our efforts to create a powerful countercuisine tend to intervene at the level of specifics, involving, for example, a certain type of animal husbandry or a particular idea about appropriate pest control. This approach continues to affirm our American assumptions that foods are first and foremost commodities. That they might be ingredients creating the building blocks of a cuisine that is located somewhere particular remains a more distant possibility. Since the present intervention strategy is piecemeal, an integration of values and practices or a foodview does not materialize. Such lack of unity often involves conflicting values and practices, and, above all, confusion about the role of the marketplace and government in affirming and promoting the taste of place. What comes first, the food as an object, or the food as representative of a place, a set of practices, or a tradition? Without a clear answer to this question, conflicting and confusing messages linking taste, place, and quality coexist. My use of "message" is intentional, for if consumers do not have commonsense knowledge of the link between taste, place, and quality, food and wine then need to *communicate* the process of going from farm to table. Conflicts arise, though, about who gets to control that communication. Meanwhile, consumers are confused about everyday choices, as well as about navigating the various claims to larger concerns, for example, what makes food or wine taste good or promote health? What is important? How can one judge? Amidst this tangled knot are numerous sustained and powerful efforts on the part of tastemakers and taste producers to bring order to the chaos, and especially to influence the various entities involved in making and regulating messages, that is, government officials, policies, and institutions.

VERMONT MAPLE SYRUP

Even in Vermont, a small, even insignificant, agricultural state when compared to powerhouses such as California and Iowa, several significant campaigns have been mounted to better communicate to consumers about the uniqueness of Vermont's food, especially maple syrup and cheese. Perhaps these attempts to link food and place are even more important here, since Vermont's bucolic working landscape has become a symbol of the state's unique character. Teaching people about the taste of place, then, is not simply good for the farm economy, but it is also beneficial for the strong tourist sector as well. A close look at efforts in Vermont reveals a central note of discord underlying them all: should we be celebrating the unique tastes of Vermont, or should we be building a brand? Taste of place and brand are very distinct framing categories for preserving, protecting, and promoting farming and food, leading to very different long-term links between taste, place, people, and food.

In the course of my work at Vermont Fresh Network (VFN), I realized that many people involved in public service in Vermont were keen on incorporating branding strategies now fully embraced by the business world as a means of building consumer loyalty to certain products.[2] The organization spent a great deal of time trying to understand how Vermont Fresh Network could transform its popular logo, a dinner plate with a farm scene in the middle, into a brand, or, in the words of Michael Jager, "an experience that delivers on a promise." Jager is a principal at Jager Di Paola Kemp Design, a firm that specializes in strategic branding for such companies as Burton Snowboards, Merrell Shoes, and Microsoft. In the increasingly crowded marketplace of goods, the more differentiated, unique, and somehow all-encompassing (of lifestyle, of values) the promise made through a brand, the more consumers will listen, take note, and, ultimately, buy, it is believed. Small nonprofits such as VFN (along with fast-food chains, state tourism offices, organic food processors, wine companies, and many others) that are trying to capture the consumers' attention and convince them to "vote with their fork" have turned to branding as a strategy. If consumers have already connected to branding, and loyally patronize companies that deliver an experience—a good, an identity, a lifestyle, or even a social vision—why not marshal those resources to make it happen locally?

Brand talk has also infiltrated government and academic arenas. During my tenure at VFN I was asked to participate in the Governor's Summit on the Vermont Destination. This effort was spearheaded by the Woodstock Foundation, a private foundation that runs the Billings Farm & Museum in Woodstock and is attempting to increase interest in Vermont's cultural heritage. The foundation's president, David Donath, was inspired by a 2004 report by the National Geographic Society that described Vermont as "tied for sixth place among the world's 115 most desirable destinations, rated according to their unspoiled attractiveness, distinctive cultural character, and the sustainability of their stewardship."[3] Donath was also struck by a National Trust for Historic Preservation report that claimed Vermont was an endangered site. For him, the summit was a means of "develop[ing] better strategies both to draw benefit from and to secure the distinctive character of the state. It is increasingly clear that the potential of the Vermont destination as an economic driver is tightly linked to the stewardship of Vermont's natural, cultural, and historical distinctiveness. To be sustainable, the relationship must be mutual, with reciprocal benefits for the economy and for stewardship."[4] This summit, then, was conceived by some as a way of coordinating a response to changing twenty-first-century economic and agricultural realities in order to build a distinctive sense of Vermont, both inside and outside the state's geographic boundaries.

The two-day event brought together people from the government, business, and nonprofit sectors to discuss the "uniqueness of Vermont," and throughout the push of building Vermont as a "brand" versus the pull of preserving Vermont's "heritage and culture" were hotly debated. We were introduced to the work of the summit with the "charge" by Vermont's governor, Jim Douglas:

The question at this Summit is how we capitalize on Vermont's distinctive mystique that is the essence of the Vermont destination—on that Vermont brand—how we develop a strategy that is comprehensive, that is forward-looking, in order to make it an economic engine for our state's future. We have to start by recognizing that a key to that strategy is preserving and protecting what we have, the natural, the cultural, the historic treasures of Vermont—the things that make this such a special place. So we have to think about the Vermont destination as a positive economic image for travelers and an image that will invite more investment in Vermont and create more and better paying jobs for Vermonters.

This charge, a vision connecting place, image, and economic viability by bundling it all into the notion of a "Vermont brand," framed the event. In particular, a group of people at the summit wanted to make sure that the Vermont brand reached out to the largest pool of possible consumers, inviting them to participate in the state's "distinctive mystique," and they cautioned against falling into, as they called it, a romantic nostalgia about the state and thus holding it back economically. As a cautionary tale, the secretary of marketing and tourism talked of an earlier debate about a national marketing campaign for the state. One faction had wanted the state's primary slogan to be "A Beckoning Country." Others, however, worried that it did not truly reflect the Vermont sensibility, and so the slogan was changed to "A Special World." The second choice, he felt, perpetuated an insularity that interfered with economic development. This fear of being too romantic, too idealistic, or too protective of a vision of Vermont that ultimately did not foster economic progress was an underlying theme in many discussions.

At the same time, the people representing the agricultural sector, the "working landscape" touted by many as crucial to Vermont's tourism sector, also had conflicting ideas about preservation and progress. Several felt that expanding potential markets for Vermont farm goods (nationally and globally) would be the most effective driver for economic development among farmers and food producers. Others, myself included, felt that this left Vermonters too much at the mercy of larger market forces without any long-term guarantees. We wondered how government policy could support the very small working farms and farmstead operations that helped create both the highly desirable and possibly endangered classifications that helped launch the summit. In the end, some basic goals were formulated, including:

- Understand Vermont is a real place, made up of real people doing real work, not a living museum.
- Appreciate that the Vermont sense of place (and brand identity) equates to a sense of well-being. It is a story of people, families, and communities making their lives in a distinctive place.
- Realize and fulfill Vermont's brand image, ensuring that it is based on the authentic and distinctive character of the Vermont Destination.[5]

These principles reflect the conceptual quandaries that arise for anyone trying to do something with "place" in a global marketplace. They articulate a need to protect what exists right now, for the "real work of the real people." Yet somehow, the scepter of economic progress always requires another layer, a fantasy bubble if you will, the "brand image" that will draw others in, or, more importantly, make them buy. This contemporary paradox in the pursuit of a taste of place in the United States, between the real practice and the perceived significance, exists clearly with Vermont's undeniably place-based food—maple syrup.

TASTING MAPLE SYRUP

Maple syrup is the food that best symbolizes a sense of place for Vermont, and for some it also represents Vermont's brand identity. Vermont is the nation's largest producer of maple syrup, in 2000 producing just over a third of the total United States crop. "Sugaring," as it is called locally, occurs throughout the state, and the number of producers is estimated at about two thousand, although that number certainly neglects hundreds of tiny family operations. Despite the market dominance of Vermont maple syrup nationally, the amount produced is not large, and a year that yields 500,000 gallons is considered a banner year.[6] The reason for the limited production is that maple syrup is really a wild food rather than a domesticated crop. The desired sap comes from a particular species of maple, the hard or rock maple (other species of maple also produce sap that can be made into syrup, but none other is as clear, sweet, and delicate as the hard or rock maple, or *Acer saccharum*). This species is found only in certain northern New World regions. Helen and Scott Nearing, who in the early days of Forest Farm made most of their "use economy money" from making maple syrup, succinctly explain in their *Maple Sugar Book* how location is all-important:

> Little or no syrup is made south of 35 degrees latitude or west of 95 degrees longitude. North Carolina, Tennessee, Iowa, and Missouri mark the south and west limits of the growth of the sugar maple. The provinces of New Brunswick and Southern Quebec in Canada mark the northern boundaries. The rock maple grows naturally in the middle Eastern district of the United States, finds the conditions it likes best and thrives there, with little the inhabitants can say, or need to do about it. It is self-seeding and self-perpetuating. It is a crop that needs neither sowing nor hoeing. Maple trees are self-supporting, need not be fed, watered, curried down, or housed. They need no cultivating, fertilizing, or spraying. They go on growing and leafing out and storing up sugar while the farm goes about his other business. In the spring the trees are standing in their old familiar places and replete with sap for the tapping.[7]

It takes on average forty years for a sugar maple tree to grow large enough to be successfully tapped. Sugar maples are tapped only during a certain period of the year, when the sap is "running," or between hard frost and bud break, usually sometime in March. Producing maple syrup is an art, and much of it lies in deciding *when* to tap the trees. If you tap too soon, the yield will be small, but if you miss the first days when the sap really starts to run, you may miss collecting what most consider to be the sweetest and clearest sap. If you tap for too long, you may introduce off flavors into your finished maple syrup. As the Nearings point out, their "idyllic picture [of sugaring] should not give the impression that sugar making is easy, or that the syrup pours from the tree full flavored and full bodied. . . . City dwellers often imagine the sap to be the same shade and flavor as maple syrup, an ambered colored fluid. Seen 'in the raw' dripping from the trees to the buckets, it is a disappointment and disillusionment to them."[8] Making maple syrup, like making wine, can be portrayed as a mythical act, but much prosaic labor is involved.

The difficulties inherent in making maple syrup (or "authentic" maple syrup) have contributed to the food's mystique, as well as to the strategies used by the state of Vermont and the people who make maple syrup to sell it in the marketplace. As with the wines of Burgundy or the cheeses of the Savoie, there are a number of different ways to make maple syrup. The process is understood to create distinct flavors, and these differences are monitored by the Vermont Agency of Agriculture and the Vermont Maple Sugar Makers' Association. Up until 2000, maple syrups were sold according to their grade: fancy, grade A, or grade B. A primary task when boiling sap into syrup is to obtain a certain level of sugar content; Vermont state requirements are slightly higher than those of any other state or Canada. Fancy syrup is the lightest, grade B the darkest. In 2000 the grading system was overhauled, because those involved in marketing Vermont maple syrup nationally felt that grade A and especially grade B had negative connotations, suggesting an inferior-quality syrup. The nomenclature was thus changed to "fancy," "medium amber," and "dark amber." Whatever name is applied to the various grades, the system for determining and labeling the syrups is uniform throughout the state: location, production levels, and production

FIGURE 13. Sugar making in Vermont. COURTESY OF SPECIAL COLLECTIONS, UNIVERSITY OF VERMONT LIBRARIES.

techniques are not incorporated in any way. All of the marketing for maple syrup is for a broad, statewide commodity food: Vermont maple syrup. The jugs, jars, or tins of syrup may list the name of the person or organization that made the syrup and where it came from, but no link is made between that information and the quality of the syrup.

Why is this? I consider this another example of America's foodview, a cultural framework that emphasizes the generic, the most known, and casts the widest net possible when trying to influence people's individual choices regarding food and beverage. In the case of Vermont, this means that blended syrups are sold in the exact same manner as those from a single sugarbush (or "maple syrup farm," if you will). However, many involved in producing and promoting maple syrup say this approach is taken because you *cannot taste a difference*. In their minds maple syrup of the same grade has a uniform flavor. They use physiological evidence to justify their cultural approach. Thus, the same dynamic between physiological taste and cultural taste exists with this truly place-based food, but with the opposite results as in France. Regulations exist, oversight occurs, and marketing campaigns are mounted. Since the underlying assumptions about what and how people taste are inverted (in France diverse flavors are linked to specific places, whereas in the United States uniform flavors are linked to mythic images), the activities and arguments are radically different.

The laws and regulations concerning maple syrup take "Vermont" as the common denominator. As is true in the regulation of most agricultural commodities in the United States, the boundaries of the state determine quality standards, even though few agricultural commodities stay within the boundaries of the state in which they were produced, or necessarily represent foods that are eaten on a day-to-day basis by residents. For maple syrup, the law states that " 'Produced in Vermont' shall mean only that maple syrup or other maple products which are manufactured in their entirety from pure, unprocessed maple sap within the state of Vermont."[9] Just as the early impetus for creating the first controlled appellations for Champagne more than one hundred years ago revolved around concerns about fraud, the Vermont laws attempt to control the "purity" of syrup sold as "Vermont maple syrup" by regulating the process by which it is created and the place where the sap is extracted and processed. The multipage "Vermont Maple Products Law" begins with definitions and continues to describe enforcement, sampling, testing, grading, labels, adulteration, advertising, violations, and penalties.

The law requires that producers obtain a license to make and sell maple syrup. Once an organization is licensed, the commissioner or inspector can enter the premises of the licensed sugar maker "for the purposes of inspecting the premises, records, equipment and inventory in a reasonable manner to determine whether the provisions of this chapter and the regulations adopted hereunder are being observed."[10] The purity of the maple syrup, according to the regulations, can be compromised by adulterating or filtering the syrup before it is graded and packaged. Article 491b, under the heading "Adulteration; Filtration," says that "maple syrup which is produced, packaged, handled or sold in this state shall not be bleached or lightened in color by artificial means except by simple filtration through cloth or paper, through a filter press or through food grade diatomaceous earth with a filter press to remove suspended solids."[11] This type of adulteration would allow the sugar maker to manipulate the grade of the syrup: fancy is generally preferred by consumers and is typically sold for a higher price.

The questions of purity regulated by the state of Vermont concern truth in advertising. One concern is the addition of artificial maple flavoring to syrup or the creation of artificial maple products. Another concern is the purchase of maple syrup from other regions, especially Quebec (the largest producer of maple syrup in the world), which is then blended with Vermont maple syrup and packaged using labels that say "100% Vermont Maple Syrup." Up until 2005 any sugar maker could use "Vermont" on a label, even if he or she blended the syrup from Vermont with syrup from other regions, but the word "Vermont" had to appear on the bottom third of the label. Studies showed, however, that this distinction meant nothing to the average consumer: if Vermont appeared anywhere on the label, it suggested it was a pure Vermont product. Now producers have to clearly indicate all the other regional sources for syrup. One newspaper reporter covering this rule change spoke to Steve Jones, general manager of Maple Grove Farms, one of twenty-three licensed syrup packers in the state, and the largest in the United States. He said, "For Maple Grove Farms of Vermont Inc. the new maple labeling rule means the company must devise a new way to label

97 maple products."¹² Jones also referred to the level of connection most Americans have to the place of origin of their food, even a food as unique as maple syrup, saying, "It's unfortunate for the state of Vermont and particularly the syrup industry because you're eliminating the word Vermont on maple syrup on our product and all over the United States. Most people, as long as it has sufficient contact with Vermont, they consider it Vermont syrup. They don't care where the tree is." Maple Grove Farms purchases syrup from New York, New Hampshire, Maine, and Canada. Jones's language also reveals something about the American foodview: he uses the term "syrup industry," and describes it as selling "maple products."¹³ This is in spite of the reality that the majority of sugar makers in the United States harvest maple sap and transform it into maple syrup as part of a diversified set of farm activities, or do it as a hobby, and that maple syrup is really a wild food, not a domesticated one.

Although maple syrup could eloquently typify the taste of place in the United States, in the end it has become part of the "Vermont brand." The regulation and marketing of maple syrup focuses on a broad, even generic, standard for flavor and purity, and always links any maple syrup—made anywhere in the state, using just about any method—to what I call "the Vermontiness of Vermont." The traditional metal containers in which the syrup is sold, and even the newer plastic bottles, depict a sugaring scene that fulfills a pastoral fantasy: A lone sugar maker taps trees using metal buckets. A horse and buggy stand nearby, poised to take the sap to a nearby sugarhouse nestled in the woods, with smoke pouring out of the chimney from the wood fire used to evaporate the sap. This pictorial representation flies in the face of Helen and Scott Nearing's much more prosaic vision from more than fifty years ago: "Sugar making is no dream of Elysian delight, with the trees 'distilling honey.' It involves arduous work, as anyone who has tried it will have found out."¹⁴ The allure of maple syrup, and by association the state of Vermont, is its mythic appeal and the way in which it evokes nostalgia for a time when most sugar makers did tap the sap with metal buckets (not plastic tubing) and used horses (not all-terrain vehicles) to transport the sap. The Vermont Maple Sugar Makers' Association and the state's Agency of Agriculture celebrate the "Elysian dream" with maple sugar festivals, sugar-on-snow parties, and open-house weekends at a number of rustic sugarhouses.

And while the Elysian dream persists, over the past fifty years, truth be told, new technologies have been developed to lessen the work. Many sugar makers now use blue plastic piping that uses gravity to bring the sap straight from the trees into the sugarhouse. The piping is strung from tree to tree in the sugarbush. Individual taps hooked into the piping allow the sap to flow out of the tree, into the piping, and down the hill to the sugarhouse, where it drips into a stainless-steel vat. A technique of reverse osmosis, which removes much of the water in the sap *before* evaporation, has also been developed, shortening the time required to turn sap into syrup. Sugar makers can purchase reverse osmosis machines, a strange amalgamation of metal chambers and tubes, which are kept in the sugarhouse. The making, grading, and selling of Vermont maple syrup thus often combines a commodity framework for "producing" maple syrup—the embrace of new technologies, and an acceptance of standard measures for evaluation—with a story that harkens to a mythic past. Is this Jager's definition of a brand, an experience that delivers on a promise? But what, exactly, is promised? With maple syrup, unlike products involved in the AOC system, the making and the selling do not have to reinforce each other; there are no regulations linking process, place, and taste. Maple syrup, then, does fulfill the guiding principles of the Governor's Summit on the Vermont Destination—realize and fulfill Vermont's brand *image,* ensuring that it is based on the authentic and distinctive character of Vermont— which in turn reflects our prevailing foodview that compartmentalizes the process from the result.

BEYOND BRAND TO TASTE OF PLACE?

But what if it is possible that maple syrup, like the wines of Burgundy and the cheeses of the Savoie, possesses a goût du terroir? More than a century ago the naturalist John Burroughs eloquently wrote of the unique taste of maple syrup, "When made in small quantities—that is, quickly from the first run of sap and properly treated—it has a wild delicacy of flavor that no other sweet can match. What you smell in freshly cut maple-wood, or taste in the blossom of the tree, is in it. It is then, indeed, the distilled essence of the tree."[15] What a shame that this "wild delicacy of flavor" has been made standard, more reliant on a color than a result of place. Are producers of Vermont maple syrup missing an opportunity to valorize the taste of place more thoroughly, to examine closely the variation in flavors of maple syrup made in the state, and ultimately to link the tastes of maple syrup to process and place?

In the early days of my research into terroir in the United States I thought about maple syrup often, but my focus was on wine and cheese, so my musings never went very far. Two years ago, however, I got into a conversation with John Elder, an environmental writer and English professor who also happens to have a sugarbush in Starksboro, near where I live. He asked me about the taste of place, with which he had become familiar while he spent time in Tuscany with olive growers. He wanted to explore the geology and geography of his sugarbush, to look for a link between his location in Starksboro and the taste of his Maggie Brook maple syrup. Our initial meeting, a casual conversation over coffee, turned into a more sustained debate about what the taste of place can mean in the rural, agricultural state of Vermont, a dialogue between a conservationist and a trained chef who also happens to research and teach, and so, perhaps inevitably, we have begun a collaborative research project on the taste of place and Vermont maple syrup.

Elder purchased 142 acres of forested hillside in 1999 and has been making maple syrup since 2000. This parcel of land is now the hub of both family and scholarly activity for Elder; as his family built the sugarhouse and began to make maple syrup, he began to write articles and book chapters on Maggie Brook Sugarworks. After hearing often of Maggie Brook, I went up to visit in the midst of sugaring season. To get to Elder's sugarhouse I drove upward and eastward. I now live at the western edge of Vermont in the Champlain Valley, the lowest-lying and most temperate region of the state (and thus known as Vermont's banana belt). There are sugarbushes in this region, but the forested hills and valleys of the spine of the Green Mountains is where the largest number of sugar maple stands can be found. The drive east is a slow climb. The mountains initially loom in the distance. By the time I got to Bristol, a small town with a longstanding sawmill, I was at the foothills of the mountains, close to Mount Abraham, one of the highest peaks in the state. I turned north, following the spine of the mountains, always casting dark shadows on this narrow valley running from south to north. In Starksboro, the next little town north of Bristol, I jogged to the right, heading up and into forested land. After several miles I reached the turnoff for Elder's road. Winding up the steep grade, I passed two small farms, one with alpacas grazing in nearby fields and another with sheep. The steep slopes, heavy forest, and hard, rocky soil of this valley are geological realities that have always shaped farming here; this is a place of hard-scrabble homesteads.

I turned onto the rough logging road leading to the sugarhouse, quickly ascending to the end of the road and the small wooden building. Most of Elder's acreage rests on the side of a steep hill. Almost exclusively forest of maple and birch with some ash, the land is wooded save for the small sugarhouse perched halfway up the hill and a nearby treehouse built by one of his sons. Elder and his sons built the sugarhouse using wood from the property. The concrete floor was poured by a friend of Elder's son, Matthew. A small room at one end of the sugarhouse contains stacked wood, ready to be loaded into the cast-iron chamber below the main evaporator. The main room has several windows, a couple of camp chairs, a shelf, and a table to store paraphernalia and snacks for the long days of sitting and watching the sap turn into syrup. Also in the main room is a filtering machine.

The evaporator dominates the building, which is roughly twenty feet by ten feet. Elder bought his evaporator from the Leader Evaporator Company in northern Vermont, the leading supplier in the United States for all types of equipment needed for making maple syrup. The company, founded in 1888, makes a variety of evaporators for operations big and small, including the "Leader Half Pint, ideal for the backyard sugar maker with 15–50 taps."[16] The Elders make maple syrup primarily the traditional way, using a wood-fired evaporator; they do not have a reverse osmosis machine, nor do they use a vacuum to get the sap out of the trees. They do, however, rely on plastic tubing and gravity to get the sap from the trees into the two large stainless-steel tanks on a platform on the edge of the sugarhouse. Plastic tubing was introduced to sugar makers about forty years ago, and in many hillside sugarbushes, the tubing has replaced the picturesque metal buckets pictured on the maple syrup labels. Using tubing alleviates the burden of moving up and down the steep hillsides with heavy metal buckets, and it eliminates the possibility of spilling precious sap on the way down to the sugarhouse. Also, many old sap buckets contain lead, and plastic tubing does not.

For Elder, sugar making is a form of conservation. He says, "Vermont is an unusual state because almost all of the state is wooded, and almost all of the property is owned by small landholders."[17] He wants to preserve Vermont's forests, but he wonders, "When forests are being fragmented all over the East, how do you not 'parcelize' the forest?" Most people who own forestland in Vermont derive revenue from allowing their trees to be harvested for timber. "Selling the logs to the mill is basically a colonial economy," according to

Elder, the globalized and industrial timber production system trapping landowners.[18] He, like the farmers and chefs concerned with keeping small-scale farming viable, is looking for a middle way.

Like countless small farmers all over the United States and beyond, then, Elder is attempting the value-added approach, and in fact he argues that conservation efforts should always focus on adding value to the forests. "Sugaring for a lot of smallholders like us is a great way to add value and make some money." The Elders make a modest amount of syrup—eighty gallons in an average year—and earn a modest amount of money. Elder says, "We put a lot of that in small glass containers—the small gift bottles get a better and better rate of return. In the end we make $2,500 in basically three concentrated weeks. It is something we do as a family. If you perceive it as recreation and a family activity, then we make plenty of money." Another enterprise of Elder's is logging and selling green-certified lumber, which earns him another few thousand dollars a year. "We are keeping in this forest because we are sugar makers. So are our neighbors," he says. He wants to create a working model for twenty-first-century small landholding. He would like to get people to hold on to their forested land, and also get new people to invest. At the same time, he says, "you don't want to supplant people. These days the big sellers are farmers."[19] They sell off their forested land so they can afford to hold on to their pastures and open lands.

So Elder's quite unique consideration of sugar making as a form of conservation, and his subsequent realization that twenty-first-century conservation needs to embrace generating measured and controllable value from the forests, led him to the goût du terroir. When we first met he had just enlisted the help of a geologist at Middlebury College, Jeff Munroe, who had agreed to do a geological map of Elder's sugarbush and to test his sap and syrup. We decided to organize a comparative tasting of a number of local maple syrups, mimicking the techniques used by wine aficionados to determine flavor profiles of wines from the same region. We started with a fairly informal tasting after a spring luncheon at my house. We were all struck by how different each of the syrups was when compared to the others. Most Americans use maple syrup only for their pancakes, even though it can be used in myriad ways. It can be used not only as a sweetener for baking, but also as a flavoring agent in savory sauces and marinades. Because of the way most Americans use it, the syrup is rarely evaluated for its ability to enhance other flavors, but is rather judged only for being "sweet," or perhaps "mapley." Everyone at the tasting agreed that there was a difference in the flavors, but how could we make sense of them, and did they relate to place? Since then we have developed an increasingly systematic approach. We now have a team of people—Elder, Munroe, myself, and Montserrat Almena-Aliste, a European food scientist who specializes in the sensory evaluation of foods—trying to determine if place influences taste in Vermont maple syrup. Our little group combines expertise in every aspect of *terroir:* culture, physiology, and environment. Like the winemakers of Burgundy or the cheese makers of the Savoie, we want to build a "dossier" that argues for the terroir of maple syrup in the Bristol-Starksboro region.

After our initial experiments we asked Almena-Aliste to help us organize the tastings so that we could truly capture any unique taste experiences. We began by doing a blind comparative tasting of maple syrups of the same grade. We tasted two syrups that came from a similar region, and then two blended maple syrups, one from Canada and one from the United States. We began to develop a vocabulary of discernment, a language for communicating with each other about the physiological sensations occurring in our mouths. Next, the geologist created a geological map of Vermont and plotted all the sugar makers listed in the Vermont Maple Sugar Makers' Association on the map. There are three major soil types in Vermont: limestone, schist, and slate. Sap and syrup from these different soil types were collected. Almena-Aliste led us through another blind tasting of these syrups;

again, we always tasted syrups of the same grade to minimize possible flavor distractions.

Munroe and his student assistant, Lee Corbett, ran a number of saps and syrups through an inductively coupled plasma spectrometer, which can determine the chemical composition of any substance that can be dissolved in liquid form. The machine has a robotic arm that reaches out, sucks up the liquid under study, rinses between samples, and then analyzes the composite parts of the sap and syrup. The initial results showed statistically significant amounts of calcium, potassium, and magnesium. Were these mineral elements contributing to the taste differences we were experiencing? We sat down and began our next tasting. Lined in front of us were three green plastic vials labeled with three-digit numbers. Only Almena-Aliste knew which number corresponded with each sugarbush. We performed a triangular test, in which two of the three vials contained the same syrup, and one was different; our goal was to determine the outlier. After three separate tastings Almena-Aliste collected our results. During one set we tasted syrup produced on limestone versus shale bedrock; another limestone versus schist; and finally shale versus schist. When the results were tabulated, in more than 50 percent of the tests Almena-Aliste had accurately tasted differences and identified the outlier. According to Almena this was a good start, but at this point our results were not statistically significant. We began to consider what other elements might play a role in taste differences and whether the test was set up correctly. Interestingly, Jeff said the syrups were chosen according to the mineral composition of the saps of each corresponding sugarbush (thus, he chose the syrups whose saps had the highest amounts of magnesium, calcium, and potassium), because he had only just run all the syrups through the spectrometer. But the morning of the tasting, when he was finally able to compare sap and syrup composition, he found that some syrups *lost* minerality and others *gained* minerality in the syrup-making process. This gave us room to consider a new set of tasting parameters based solely on the mineral content of the final syrups rather than the saps. We also discussed the significance of how the sap was made into syrup: Reverse osmosis? Propane or wood fire? Large- or small-scale production? The more maple syrup we taste, the more I am reminded of Yolande Noël's characterization of terroir and the taste of place as a double helix: we are beginning to unlock certain secrets, but are we moving inward or expanding ever upward and outward? We recently did a series of triangular tests with sixty people using maple syrup from trees growing exclusively on limestone, schist, or shale. The results were significant. Participants were actually able to taste bedrock, or at least variations in syrups from different bedrocks.

Elder has begun to talk to other sugar makers in his region to discover the "local knowledge" linking place and taste; he is particularly interested in the evaporation process and in the way the sugarbush is managed. I am reaching out to the Agency of Agriculture, hoping to learn more about the history of the grading process, and also documenting both traditional and contemporary sugaring practices.

In our second year of research we again collected maple syrup from more than twenty sugar makers, all of whom had a sugarbush primarily on either shale, schist, or limestone bedrock. We began to ask the sugar makers a series of questions about how they transform forty gallons of sap into one gallon of maple syrup. We also asked each sugar maker what they think influences the final flavor of maple syrup. Interestingly, all identified an environmental factor. Some said soil, some said weather conditions, and others said north- or south-facing slope. A chemist, Molly Costanza-Robinson, has now joined our team, and she is making maple syrup under controlled conditions in her laboratory and looking at the underlying chemical composition of syrup from the three different bedrocks. We still get together on a regular basis to taste various maple syrups, working to build a sensory vocabulary based on place.

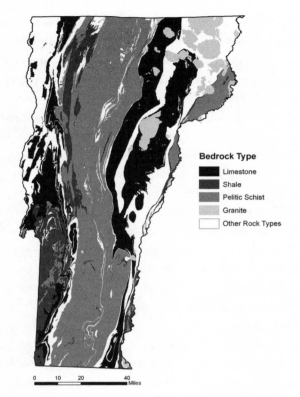

FIGURE 14. Bedrock map of Vermont. COURTESY OF LEE CORBETT.

Henry Marckres, who works for the Vermont Agency of Agriculture and as part of his duties works with the state's sugar makers, has also joined the research team. At one tasting, during which the team, led by Almena-Aliste, tasted maple syrups from the 2007 season, we started to talk about the persistence of tradition in the taste of maple syrup. I wondered if syrup taste profiles were understood to be typical over long periods of time, as AOC cheeses in France are crafted to retain a characteristic flavor profile. Marckres then pointed out that until the late 1940s, the majority of fluid maple syrup made in the state was in fact made into maple sugar, and that this crystalline form of maple dominated in the state for centuries, which clarifies why "sugar maker" and "sugarbush" are the preferred words related to an activity that today usually creates a product more like honey than sugar. The decreasing cost of refined cane sugar over the course of the twentieth century, Marckres said, made the production of maple sugar less lucrative, and there was a concerted effort in the state to promote the syrup rather than the sugar form of maple. So even with maple syrup, the food most clearly identified with Vermont, the vagaries of commercial markets (local, national, and global) have shaped everyday practices. And thus perhaps the terroir of maple syrup allows not recourse to the state's Elysian past, but rather a twenty-first-century method for building the taste of place.

Although this collaboration is just beginning, we hope to develop an argument for maple syrup's taste of place. To go from this idea to reality, of course, we will have to navigate the government agency that oversees both the production and sales of maple syrup, and that relies on Vermont's brand image to sell it. Perhaps our biggest challenge, however, will be changing the minds of American consumers: if it is hard to absorb ideas linking quality and place with wine, which is already established as a different type of commodity, how can it be achieved with maple syrup, chiefly considered limited to the domain of Sunday morning breakfasts?

ROCAMADOUR OR CABÉCOU?

To contrast the French and American foodviews without considering the ways that the globalization of the marketplace has also influenced practices and values in France would be naïve, a descent into a fantasy of "France, the ideal food culture." As the outcry in Aniane over the prospect of creating a grand cru winery on public lands indicates, everyone involved in the small-scale production of artisanal foods and beverages can feel as if they are under assault, no matter where they live. In France, the allure of the brand, or *le marc*, is strong, and branding is applied in attempts to sell all manner of goods, including foods and beverages. In the movie *Mondovino*, for example, several French winemakers mention the contemporary fascination with *le marc* as a sign of changes in the wine business, and this, for them, is associated with a sense of loss.

Creating a unique experience with every purchase has influenced even the protected world of the *appellations d'origine contrôlée*. Early in my research into terroir, during the spring of 2000, I spent several weeks in Bordeaux and regions to the east, the ur-region for the appellation system and also an area known for a rich regional cuisine. As I visited numerous markets and ate at local restaurants, I noted the widespread use of small fresh goat cheeses, called cabécou, especially in a traditional salad that included frisée (a type of escarole), walnuts, and a warm disc of the mild cheese. At one point my husband and I decided to visit the nearby Cahors region, the site of an AOC wine appellation, and also to visit Rocamadour to investigate a relatively new AOC cheese, awarded the appellation in 1996 (another regional cheese, Roquefort, by contrast, was the first cheese awarded AOC status, in 1925). Since I had yet to encounter a cheese named "Rocamadour," we went to find out more about the new AOC cheese.

The drive from the heart of the Dordogne east into the Lot region was beautiful, a gradual transition from the lush, green Dordogne River valley up into a more arid and open plateau. The plateau is made of a series of causses, unique geological formations of limestone plateaus punctuated by deep river valleys, especially that of the Lot River, which snakes through the entire region. The causses do not nurture much vegetation, and are primarily barren and marked by deep rainfall-created chasms, locally known as *igues*. Each plateau, or causse, is named: the Causse de Martel, the Causse de Cahors, the Causse de Quercy. The causses have long been perfect grazing grounds for sheep and goats, and thus the region is known for many distinctive cheeses.

After a few hours we arrived in the town of Rocamadour, or, more accurately, at the top of Rocamadour, for it is a medieval town built into the side of limestone cliffs along the Lot River. When we pulled into the town we saw parking lot after parking lot and, in the distance, a huge medieval church. Having done little advance research on the town's history, we stumbled onto one of the tourist sites most visited by the French, second only to Mont Saint-Michel. The town is named for Saint Amadour, also known as Roc d'Amadour, but for centuries the main attraction of the town has been the shrine to the Black Virgin, possibly carved by Saint Amadour, whose body was found in a cave on the cliff. Traditionally, pilgrims have climbed the 216 steps leading from the medieval town up to the Notre Dame church on their knees, passing the stations of the cross as they ascend. We decided to park and walk down the steep staircase hugging the cliffs. We ended up on a tiny street lined with limestone buildings, now almost all transformed into tourist shops. We wandered around looking for cheese, or perhaps a cheese maker—anything that would link the dramatic location with the AOC-designated food. We had no luck. Puzzled, we left and proceeded on to Cahors, the seat of the AOC wine and also home to the region's Maison de l'Agriculture.

At the Maison de l'Agriculture I explained my confusion to an agricultural researcher. Why were there no goats, no cheese makers, no Rocamadour cheese in Rocamadour? He smiled and explained that Rocamadour cheese is in fact the very cabécou we had been eating for weeks! *Cabécou* is the name for a small fresh goat cheese in Occitan, a local dialect. When the dossier for AOC designation was accepted by the INAO, the decision was made to call this AOC cheese *cabécou de Rocamadour*, since this name was recognized throughout France. Also, by including Rocamadour in the name, this cheese could be differentiated from other cabécou-style goat cheeses made throughout the Dordogne and Lot regions. In fact, the term *cabécou* is completely left off all the packaging, which highlights the town of Rocamadour and also includes a drawing of a goat's head. My field notes from before we took the trip from the Dordogne to the Causse de Quercy reveal my mistake in thinking Rocamadour cheese was any different from the cabécou. This AOC cheese has shifted meaning in the journey from local food to labeled commodity. I was eating it every day. As I wrote in my field notes, "There is one AOC cheese, Rocamadour. In the region 'cabécous' are also made, a very small disk of goat cheese sold fresh and often served baked on bread with a salad. Though still very agricultural, the Dordogne's primary industry these days is tourism, as much for the French as foreigners."

As I left the office I picked up a promotional packet for cabécou de Rocamadour in the lobby. Five glossy information sheets were enclosed: "A Small History of a Great Cheese," "The Conditions of Production," "The Economic Influence," "What Is an AOC?" and "The Region of Delimitation." On the left-hand side of each sheet an old etching of the town of Rocamadour takes up a narrow column from top to bottom, showing the church at the top of cliff, the buildings perched on the side, and, at the bottom, the Dordogne River. This strategically placed etching, probably from the nineteenth century, intends to link the present food to the past just as the wintry scenes of plow horses pulling the sap to the sugarhouse do for maple syrup. The "Small History of a Great Cheese" is truly small, consisting of one short paragraph. "Formerly called 'cabécou de Rocamadour,' for what it signifies in Occitan *[ce qui signifie en Occitan]*: a small goat cheese, it is one of the oldest goods of the Causses de Quercy. In a fifteenth-century monograph written by J. Meulet, the cheeses of 'Rocamadour' were cited as the way tenant farmers could pay their taxes. Thus, the tenancy agreement between the largest landholder in the region, the bishop of Evreux, and his vassals fixed the value of the tithe in cheese."[20] So, a cheese with a lineage back to the everyday life of the region's *paysans,* who made cheese simply to preserve the excess milk of their goats, eventually lost the connection to Rocamadour, the site of the people's servitude to the medieval Catholic church (with its subsequent decline in power over ensuing centuries), but now, in the early twenty-first century, the cheese becomes associated yet again with Rocamadour. Perhaps this is a fitting, rather than ironic, end for cabécou, for hasn't the chase for consumer markets become the new tyranny of the modern *paysan*? If thousands of people stream to Rocamadour each year on their tour of Europe, why not re-create the cabécou de Rocamadour as a way to enlighten people from around the nation and the globe about the unique tastes of the cheese?

"The Conditions of Production" outlines the specific technical and environmental conditions for making the cheese that enabled it to be awarded AOC status in 1996. Among these are "the boundaries of the appellation enclose a precise terroir, unified by geological (soil and vegetation), climatic (altitude, rainfall), and human (traditional practices) similarity; only Alpine or Saanen goats with a maximum of ten animals per hectare; a respect for tradition in making Rocamadour, including manually creating a round disc with a mold and aging in caves." These detailed conditions for production explain why the decision to rename cabécou as cabécou de Rocamadour is not simply selling the sizzle but not the steak, and distinguishes the French *savoir vivre* when it comes to artisanal practices and small-scale farming. There is a *method* to the process before the marketing begins. Today 18,000 goats produce more than five million liters of milk that are transformed into cabécou by the cooperative of producers, including forty farmsteads and five companies that blend milk to make the cheese.[21] Each year approximately thirteen million cabécous de Rocamadour are made, with more than half coming directly from farmsteads and the rest from small-scale artisanal enterprises.

Linking the celebration of local cuisine to regional tourism has a long history in France, as shown by Curnonsky's numerous regional cookbooks and guides, the red Michelin guides, and many other regional cookbooks. Regions like Provence, Alsace-Lorraine, and Normandy have long embraced their regional identity through their food, but over the past twenty-five years other regions have, too. The Dordogne and Lot regions have expanded their endeavors, attracting many urbanites from other parts of France, the United Kingdom, and beyond who purchase second homes and take summer vacations there. Also, the many medieval and prehistoric sites in the Dordogne, including the famous Caves of Lascaux, attract many school tours and families during the summer. In Castelnaud-la-Chapelle, a medieval hill town in the Dordogne, the castle at the top of the hill became the Museum of Medieval Warfare in 1985. Outside the castle various instruments of medieval warfare have been reconstructed. In the summer, medieval reenactments are staged, and evening tours of the castle are available. As publicity materials state, "During the entertaining one-hour tour throughout the castle, Jeannette, Castelnaud's cook, who is as good with words as she is with food, tells marvelous tales of château battles."[22]

Some longtime residents of the Dordogne feel that the traditional foods of the region—foie gras, truffles, cabécous—have been swallowed up by the tourism industry, victims of the development of a regional theme park. In an interview, the operators of a small press that prints books related to the Dordogne, including cookbooks, argued that the emphasis on terroir has increased in the past thirty years; people are searching for their *racines,* or roots, as an antidote to their increasingly fast-paced lives. They defined terroir as, first, a form of nostalgia for a sense of identification with a region that people have lost due to urbanization, and, second, a way to create a brand for products that capitalizes on this nostalgia in the marketplace. Taste producers, such as the cheese makers who compiled the dossier for Rocamadour and the agriculture officials overseeing the process, are acting in much the same manner as the sugar makers and agriculture officials in Vermont. As these Dordogne residents put it, "These people are trying to add value [*valoriser*] to products as a way to sell them in the marketplace."[23] Lifelong residents of the region, they see the same mix of myth making and market savvy in the Dordogne that I see in Vermont.

In the final analysis, should their perhaps jaded sensibility be ours as well? Are the stories of Vermont maple syrup and cabécou de Rocamadour new versions of the children's classic "The Emperor's New Clothes"? Or, to use modern American parlance, are we being sold a bill of goods? Should we adopt the same skepticism when purchasing place-specific food and drink as we do when buying a used car? I think not, as long as the primary explanation for *why* we should purchase the quart of medium amber syrup or the disc of goat cheese is not based on abstract notions of authenticity or distinction. Rather, we should buy it for the possibility of an exquisite taste sensation, an experience that will lift us above the Aunt Jemima and Kraft Cracker Barrel. We should also make these purchases because by choosing the pure Vermont syrup or the cabécou we are voting for a future that includes a strong localized agrarian and culinary culture around the globe.

SLOW FOOD

If the ties that bind maple syrup in Vermont and goat cheese in the Dordogne and the Lot are physiological and cultural tastes that emerge from these specific places, it would be remiss not to consider the successful organization Slow Food, dedicated to such tastes. This nonprofit organization began as a loose network of people in the Piedmont region of northern Italy. Its members wanted to promote the great tastes of that region, often best known for the industrial activities of Turin and its environs, even though agriculture is a major economic engine of the area. First known as Arcigola (which could be translated as "arch gluttony"), the organization was renamed Slow Food in 1989, when the charismatic journalist and political activist Carlo Petrini took the helm and membership increased to more than

11,000. As Petrini points out in his slim but influential book *Slow Food: The Case for Taste,* Slow Food's publications and activities were consciously "subversive" from the very beginning. He uses as an example the organization's first guide to Italy's traditional *osterias* (restaurants, similar to French bistros). In that guide, Petrini writes, the *osterias* used "subversive terms like 'tradition,' 'simplicity,' 'friendliness,' 'moderate prices,' and above all *territory*—a word I will use throughout this book in exactly the same sense as the French word *terroir:* the combination of natural factors (soil, water, slope, height above the sea level, vegetation, microclimate) and human ones (tradition and practice of cultivation) that gives a unique character to each small agricultural locality and the food grown, raised, made, and cooked there."[24] Petrini goes on to say that the main impetus for the organization was a "critical reaction to incipient globalization"; the larger political and economic forces shaping everyday values and practices in Piedmont and Italy more generally convinced him and his fellow organizers of the importance of the taste of place. Petrini locates Slow Food's origins in a Roman piazza, where he and other members of Arcigola were protesting the opening of a McDonald's by creating an anti–fast food manifesto. And Slow Food has brilliantly intervened in the global debate about our industrial and global food system, creating a worldwide network of farmers, artisans, and consumers who ally themselves by their "slowness" with respect to food and drink.

The headquarters of Slow Food International is located in Bra, a small city in the southern part of Piedmont, a region of Italy with both a rich winemaking tradition (renowned wines such as barolo, barbaresco and nebbiolo are made here) and modern industrial activity (nearby Turin is the world headquarters for Fiat). Driving south from Turin to Bra, the landscape is flat; this region is known for growing wheat, rice, and fodder for cows and pigs. The view is not necessarily bucolic: the flat landscape is frequently interrupted by industrial warehouses and production facilities. As you move farther south, the landscape gets lusher and rolling hills begin to appear. This is the edge of wine country, and towns like Alba, Cuneo, and Asti are not far away. Bra has long been a market town for the surrounding agricultural areas, as well as a hub for the leather industry, and many tanneries were located there through World War II.[25] The offices of Slow Food are located on a small, narrow, cobblestone side street near the center of town. Some are in a medieval stone building at the top of the street, and others are located farther down the street in a renovated stable. The organization now has more than 80,000 members worldwide, and it spreads its mission with publications, conferences, tastings, and, more recently, the creation of the University of Gastronomic Sciences.

Slow Food continues to publish guides to food, wine, and restaurants. In addition to the Italian guides to regional food and wine, the organization now publishes a guide to New York and San Francisco. Every other year Slow Food transforms a former Fiat factory in Turin into a festival of slowness with the Salone del Gusto, a multiday event celebrating slow food from around the world. In 2002 more than 130,000 people attended the event, and the numbers steadily increased in 2004 and 2006. At these events hundreds of artisans from all over Europe and beyond set up booths where attendees can taste and learn about the cheeses, beers, wines, olive oils, and more on display. In addition to the booths there are many scheduled events, including a number of *laboratori del gusto,* or taste workshops, much like the one I attended in the Mas de Saporta in the Languedoc. Here people are encouraged not only to use their sight, smell, and touch to discern unique tastes, but also to consider the food's connection to the earth. The Salone del Gusto, like France's Semaine du Goût and the new Ateliers du Goût and Vermont Fresh Network's Annual Forum and Farmers' Dinners, bring farmers, chefs, and consumers together and creates a lesson in taste education, because, as Petrini says, "the organoleptic profile of the food we eat (in other words, how it strikes our organs) is being constantly impoverished."[26]

In 2004 Slow Food launched Terra Madre, or Mother Earth, a multiday event for people from around the world who are committed to making food and drink slowly. To participate in this event one must meet specific criteria, all of which are related to being involved in a "food community." All those nominated are vetted by the Slow Food organization, which then chooses delegates. "It sounds like the United Nations of artisanal food production. I get to have a whole week to get a perspective on the whole world," said Meghan Sheradin, executive director of Vermont Fresh Network, when she was planning to attend the 2006 Terra Madre.[27] A number of other delegates from Vermont also attended the event, including Enid Wonnacott, from Northeast Organic Farming Association (NOFA-VT), and John Elder and his family, representing Maggie Brook Sugarworks. Enid organized a "farm community," made up of a group of Vermont organic farmers, to attend. Once the delegates arrived, they were housed in people's homes throughout the region. More than six thousand delegates came from around the world to meet and to celebrate, in Petrini's words, "the unique character to each small agricultural locality and the food grown, raised, made, and cooked there."[28] Such an event might just symbolize the possibilities for twenty-first-century terroir: global in vision, local in execution, and embodying aesthetic and entrepreneurial ideals.

The Slow Food Manifesto, approved by the delegates at the founding conference of the International Slow Food Movement for the Defense of and the Right to Pleasure, states, "In the name of productivity, Fast Life has changed our way of being and threatens our environment and our landscapes. So Slow Food is the only truly progressive answer. That is what real culture is all about: developing taste rather than demeaning it. And what better way to set about this than an international exchange of experiences, knowledge and projects? Slow Food guarantees a better future."[29] In all its efforts, Slow Food has linked taste, place, and culture. And although many of the organization's ends are economic (developing better markets and creating a more informed public to enable the preservation of artisanal food and wine), the means are definitely sensual and aesthetic: "The primary instrument that, when trained, can make it possible for anyone to choose an adequate and enjoyable diet are our senses. . . . The education of taste is the Slow way to resist McDonaldization."[30]

The AOC system emerged as a regionally based method for protecting French food and drink in the international marketplace. By 1960 Italy had adopted a remarkably similar set of laws and regulations to regulate winemaking, called the Denominazione d'Origine Controllata. The global reach of Slow Food promises to help extend the values and practices of the AOC and DOC, for the mission of Slow Food makes all the same assumptions as does the AOC system about why foods like syrup and goat cheese are important, assumptions about the need to make recourse to discernment and location. However, Slow Food also tends to rely on assumptions about tradition and, by association, authenticity when making arguments for why certain foods and drinks need to be championed. In Italy, where the peasant agrarian tradition still maintains a lot of cultural capital (as it does in France), where small-scale agriculture and the production of artisanal foods and wines remain a vital component of the agricultural economy, and where they have a system of controlled appellations modeled after the French AOC, discussing the lineage and authenticity of Parma ham and Parmigiano-Reggiano might make good sense.

But as the organization becomes global and seeks to make convincing arguments about the importance of both scientific and cultural terroir, these arguments need to be inflected with the values and practices of the home cultures. Does Slow Food really take account of the global possibilities for terroir? Carlo Petrini, in an editorial in the Italian newspaper *La Stampa*, talks about the threat to the European winemaking tradition by wine production in other countries. As he points out, 200 million of the 260 million hectoliters of wine produced in the world still come from Europe (with three

countries—France, Italy, and Spain—responsible for 75 percent of that total), but wine is now made "in over 70 countries from all five continents."[31]
The editorial, ostensibly concerning threats to European winemaking, reveal Petrini's deeper assumptions about the importance of traditional practices, which permeate the mission of Slow Food. He feels that winemaking
in Europe is in decline due to increased competition from these new ar-
rivals. He claims, "Though brought by European immigrants, it only started
to make a significant mark in the 1970's—truly an instant compared to old
Europe's millennia-old wine culture."[32] He characterizes the winemaking in
these non-European locations (he lists California, Argentina, Chile, South
Africa, Australia, and New Zealand) as being focused on "maximum profit
criteria . . . [combined with] a blind faith in technology [that] led many winemakers to think that wine could be created in the cellar."[33] He feels that this
approach, combined with legislation that is "very lax" compared to that in
Italy, where winemaking "has always been strictly regulated by official bod-
ies, controls, and certification systems," means that non-European wines
have very little personality.[34]

But isn't Petrini being very selective in his use of the past to explain sensory differences between European and non-European wines? Yes, wine has
been made in Europe for thousands of years, but those strict regulations
that he says have "always" been in existence are less than a century old. And
a major impetus for creating those regulations was to have better oversight
over poorly made wines being produced in Europe, to create a distinction
between quality wine and plonk. He concludes with a lyrical evocation of
terroir, saying that "whether the vineyards are planted in the coastal climate
of Bordeaux or . . . in the hills of Piedmont and Tuscany, it is here that you
can experience the history, climate, the land, or in a single word, the 'terroir'
that have defined a cultural, economic and human story of wine." So his
more global articulation of terroir in *Slow Food* has transformed in this instance into a more Euro-nationalist definition, perhaps because the European

wine industry has been suffering financial difficulties over the past five years because of overproduction and the high value of the euro compared to the U.S. dollar. But although Petrini and his Slow Food compatriots, like many in France, believe in a brand of historical determinism, articulated as the authenticity and tradition needed to create food and drink that taste good, neither he nor the organization is a cheap sentimentalist. He concludes his editorial on a pragmatic note: "But we cannot remain dazzled by our glorious past. European producers need to join forces to meet the challenge of products that are commercially attractive but, apart from a few rare exceptions, are nothing to get really excited about."[35] The time has come, it seems, for Europeans to fight.

But what of the legions of global members of Slow Food—in the United States, Australia, and New Zealand, for example—who are both producers and consumers? What are they to think of Petrini's recent shift to a Euro-nationalist definition of terroir? Slow Food awards people from all over the world for their efforts to preserve traditional foods—American chestnuts and Argentinean potatoes, for example—but it does not concern itself with wine from these locations, even though it has been made in both these nations for at least a century. In the end, these sensory objects, the handiwork of various people and places, whether it is syrup, cheese, or wine, must always jostle for attention in the global marketplace, made knowable somehow, whether by individuals, organizations, or governments.

EPILOGUE

IN THE MIDDLE OF THE DOCUMENTARY *MONDOVINO*, A TELLING SCENE REVEALS the global possibilities for the taste of place. Neil Rosenthal, a New York wine importer, and J. M. Baptiste, a Haitian immigrant working in Rosenthal's warehouse, both articulate their perspective on *terroir* with director Jonathan Nossiter. Rosenthal, who makes his living importing European wine and selling it to Americans, must be fluent in the language of terroir in order to sell potential buyers on the quality of the wines he represents. However, he explicitly rejects the language of connoisseurship. He says, "For me, enjoying the greatness of wine doesn't have anything to do with some sort of snobbish quality about life." He continues by making the association between wine and farming, saying, "Just the notion that wine is an agricultural product means that it must have a very specific taste related to where it is produced. This is important. To me there is nothing hidebound about this." Rosenthal, the son of a Brooklyn pharmacist whose family never drank wine, now champions the taste of place in wine. His vision is inclusive, not exclusive. "This [terroir] is an absolutely critical notion for expressing the entire panoply, the entire joy of life," he explains.

In the subsequent scene Nossiter and Rosenthal, standing in the middle of a warehouse stacked high with boxes of wine, talk to Baptiste and his co-worker about terroir. Baptiste says, "I have got an example [of terroir] from my country. We have a mango tree that might have two different tastes; the side where the sun comes up in the morning tastes different from the side where the sun goes down in the afternoon. So that is one thing. And then the same tree over here, you may have some kind of terroir right here, and over here one step there might be another tree with a different kind of terroir. So I understand that." By working at the wine warehouse, Baptiste has been introduced to a way of knowing food and drink that allows him to interpret Haitian local knowledge in a new way, bringing the mango under the taste-of-place umbrella. Because our food and drink come from the earth, they must somehow speak to those origins. This is perhaps the universal element of terroir. If you possess the local knowledge, by birth or design, the taste of place can reside anywhere. All that is needed to cultivate it is a certain attention to the environment where the food and drink are grown, the skill to nurture those grapes, mangoes, or other products, and, finally, the ability to discern their local tastes in the mouth. In the course of my research, people told me of the terroir they had discovered in Sri Lankan jaggery, in Maine potatoes, and in Mexican tequila, to name just a few items.

Local environments and practices do affect our physiological taste experiences, but particular stories show that the different emphasis placed upon terroir and the acclaim awarded to it also depend, above all, on how much tasting terroir matters to everyone involved in farming, cooking, eating, and drinking. If place and taste matter in a certain context—say an entire culture, like in France, or a group of dedicated believers, like in California, or a cadre of trained professionals, like winemakers around the globe—then the taste of place can thrive and inform both practices and values. If other concerns—market forces, aesthetic ideals, cultural capital, competing values— seem more paramount, however, then this mode of discernment takes a back seat or disappears altogether. Thus, in any location, including France and certainly the United States, the engagement with this foodview is not universally held, nor is it the only framing mechanism for discerning taste. In France, the "molecular gastronomy" promoted by Hervé This has become quite the trend, with chefs like Heston Blumenthal following the lead of Spanish chef Ferran Adrià and parsing individual ingredients such as potatoes, mangoes, and jaggery to the extent that not only are their geographic origins obscured, but their botanical ones are, too. And in the United States the discourse that dismisses paying too much attention to what we taste in our mouth remains powerful. As Gene Kahn, the founder and former president of Cascadian Farms, states in an article on the rising interest in organic foods in America, "This is just lunch for most people. *Just lunch.* We can call it sacred, we can talk about communion, but it's just lunch."[1]

Yet the taste of place does matter, perhaps even more now than it did a hundred years ago, when French citizens—agrarian activists like the *vignerons* of Champagne, or champions of France's *cuisines du terroir* like Curnonsky and Austin de Croze, or political insiders like Joseph Capus— helped make a local understanding a culture's foodview. Our times are characterized by the industrialization and globalization of our food supply: in Europe and the United States eating has never been less connected to where people live and how people farm, whereas in Mexico, farming has never had less to do with what people who live there actually eat. If we want to have a relationship to food based on location, we must *make it happen,* for tasting place and eating locally now more than ever require the "truant freedom of practices" described by Michel de Certeau and Luce Giard. Tasting place is an intervention into a world of food and wine that is now globally organized. This global structure always pushes us in other directions, toward universal commodities universally located and anonymously created.

But what should the taste of place look like in our era, and how should it develop in the future? Should our primary guide be the language of discernment, the organization of practices, and the agrarian and culinary values developed in France? Should citizens around the globe—Randall Grahm in California, Odessa Piper in Wisconsin, John Elder in Vermont, Carlo Petrini in Italy, J. M. Baptiste in Haiti—seek to incorporate the French foodview into their own vision, in effect creating a global community of local tastes, tastemakers, and taste producers? Yes. And no. Yes, there is much cultural work to be done to create foodviews that place value on where food comes from, how it is grown or raised, and how it tastes. The combination of culture, environment, and agriculture that undergirds terroir, and the long-standing involvement of the French state in keeping those values and practices viable (even as the marketplace and the organization of social life have changed drastically), is an admirable model. Also, the collective tradition embedded in the AOC process, which requires groups of farmers, winemakers, or cheese makers to work together to demonstrate the uniqueness of their potatoes or wine or cheese, helps guarantee that these products will not simply be commodities in the global marketplace but will remain rooted in place and communities.

However, there are pitfalls to the French foodview, and particularly to their contemporary definition of terroir. As other scholars have noted, the AOC system and all its associated efforts, as well as the overall anti-globalization and anti–free market stance of the French, leads to a nostalgia for the past and difficulties in imagining the future: "This has far-reaching consequences in the search for an identity fixed in a historical continuum which would dispel the fears of coping with rapid social change. For ironically, the process of *labélisation* serves only to distance the past: as a consequence, heritage becomes a fixed institutionalised fact and any organic relationship to the past is lost."[2]

The French taste of place remains primarily essentialist, a fundamentalist rally for the importance of "location, location, location." Terroir, as defined by the French, can be static; there are few opportunities for bricolage, or tinkering, and making do on French soil. Because of this, many of the most innovative winemakers in France today do not seek to participate in the AOC system. There are a number of winemakers in Bordeaux, called *garagistes,* who buy grapes from different Bordeaux appellations and then blend them in their garages. Using their own criteria for tasting terroir, they create new wines in new bottles. Other vintners in France have embraced Rudolf Steiner's principles of biodynamic farming—adopting organic practices, instituting homeopathic applications, and following the lunar cycle in their vineyards—whether they are working within a designated appellation or not, and whether other nearby winemakers agree with these practices or not.

Is there a twenty-first-century model for tasting terroir that can take the best of the French foodview and yet also include the many global entrepreneurial efforts to localize taste, as well as the realities of contemporary markets and social life? Many people invested in tasting terroir and making sure such tastes can be found in the future end up stopping short of such claims, usually because of the past. The weight of history ends up serving as the gatekeeper for truly tasting terroir, requiring a commitment to the power of tradition, heritage, and experience for any local tastes, anywhere. According to this view the lack of a long agrarian tradition in the United States, and the swift transition from small-scale peasant farms to large commodity farms, dooms us to a long, slow walk toward terroir; only the passage of time will give us the customs and know-how necessary to really taste place. But must we adopt this fundamentalist position? Why can't we take back an original definition of terroir, the earth from the point of view of agriculture? Why can't we rescue terroir from the prison of essentialism, a highly problematic endeavor as seen in the nationalistic and fundamentalist movements of the past century?

Tasting terroir means having a sensibility, adopting a set of framing values that inform agricultural practices and shape physiological tastes. The people growing the potatoes and mangoes, making the wine and cheese, and cooking the bouillabaisse and mushroom lentil salad can enable us all to taste place if they are given the cultural tools and structures. This vision of the taste of place certainly embraces Gustavo Esteva and Madhu Suri Prakash's call for a "grassroots postmodernism," an orientation that neither clings to the past nor is mired in the present but looks toward the future. But will these people have the necessary tools and structures? Some of the depth of *terroir* in France—developed over time and across geographic space—can certainly be attributed to the influence of the French state in the form of laws, regulations, and subsidies. In the global marketplace, however, national attempts to control and support specific markets are increasingly under assault, in part because of the increased importance of supranational entities such as the European Union, NAFTA, and the World Trade Organization. And as the story of the increased corporate interest and control over organic production in the United States demonstrates, new methods of capturing consumer markets are always vulnerable to the consolidating and industrializing impulses of modern capitalism. The next chapter of the story of the taste of place will have to include some instrumental means for continuing to make local food and drink more than commodities, through economic incentives, research and policy priorities, and cultural programs.

Randall Grahm says terroir is "something like a Platonic form, or perhaps more concretely, a beautiful, ordered waveform," or perhaps a sensual double helix.[3] In this sense, this word is ultimately untranslatable because it never refers to specifics, only to universals: the earth, the human condition, the relationship between nature and culture. Could unlocking the secret language of terroir offer up the same possibilities as the once unknown language of DNA? Perhaps the taste of place is best understood, as Grahm sees it, as an aspiration, a desire to make and appreciate food and wine with place always in mind. Grahm grounds the universality of terroir by associating it with practices, claiming that there is no "terroir extract" or terroir formula. Instead, there is only "terroir intelligence: [this] does not entirely repose in the site itself, of course, but within the relationship that exists between the land and those who have farmed that land over generations."[4] The only way to unlock the secret language is to keep working to create the taste of place.

The last time I spoke to Mark W. Davis, years after we shared an office together at the New England Culinary Institute and shortly before he left Vermont for warmer climes, we shared a glass of wine and a plate of Vermont cheeses at Smokejack's restaurant in Burlington. His passion for the importance of terroir in understanding wine was a bit more muted than it had been previously, for he had turned his attention to biodynamic practices as the "next new thing" in the wine world. He was increasingly looking for certain people and their wines rather than a certain region writ large as the greatest guarantor of high-quality wines. He continued to believe in terroir, however, saying, "Terroir is character. It is the triumph of diversity over homogeneity." If terroir exists more as an aspiration than as a guarantee, other practices, such as biodynamic vineyard practices or new methods of making farmstead cheeses, can be placed under its umbrella. In the end, he said, "Terroir is there, but it is not there." Or, the taste of place exists, as long as it matters.

APPENDIX

THE FRENCH GOVERNMENT ESTABLISHED THE APPELLATION D'ORIGINE CON-
trôlée (or AOC) system in 1935. Initially the AOC classification, administered by the French Ministry of Agriculture, was designed solely to protect
specific wines. The system, however, proved economically successful, and
by 1990 AOC status had been extended to include dairy and other agricultural products. Following France's example, Italy established its own system
of classification, called the Denominazione di Origine Controllata. Instituted in 1963, the DOC system, like the AOC system, involved the place-
ment of a quality assurance label on food products, especially wines. In the
1970s, Spain, South Africa, and Germany established agricultural classification systems of their own. Spain modeled its system, the Denominación de
Origen, on the Italian system, and applied it to wines and other foodstuffs.
South Africa has a system for classifying wines based on location of production, while Germany's system classifies wines based on the ripeness of
grapes. The United States also got on board in the 1970s, creating American
Viticultural Areas; the AVA designation is applied to grape-growing regions
in the United States based on geographic features and does not take into
consideration traditional practices or production limits. In 1986 Portugal
instituted its own system for classifying wines, known as the Denominação

de Origem Controlada. The newest system of classification belongs to Austria. In 2001, Austria established the Districtus Austriae Contrallatus, an origin-based system that combines a denomination of origin with a clear taste profile. Recognizing the importance of protecting place-specific food and drink, the European Union established a system of protection for geographic names known as the Protected Designation of Origin (PDO) in 1992. Possessing PDO status guarantees a close link between the product and the *terroir;* award of the PDO label means the product cannot be reproduced outside the designated territory.

FRENCH AOC PRODUCTS

CHEESES
Abondance
Banon
Beaufort
Bleu d'Auvergne
Bleu des Causses
Bleu du Haut-Jura or de
   Gex or de Septmoncel
Bleu du Vercors—Sassenage
Brie de Meaux
Brie de Melun
Brocciu Corse or Brocciu
Cabecou
Camembert de Normandie
Cantal or Fourme de
   Cantal or Cantalet
Chabichou du Poitou
Chaource
Chevrotin
Comté
Crottin de Chavignol or
   Chavignol

Epoisses de Bourgogne
Fourme d'Ambert or
   Fourme de Montbrison
Laguiole
Langres
Livarot
Maroilles or Marolles
Mont d'or or Vacherin du
   Haut-Doubs
Morbier
Munster or Munster-
   Géromé
Neufchâtel
Ossau-Iraty
Pélardon
Picodon de l'Ardèche or
   Picodon de la Drôme
Pont-l'Evêque
Pouligny-Sainte-Pierre
Reblochon or Reblochon
   de Savoie
Rocamadour

Roquefort
Roue de Brie
Sainte-Maure de Touraine
Sainte-Nectaire
Salers
Selles-sur-Cher
Valençay

Table Olives
Olives cassées de la Vallée
   des Baux-de-Provence
Olives de Nice
Olives de Nîmes
Olives noires de la Vallée
   des Baux-de-Provence
Olives noires de Nyons

FRUITS, VEGETABLES,
AND CEREALS
Chasselas de Moissac
   (grape)
Coco de Paimpol (bean)

Lentille verte du Puy
  (lentil)
Muscat du Ventoux (grape)
Noix de Grenoble (nut)
Noix du Périgord (nut)
Olive de Nice (olive)
Piment d'Espelette (chili
  pepper)
Pomme de terre de l'Île de
  Ré (potato)

FRESH MEAT AND OFFAL
Dinde de Bresse (poultry)
Taureau de Camargue
  (beef)

PRODUCTS OF ANIMAL
ORIGIN
Crème d'Isigny (fresh
  cream)
Miel de Corse—Mele de
  Corsica (honey)
Miel de Sapin des Voges
  (honey)

DRINKS
Cornouaille (hard cider)
Domfront (alcoholic
  sparkling drink)
Pays d'Auge or Pays
  d'Auge-Cambremer
  (hard cider)

OILS AND FATS/OLIVE OIL
Beurre Charentes-Poitou
  or Beurre des
  Charentes or Beurre

des Deux-Sèvres
  (butter)
Beurre d'Isigny (butter)
Huile d'olive d'Aix-en-
  Provence (olive oil)
Huile d'olive de Corse
  (olive oil)
Huile d'olive de Haute-
  Provence (olive oil)
Huile d'olive de la Vallée
  des Baux-de-Provence
  (olive oil)
Huile d'olive de Nice
  (olive oil)
Huile d'olive de Nîmes
  (olive oil)
Huile d'olive de Nyons
  (olive oil)

NONFOOD PRODUCTS
Foin de Crau (hay)
Huile essentielle de
  lavande de Haute-
  Provence (essential oil)

WINE
*Unless otherwise noted, all
wines have AOC status.
AOVDQS indicates Appella-
tion d'Origine Vin de Qualité Supérieure.*

Alsace
Alsace Chasselas or
  Gutedel
Alsace Gewurztraminer
Alsace Grand Cru

Alsace Pinot or Klevner
Alsace Pinot Noir
Alsace Riesling
Alsace Sylvaner
Alsace Tokay–Pinot Gris
Crémant d'Alsace

Beaujolais
Beaujolais
Beaujolais Supérieur
Beaujolais-Villages
Brouilly
Chénas
Chiroubles
Coteaux du Lyonnais
Côte de Brouilly
Fleurie
Julienas
Morgon
Moulin à Vent
Régnié
Saint-Amour

Bordeaux
Barsac
Blaye
Bordeaux Clairet
Bordeaux Côtes de Francs
Bordeaux Rose
Bordeaux Sec
Bordeaux Supérieur
Cadillac
Canon-Fronsac
Cerons
Côtes de Blaye
Côtes de Bourg
Côtes de Castillon

Crémant de Bordeaux
Entre-deux-Mers
Fronsac
Graves
Graves de Vayres
Graves Supérieures
Haut-Médoc
Lalande de Pomerol
Listrac-Médoc
Loupiac
Margaux
Montagne Saint-Emilion
Moulis en Médoc
Pauillac
Pessac Léognan
Pomerol
Premières Côtes de Blaye
Premières Côtes de
   Bordeaux
Puisseguin Saint-Emilion
Sainte-Croix-du-Mont
Sainte-Foix-Bordeaux
Saint-Emilion
Saint-Emilion Grand Cru
Saint-Estèphe
Saint-Georges Saint-
   Emilion
Saint-Julien
Sauternes

Burgundy
Aloxe-Corton
Auxey-Duresses
Batard-Montrachet
Beaune
Bienvenue Bâtard-
   Montrachet

Blagny
Bonnes-Mares
Bourgogne
Bourgogne Aligoté
Bourgogne Aligoté
   Bouzeron
Bourgogne Chitry
Bourgogne Claret
Bourgogne Côte
   Chalonnaise
Bourgogne Côte Saint-
   Jacques
Bourgogne Côtes
   d'Auxerre
Bourgogne Côtes du
   Couchois
Bourgogne Coulanges-la-
   Vineuse
Bourgogne Epineuil
Bourgogne Grand
   Ordinaire
Bourgogne Hautes-
   Côtes de Beaune
Bourgogne Hautes-
   Côtes de Nuits
Bourgogne la Chapelle
   Notre-Dame
Bourgogne le Chapitre
Bourgogne Montrecul
Bourgogne Mousseux
Bourgogne Passetoutgrain
Bourgogne Vézelay
Chablis
Chablis Grand Cru
Chablis Premier Cru
Chambertin
Chambertin-Clos de Bèze

Chambolle Musigny
Chapelle-Chambertin
Chassagne-Montrachet
Chevalier-Montrachet
Chorey-les-Beaune
Clos de la Roche
Clos des Lambrays
Clos de Tart
Clos de Vougeot
Clos Saint-Denis
Corton
Corton-Charlemagne
Côte de Beaune
Côte de Beaune Blanc
Côte de Beaune Villages
Côte de Nuits—Villages
Crémant de Bourgogne
Criots Bâtard-Montrachet
Echezeaux
Fixin
Gevrey-Chambertin
Givry
Grands-Echezeaux
Griotte-Chambertin
Irancy
Ladoix
La Grande Rue
La Romanée
La Tâche
Latricières-Chambertin
Mâcon
Mâcon Supérieur
Mâcon-Villages
Maranges
Marsannay
Mazis-Chambertin
Mazoyères-Chambertin

Mercurey
Meursault
Montagny
Monthelie
Montrachet
Morey-Saint-Denis
Nuit-Saint-Georges
Pernand-Vergelesses
Petit Chablis
Pommard
Pouilly-Fuissé
Pouilly-Loche
Pouilly-Vinzelles
Puligny-Montrachet
Richebourg
Romanée-Conti
Romanée-Saint-Vivant
Ruchottes-Chambertin
Rully
Saint-Aubin
Saint-Bris
Saint-Romain
Saint-Véran
Santenay
Savigny-les-Beaune
Viré-Clessé
Volnay
Vosne-Romanée
Vougeot

Côtes du Rhône
Beaumes de Venise
Château-Grillet
Châteauneuf-du-Pape
Clairette de die
Condrieu
Cornas

Coteaux de Pierrevert
Coteaux du Tricastin
Côte Rôtie
Côtes du Lubéron
Côtes du Rhône
Côtes du Rhône-Villages
Côtes du Ventoux
Côtes du Vivarais
  (AOVDQS)
Crozes-Hermitage
Gigondas
Hermitage
Lirac
Muscate de Beaumes-
  de-Venise
Saint-Joseph
Saint-Peray
Tavel
Vacqueyras
Vinsobres

Languedoc-Roussillon
Banyuls
Banyuls Grand Cru
Blanquette de Limoux
Cabardes (AOVDQS)
Clairette de Bellegarde
Clairette du Languedoc
Collioure
Corbières
Costières de Nîmes
Coteaux du Languedoc
Côtes de la Malepère
Côtes du Roussillon
Côtes du Roussillon-
  Villages
Faugeres

Fitou
Limoux
Maury
Minervois
Muscat de Lunel
Muscat de Mireval
Muscat de Rivesaltes
Muscat de Saint-Jean de
  Minervois
Picpoul de Pinet
Rivesaltes
Saint-Chinian

Loire
Anjou
Anjou-Coteaux de la
  Loire
Anjou-Gamay
Anjou-Villages
Bonnezeaux
Bourgueil
Cabernet d'Anjou
Châteaumeillant
  (AOVDQS)
Chaume
Cheverny
Chinon
Coteaux d'Ancenis
Coteaux de l'Aubance
Coteaux du Giennois
  (AOVDQS)
Côte Roannaise
Côtes d'Auvergne
  (AOVDQS)
Côtes du Forez
  (AOVDQS)
Cour-Cheverny

Fiefs Vendéens
(AOVDQS)
Gros Plant (AOVDQS)
Haut-Poitou
(AOVDQS)
Jasnières
Menetou-Salon
Montlouis
Muscadet
Muscadet Côtes de
Grand-Lieu
Muscadet des Coteaux de
la Loire
Muscadet de Sèvre-
et-Maine
Pouilly-Fumé
Pouilly-sur-Loire
Quarts de Chaume
Quincy
Reuilly
Rose d'Anjou
Rosé de Loire
Saint-Nicolas-de-
Bourgueil
Saint-Pourçain (AOVDQS)
Sancerre
Saumur
Saumur-Champigny
Saumur Sec Blanc
Savennières
Savennières Coulée-
de-Serrant
Savennières Roches-
aux-Moines
Touraine

Touraine Amboise
Touraine-Azay-le-Rideau
Touraine-Mesland
Valençay (AOVDQS)
Vouvray

Provence and Corsica
Ajaccio
Bandol
Bellet
Cassis
Coteaux d'Aix
Coteaux Varois en Provence
Côtes de Provence
Muscat du Cap Corse
Pallette
Patrimonio
Vin de Corse

Southwest
Bearn
Bergerac
Bergerac Sec
Buzet
Cahors
Côtes de Bergerac
Côtes de Bergerac
Moelleux
Côtes de Duras
Côtes de Saint-Mont
(AOVDQS)
Côtes du Marmandais
Fronton
Gaillac
Haut-Montravel
Irouléguy

Jurançon
Jurançon Sec
Madiran
Marcillac
Monbazillac
Montravel
Pacherenc du Vic-Bilh
Pécharmant
Saussignac
Tursan (AOVDQS)

Other Regions
Arbois (Jura)
Arbois Pupillin (Jura)
Bugey (AOVDQS)
(Rhône-Alps)
Champagne
(Champagne)
Château-Chalon (Jura)
Côtes de Toul (AOVDQS)
(Est)
Côtes du Jura (Jura)
Couteaux Champenois
(Champagne)
Crémant du Jura (Jura)
L'etoile (Jura)
Moselle (AOVDQS)
(Est)
Pineau des Charentes
(Charentes)
Rose de Riceys
(Champagne)
Roussette de Savoie
(Savoie)
Vin de Savoie
(Savoie)

EUROPEAN UNION PROTECTED DESIGNATION OF ORIGIN PRODUCTS

AUSTRIA
Cheeses
Gailtaler Almkäse
Tiroler Almkäse or Tiroler
    Alpkäse
Tiroler Bergkäse
Tiroler Graukäse
Vorarlberger Alpkäse
Vorarlberger Bergkäse

Fruit, Vegetables,
and Cereals
Wachauer Marille
    (apricot)
Waldviertler Graumohn
    (poppy seed)

BELGIUM
Cheeses
Fromage de Herve

Oils and Fats/Olive Oil
Beurre d'Ardenne (butter)

FINLAND
Fruit, Vegetables,
and Cereals
Lapin Puikula (potato)

GERMANY
Cheeses
Allgäuer Bergkäse
Allgäuer Emmentaler
Altenburger Ziegenkäse
Odenwälder Frühstück-
    skäse

Fresh Meat and Offal
Diepholzer Moorschnucke
    (lamb/mutton)
Lüneburger Heidschnucke
    (lamb/mutton)

Drinks (Water)
Bad Hersfelder
    Naturquelle
Bad Niedernauer Quelle
Bad Pyrmonter
Birresborner
Bissinger Auerquelle
Blankenburger Wiesen-
    quelle
Caldener
    Mineralbrunnen
Ensinger Mineralquelle
Felsenquelle Beiseförth
Gemminger
    Mineralquelle
Göppinger Quelle
Graf Meinhard Quelle
Giessen
Haaner Felsenquelle
Haltern Quelle
Höllen Sprudel
Katlenburger
    Burgbergquelle
Kißlegger Mineralquelle
Leisslinger Mineral-
    brunnen
Lieler Quelle
Löwensteiner Mineral-
    quelle

Rhenser Mineralbrunnen
Rilchinger Armandus
    Quelle
Rilchinger Gräfin
    Mariannen-Quelle
Schwollener Sprudel
Siegsdorfer Petrusquelle
Steinsieker Mineralwasser
Teinacher Mineralquellen
Überkinger Mineral-
    quellen
Vesalia Quelle
Wernigeröder Mineral-
    brunnen
Wildenrath Quelle

GREECE
Cheeses
Anevato
Batzos
Feta
Formaella Arachovas
    Parnassou
Galotyri
Graviera Agrafon
Graviera Kritis
Graviera Naxou
Kalathaki Limnou
Kasseri
Katiki Domokou
Kefalograviera
Kopanisti
Ladotyri Mytilinis
Manouri
Metsovone

Pichtogalo Chanion
San Michali
Sfela
Xynomyzithra Kritis

Table Olives
Kalamata
Konservolia Amfissis
Konservolia Atalantis
Konservolia Piliou Volou
Konservolia Rovion
Konservolia Stilidas
Trumba-Ambadai
    Rethimno Crète
Trumba Quios
Trumba Thasu

Fruit, Vegetables,
and Cereals
Aktinidio Sperchiou
    (kiwifruit)
Corinthiaki Stafida Vostitsa
    (grape)
Fistiki Aeginas
    (pistachio)
Fistiki Megaron (pistachio)
Kelifoto fistiki Phtiotidas
    (pistachio)
Kerasia Tragana
    Rodochoriou (cherry)
Mila Delicious Pilafa
    Tripolos (apple)
Mila Zagora Piliou (apple)
Portokalia Maleme Hanion
    Kritis (orange)
Rodakina Naoussas
    (peach)

Tsakoniki Melintzana
    Leonidiou (eggplant)
Xera Syka Kymis (fig)

Fresh Fish, Mollusks,
and Crustaceans
Avgotaracho Messo-
    longhiou (fish eggs)

Products of Animal Origin
Meli Elatis Menalou
    Vanilia (honey)

Oils and Fats/Olive Oil
Apokoronas Hanion Kritis
    (olive oil)
Archanes Iraklio Kritis
    (olive oil)
Exeretiko partheno eleo-
    lado: "Thrapsano"
    (olive oil)
Finiki Lakonias (olive oil)
Kalamata (olive oil)
Kolymvari Hanion Kritis
    (olive oil)
Kranidi Argolidas
    (olive oil)
Krokees Lakonias
    (olive oil)
Lygourgio Asklipiou
    (olive oil)
Petrina Lakonias (olive oil)
Peza Iraklio Kritis
    (olive oil)
Sitia Lasithi Kritis
    (olive oil)
Viannos Iraklio Kritis
    (olive oil)

Vorios Mylopotamos
    Rethymnis Kritis
    (olive oil)

Nonfood Products
Krokos Kozanis (saffron)
Mastiha Chiou (gum)
Mastihelaio Chiou
    (mastic oil)
Tsikla Chiou (gum)

IRELAND
Cheeses
Imokilly Regato

ITALY
Cheeses
Asiago
Bitto
Bra
Caciocavallo Silano
Canestrato Pugliese
Casciotta d'Urbino
Castelmagno
Fiore Sardo
Fontina
Formai de Mut dell'alta
    Valle Brembana
Gorgonzola
Grana Padano
Montasio
Monte Veronese
Mozzarella di Bufala
    Campana
Murazzano
Parmigiano-Reggiano
Pecorino Romano

Pecorino Sardo

Pecorino Siciliano

Pecorino Toscano

Provolone Valpadana

Quartirolo Lombardo

Ragusano

Raschera

Robiola di Roccaverano

Spressa delle Giudicarie

Taleggio

Toma Piemontese

Valle d'Aosta Fromadzo

Valtellina Casera

Table Olives

La Bella della Daunia

Nocellara del Belice

Fruit, Vegetables,
and Cereals

Asparago Bianco di
Bassano (asparagus)

Basilico Genovese
(basil)

Castagna Cineo (chestnut)

Farina di Neccio della
Garfagnana (chestnut
flour)

Fico Bianco del
Cilento (fig)

Ficodindia dell'Etna
(Indian fig)

Marrone di San Zeno
(chestnut)

Mela Val di Non (apple)

Oliva Ascolana del Piceno
(olive)

Pomodoro S. Marzano
dell'Agro Sarnese-
Nocerino (tomato)

Bread, Pastry, Cakes,
Confectionery, and Biscuits

Pane di Altamura (bread)

Meat-Based Products

Capocollo di Calabria
(pork)

Coppa Piacentina (pork)

Culatello di Zibello
(pork)

Pancetta di Calabria
(pork)

Pancetta Piacentina
(pork)

Prosciutto di Carpegna
(ham)

Prosciutto di Modena
(ham)

Prosciutto di Parma
(ham)

Prosciutto di San Daniele
(ham)

Prosciutto di Veneto
Berico-Euganeo (ham)

Prosciutto Toscano (ham)

Salame Brianza (pork)

Salame di Varzi (pork)

Salame Piacentino (pork)

Salamini Italiani alla
Cacciatore (pork)

Salsiccia di Calabria (pork)

Soppressata di Calabria
(pork)

Sopressa Vicentina (pork)

Valle d'Aosta Jambon de
Bosses (ham)

Valle d'Aosta Lard d'Arnad
(ham)

Products of Animal
Origin

Miele della Lunigiana
(honey)

Ricotta Romana (milk
product)

Oils and Fats/Olive Oil

Alto Crotonese (olive oil)

Aprutino Pescarese
(olive oil)

Brisighella (olive oil)

Bruzio (olive oil)

Canino (olive oil)

Cartoceto (olive oil)

Chianti Classico (olive oil)

Cilento (olive oil)

Collina di Brindisi
(olive oil)

Colline di Romagna
(olive oil)

Colline Salernitane
(olive oil)

Colline Teatine (olive oil)

Dauno (olive oil)

Garda (olive oil)

Laghi Lombardi (olive oil)

Lametia (olive oil)

Lucca (olive oil)

Molise (olive oil)

Monte Etna (olive oil)

Monti Iblei (olive oil)
Penisola Sorrentina
 (olive oil)
Pretuziano delle Colline
 Teramane (olive oil)
Riviera Ligure (olive oil)
Sabina (olive oil)
Tergeste (olive oil)
Terra di Bari (olive oil)
Terra d'Otranto (olive oil)
Terre di Siena (olive oil)
Terre Tarantine (olive oil)
Toscano (olive oil)
Tuscia (olive oil)
Umbria (olive oil)
Valdemone (olive oil)
Val di Mazara (olive oil)
Valle del Belice (olive oil)
Valli Trapanesi (olive oil)
"Veneto Valpolicella,"
 "Veneto Euganei e
 Berici," and "Veneto del
 Grappa" (olive oils)

Nonfood Products
Aceto balsamico
 tradizionale di Modena
 (vinegar)
Aceto balsamico
 tradizionale di Reggio
 Emilia (vinegar)
Bergamotto di Reggio
 Calabria (essential oil)

Other Products
Zafferano del' Aquila
 (saffron)

Zafferano di San
 Gimignano (saffron)

LUXEMBOURG
Products of Animal Origin
Miel luxembourgeois de
 marque nationale
 (honey)

Oils and Fats/Olive Oil
Beurre rose de la marque
 nationale grand duché
 de Luxembourg (butter)

NETHERLANDS
Cheeses
Boeren-Leidse met
 sleutels
Kanterkaas, Kanter-
 nagelkaas, or
 Kanterkomijnekaas
Noord-Hollandse
 Edammer
Noord-Hollandse
 Gouda

Fruit, Vegetables,
and Cereals
Opperdoezer Ronde
 (potato)

PORTUGAL
Cheeses
Queijo de Azeitão
Queijo de Cabra
 Transmontano
Queijo de Évora
Queijo de Nisa

Queijo do Pico
Queijo Rabaçal
Queijo São Jorge
Queijos da Beira Baixa
Queijo Serpa
Queijo Serra da Estrela
Queijo Terrincho

Table Olives
Azeitona de conserva
 Negrinha de Freixo

Fruit, Vegetables,
and Cereals
Ameixa d'Elvas (plum)
Amêndoa Douro (almond)
Ananas dos Açores/São
 Miguel (pineapple)
Anona da Madeira
 (cherimoya)
Castanha da Terra Fria
 (chestnut)
Castanha de Marvão–
 Portalegre (chestnut)
Castanha de Padrela
 (chestnut)
Castanha dos Soutos da
 Lapa (chestnut)
Cereja de São Julião–
 Portalegre (cherry)
Maçã Bravo de Esmolfe
 (apple)
Maracuja dos Açores or
 S. Miguel (passion
 fruit)
Pêra Rocha do Oeste
 (perry)

Fresh Meat and Offal
Borrego Serra da Estrela
(lamb/mutton)
Borrego Terrincho
(lamb/mutton)
Cabrito Transmontano
(goat)
Carnalentejana (beef)
Carne Arouquesa (beef)
Carne Barrosã (beef)
Carne Cachena da Peneda
(beef)
Carne da Charneca (beef)
Carne de Porco Alentejano
(pig)
Carne Marinhoa (beef)
Carne Maronesa (beef)
Carne Mertolenga (beef)
Carne Mirandesa (beef)
Cordeiro Bragançano
(lamb/mutton)

Meat-Based Products
Presunto de Barrancos
(ham)

*Products of Animal
Origin*
Mel da Serra da Lousã
(honey)
Mel da Serra de
Monchique (honey)
Mel das Terras Altas do
Minho (honey)
Mel da Terra Quente
(honey)
Mel de Barroso (honey)

Mel do Alentejo (honey)
Mel do Parque de Monte-
zinho (honey)
Mel do Ribatejo Norte
(honey)
Mel dos Açores (honey)
Requeijão Serra da Estrela
(milk product)

Oils and Fats/Olive Oil
Azeite de Moura
(olive oil)
Azeite de Trás-os-Montes
(olive oil)
Azeite do Ribatejo
(olive oil)
Azeites da Beira Interior
(olive oil)
Azeites do Norte Alente-
jano (olive oil)

SPAIN
Cheeses
Cabrales
Idiazábal
Mahón
Picón Bejes-Tresviso
Queso de Cantabria
Queso de l'Alt Urgell y la
Cerdanya
Queso de la Serena
Queso de Murcia
Queso Ibores
Queso Majorero
Queso Manchego
Queso Palmero or Queso
de la Palma

Queso Tetilla
Queso Zamorano
Quesucos de Liébana
Roncal
Torta del Casar

*Fruit, Vegetables,
and Cereals*
Alcachofa de Benicarló or
Carxofa de Benicarló
(artichoke)
Arroz de Valencia or Arròs
de València (rice)
Avellana de Reus (hazelnut)
Calasparra (rice)
Chufa de Valencia
(tiger nut)
Kaki Ribera del Xúquer
(persimmon)
Manzana Reineta del
Bierzo (apple)
Melocotón de Calanda
(peach)
Nísperos Callosa d'En
Sarriá (medlar)
Pera de Jumilla (pear)
Peras de Rincón de Soto
(pear)
Pimientos del Piquillo de
Lodosa (pimiento)
Uva de mesa embolsada
"Vinalopó" (grape)

Meat-Based Products
Dehesa de Extremadura
(ham)
Guijuelo (ham)

Jamón de Huelva (ham)

Jamón de Teruel (ham)

Products of Animal Origin

Miel de Granada (honey)

Miel de la Alcarria (honey)

Oils and Fats/Olive Oil

Aceite de la Rioja (olive oil)

Aceite del Bajo Aragón
(olive oil)

Aceite de Mallorca, Aceite
mallorquín, Oli de
Mallorca, or Oli
mallorquí (olive oil)

"Aceite de Terra" or
"Oli de Terra Alta"
(olive oil)

Antequera (olive oil)

Baena (olive oil)

Les Garrigues (olive oil)

Mantequilla de l'Alt Urgell
y la Cerdanya or Man-
tega de l'Alt Urgell i la
Cerdanya (butter)

Montes de Granada
(olive oil)

Montes de Toledo
(olive oil)

Priego de Córdoba
(olive oil)

Sierra de Cádiz (olive oil)

Sierra de Cazorla (olive oil)

Sierra de Segura (olive oil)

Sierra Mágina (olive oil)

Siurana (olive oil)

Other Products

Azafrán de la Mancha
(saffron)

Pimentón de Murcia
(paprika)

"Sidra de Asturias" or
"Sidra d'Asturies" (cider)

UNITED KINGDOM

Cheeses

Beacon Fell traditional
Lancashire

Bonchester

Buxton blue

Dovedale

Single Gloucester

Swaledale or Swaledale
ewes'

West Country farmhouse
Cheddar

White Stilton or Blue
Stilton

*Fruit, Vegetables,
and Cereals*

Jersey Royal potatoes

*Fresh Meat and
Offal*

Orkney beef

Orkney lamb

Shetland lamb

*Products of Animal
Origin*

Cornish clotted
cream

NOTES

PREFACE

1 Julia Moskin, "Maine Is Busy Praising the Potato," *New York Times*, November 30, 2005, D6.

2 Translation: "This wine has a local [or site-specific] taste; I don't smell the place."

3 In combining such cultural activities, my approach differs somewhat from Lévi-Strauss's more exclusively symbolic focus.

4 Frank Bruni, "Having Your Ethics and Eating Them, Too," *New York Times*, November 30, 2005, D12.

5 Ibid.

6 Ibid.

7 Ibid.

INTRODUCTION

1 Anthropologists are researchers of the everyday, trying to capture the meaning of quotidian choices and seeking to understand what they tell us about culture, the shared values, meanings, and practices that shape us all. Culture may seem an abstract idea, but once one is trained to see the commonalities beneath the surface of individual behaviors, especially in a community, the connection between the individual and culture becomes apparent. Strategies for capturing the significance of the everyday vary greatly from person to person, but I have always sought to find out what matters most to my "tribe," people whose work

revolves around food and wine. Though perhaps not as exotic as desert-dwelling Bedouins or hunter-gatherers from the rainforests of Colombia, my colleagues for the eight years I worked at the culinary school guided me through the taste-of-place jungle on an exploration that ultimately went far beyond the human physiology of taste and into the external world of culture and environment.

2 Pradeep Jeganathan, "A Space for Violence," in *Community, Gender, and Violence: Subaltern Studies XI*, ed. Partha Chatterjee and Pradeep Jeganathan (New York: Columbia University Press, 2001), p. 65.

3 Many scholars have considered the implications of what Claude Fischler first aptly calls "the homnivore's dilemma." See Claude Fischler, *L'Homnivore* (Paris: Odile Jacob, 2000); E. N. Anderson, *Everyone Eats: Understanding Food and Culture* (New York: New York University Press, 2005); and Michael Pollan, *The Omnivore's Dilemma: A Natural History of Four Meals* (New York: Penguin, 2005).

4 This volume explores this process of discernment as the result of individual and group will as it evolved in France, and how it continues to evolve there and in the United States as well.

5 *Concise Oxford French Dictionary* (Oxford: Oxford University Press, 1980).

6 *American Heritage Dictionary of the English Language*, 4th edition (Boston: Houghton Mifflin, 2000).

7 Michel de Certeau and Luce Giard, *Culture in the Plural* (Minneapolis: University of Minnesota Press, 1998), p. 185.

8 Ibid.

9 "A Tale of Two Frances," *The Economist*, March 30, 2006, pp. 22–24.

10 See Harvey Levenstein, *The Paradox of Plenty: A History of Eating in Modern America* (Berkeley: University of California Press, 2003).

11 Ted Lewellen, *The Anthropology of Globalization: Cultural Anthropology Enters the Twenty-first Century* (Westport, CT: Bergin & Garvey, 2002), p. 3.

ONE. PLACE MATTERS

1 Olivier de Serres, *Le théâtre d'agriculture et mesnage des champs* (Paris: Publiée par la Société d'Agriculture de la Seine, 1805).

2 Julia Csergo, "The Regionalization of Cuisines," in *Food: A Culinary History*, ed. J. L. Flandrin and M. Montanari (New York: Columbia University Press, 1999), p. 502.

3   Aglae Adanson, *La cuisinière de la campagne et de la ville* (Paris: Audot, 1827), p. 56.

4   Kyri Watson Claflin, "A Cuisine High and Low: Charles Fourier's Gastrosophy as an Interpretation of the Past and Vision for the Future," unpublished paper.

5   Thanks to Kolleen Guy for pointing out the importance of Vidal de la Blache.

6   Jean-Yves Guiomar, "Vidal de la Blache's Geography of France," in *Realms of Memory: Rethinking the French Past,* ed. Pierre Nora (New York: Columbia University Press, 1996), pp. 187–88.

7   Ibid.

8   Kolleen Guy, *When Champagne Became French* (Baltimore, MD: Johns Hopkins University Press, 2003), p. 150.

9   Institut National des Appellations d'Origine, "Les Fondements de l'appellation," www.inao.gouv.fr/public/home.php (accessed October 4, 2006).

10 Ibid.

11 Ibid.

12 Ibid.

13 *L'appellation d'origine contrôlée: Vins et eaux de vie* (Paris: Réalisation Euro-Impressions, 1998), p. 25.

14 Institut National des Appellations d'Origine, "Les fondements de l'appellation," www.inao.gouv.fr/public/home.php (accessed October 4, 2006).

15 Ibid.

16 Ibid.

17 Ibid.

18 INAO, Official literature, 1999.

19 Elizabeth Barham, "Translating Terroir: The Global Challenge of French AOC Labeling," *Journal of Rural Studies* 19 (2003): 130.

20 Ibid., p. 132.

21 Ibid., pp. 133–34.

22 Ibid., p. 135.

23 Official literature, 1999.

24 Barham, "Translating Terroir," p. 132.

25 Jim Chen, "A Sober Look at Appellations of Origin: How the United States Will Crash France's Wine and Cheese Party," *Minnesota Journal of Global Trade* 5, no. 1 (1996): 35.

26 Ibid., p. 37.

27 Sarah Blowen, Marion Demossier, and Jeanine Picard, *Recollections of France: Memories, Identities, and Heritage in Contemporary France* (New York: Berghahn Books, 2002), p. 9.

28 Stephen Mennell, *All Manners of Food: England and France from the Middle Ages to the Present* (Champaign: University of Illinois Press, 1995), pp. 45–47.

29 Ibid., p. 148.

30 Olwen Hufton, "Social Conflict and the Grain Supply in Eighteenth-Century France," in *Hunger and History,* ed. Robert Rothberg and Theodore Rabb (Cambridge: Cambridge University Press, 1985), p. 106.

31 Ibid.

32 Priscilla Parkhurst Ferguson, *Accounting for Taste: The Triumph of French Cuisine* (Chicago: University of Chicago Press, 2004), p. 25.

33 Madame Pampille, *Les bons plats de France: Cuisine régionale* (Paris: Fayard, 1918), pp. 23–24.

34 Ibid., p. 24.

35 Ibid., p. 143.

36 Curnonsky, *Recettes de provinces de France* (Paris: Productions de Paris, 1953), pp. 14–16.

37 Ibid., p. 27.

38 Stephen Harp, *Marketing Michelin: Advertising and Cultural Identity in Twentieth-Century France* (Baltimore, MD: Johns Hopkins University Press, 2001).

39 Association des Amis de Curnonsky, *Curnonsky et ses amis* (Paris: Librairie Edgar Soete, 1979), pp. 130–38.

40 Curnonsky, *Traditional Recipes of the Provinces of France* (New York: Doubleday, 1961), p. 15.

41 Edmond Richardin, *La cuisine française du XIVe au XXe siècle* (Paris: Editions de l'Art et Littérature, 1913).

42 Curnonsky and Austin de Croze, *Le trésor gastronomique* (Paris: Librairie Delagrave, 1933), p. 1.

43 Ibid.

44 Blowen, Demossier, and Picard, *Recollections of France,* p. 146.

45 Jean Fulbert-Dumonteil, *Le Perigord gourmand* (Castelnaud: L'Hydre, 1996), pp. 40–41.

46 www.ambafrance-us.org/atoz/agriculture.asp (accessed June 19, 2007).

47 Ibid.

48 Thanks to Susan Carol Rogers for pointing this out to me.

49 See Eugen Weber, *Peasants into Frenchman: The Modernization of Rural France, 1870–1914* (Stanford, CA: Stanford University Press, 1976).

50 Deborah Reed-Danahy and Susan Carol Rogers, "Introduction," special issue, *Anthropological Quarterly* 60 (1987): 51.

51 Susan Carol Rogers. "Good to Think: The 'Peasant' in Contemporary France," *Anthropological Quarterly* 60 (1987): 56.

52 James R. Lehning, *Peasant and French: Cultural Contact in Rural France during the Nineteenth Century* (Cambridge: Cambridge University Press, 1995).

53 Ibid., p. 206.

54 Armand Fremont, "The Land," in *Realms of Memory: Rethinking the French Past,* ed. Pierre Nora (New York: Columbia University Press, 1996), p. 17.

55 Ibid., p. 34.

56 Roger Cohen, "Heartburn: Fearful over the Future, Europe Seizes on Food," *New York Times,* August 29, 1999.

57 I did archival research, interviewed wine experts and winemakers, and visited vineyards, markets, and more.

58 *La Semaine du Goût,* www.legoût.com (accessed March 21, 2006).

59 Ibid.

60 Ibid.

61 Association Nationale des Sites Remarquables du Goût, http://uk.franceguide.com/adherents/fiche_atf.asp?idatf=1949 (accessed March 22, 2006).

62 Press release, January 2006, www.inao.gouv.fr/ (accessed March 2006).

63 Barham, "Translating Terroir," p. 136.

64 Kyri Watson Claflin, "Culture, Politics and Modernization in Paris Provisioning, 1880–1920," Ph.D. diss., Boston University, 2006, p. 11.

65 Barham, "Translating Terroir," p. 134.

66 Arjun Appadurai, *Modernity at Large: Cultural Dimensions of Globalization* (Minneapolis: University of Minnesota Press, 1996).

TWO. "WINE IS DEAD! LONG LIVE WINE!"

1 Mary Douglas, *Purity and Danger: An Analysis of the Concepts of Pollution and Taboo* (Boston: Ark Paperbacks, 1985), p. 35.

2   *The Oxford Companion to Wine*, 2nd ed., ed. Jancis Robinson (Oxford: Oxford University Press, 1999), p. 490.

3   Jean-Antoine Chaptal, *L'art de faire le vin* (Marseille: Jeanne Laffitte, 1819), pp. 1–2.

4   Emile Peynaud, *The Taste of Wine: The Art and Science of Wine Appreciation* (New York: John Wiley & Sons, 1996), p. 230.

5   *The Oxford Companion to Wine*, p. 700.

6   "Journal Officiel de la République Française," *L'appellation d'origine contrôlée: Vins et eaux de vie* (Paris: Réalisation Euro-Impressions, 1998), pp. 4–5.

7   Ibid., p. 67.

8   Ibid., p. 69.

9   James Wilson, *Terroir: The Role of Geology, Climate, and Culture in the Making of French Wines* (Berkeley: University of California Press, 1999), p. 72.

10 *The Wines and Winelands of France: Geological Journeys*, ed. Charles Pomerol (London: Robertson McCarta, 1989), p. 19.

11 *L'appellation d'origine contrôlée: Vins et eaux de vie*, pp. 69–71.

12 Emmanuelle Vaudour, "The Quality of Grapes and Wine in Relation to Geography: Notions of Terroir at Various Scales," *Journal of Wine Research* 13 (August 2002): 119.

13 Timothy J. Tomasik, "Certeau à la Carte: Translating Discursive Terroir in the Practice of Everyday Life: Living and Cooking," *The South Atlantic Quarterly* 100 (Spring 2001): 523.

14 During the nineteenth and early twentieth centuries, saying a wine had the goût du terroir was not considered a compliment. But over time France has come to celebrate and promote the goût du terroir of wine and food. Following this tradition, the Mondavi family hoped to make a premium wine with a distinctive goût du terroir.

15 Telephone interview with Tim Mondavi, August 2003.

16 http://perso.club-internet.fr/verab/fr/projet.htm (accessed August 2003).

17 Jon Henley, "Villagers Rebel against Sale of Vineyard to Depardieu," *The Guardian*, February 8, 2003.

18 Vaudour, "The Quality of Grapes and Wine in Relation to Geography," p. 120.

19 Robert Mondavi Winery, www.mondavi.com (accessed May 2006).

20 Telephone interview with Tim Mondavi, August 3, 2003.

21 Telephone interview with David Pearson, August 13, 2003.

22 Telephone interview with Tim Mondavi, August 3, 2003.

23 Judy Ridgway, *The Little Red Wine Guide* (Paris: Les Arenes, 2000).

24 Ibid.

25 Mas de Daumas Gassac promotional brochure.

26 Vaudour, "The Quality of Grapes and Wine in Relation to Geography," p. 119.

27 Mas de Daumas Gassac promotional brochure.

28 Ibid.

29 Interview with Aimé Guibert, March 15, 2003, Aniane, France.

30 Telephone interviews with Gilles de Chambure, director of wine education at Mondavi Family Vineyard, August 1, 2003, and David Pearson, August 13, 2003.

31 Aveyron, "Aimé Guibert, Owner and Founder of Daumas Gassac," www .aveyron.com/accueil/daumas.html (accessed May 2006).

32 Interview with Chantal Borrida, March 15, 2003, Aniane, France.

33 Ibid.

34 Interview with Alain Carbonneau, March 5, 2003, Montpellier, France. See also "La notion complexe de terroir," *Progrès agricole et viticole* 2 (1995): 122.

35 A May 2001 article in the local newspaper *La Gazette*, "Why They Kicked the Americans out of Aniane," confirms this view in interviews with Aniane residents. Christophe, a thirty-five-year-old born and bred in Aniane, says, "Once they destroyed the woods in this fashion, they would not have stopped for anything. Nature is important." "We used to live in Montpellier. When we made the decision to live in the country, it was not to see it vanish," states Ursula. See Hélène Tauzin, "Pourquoi ils ont boute l'americains hors d'Aniane," *La Gazette* no. 680, May 18–24, 2001, p. 9.

36 http://perso.club-internet.fr/verab/fr/projet.htm (accessed August 2003).

37 Telephone interview with David Pearson, August 13, 2003.

38 http://perso.club-internet.fr/verab/fr/projet.htm (accessed August 2003).

39 Philip H. Gordon and Sophie Meunier, *The French Challenge* (Washington, DC: Brookings Institute Press, 2001), pp. 41–43.

40 Ibid., pp. 55–60.

41 Interview with Manuel Diaz, March 15, 2003, Aniane, France.

42 Interview with Aimé Guibert, March 15, 2003, Aniane, France.

43 Telephone interview with Tim Mondavi, August 13, 2003.

44 Josie Butchart, "Depardieu Resisted in the Languedoc," February 5, 2002, www.decanter.com (accessed August 2003).

45 Telephone interview with David Pearson, August 13, 2003.

THREE. CALIFORNIA DREAMING

1 The Egyptians were the first to record their winemaking and wine-drinking activities, and tomb paintings from Thebes trace the whole winemaking process. In these paintings grapes are picked from high, arching arbors. The grapes are depicted being crushed and then stored in large earthenware vessels to ferment.

2 Jancis Robinson, ed., *The Oxford Companion to Wine*, 2nd ed. (Oxford: Oxford University Press, 1999), p. 594.

3 Ibid., p. 285.

4 Ibid.

5 Ibid.

6 Ibid., p. 726.

7 George Husmann, *American Grape Growing and Wine Making* (New York: Orange Judd Co., 1880), p. v.

8 Ibid., p. vi.

9 Ibid., pp. 28–29.

10 John Hutchinson, "Northern California from Haraszthy to the Beginnings of Prohibition," in *The Book of California Wine*, ed. Davis Muscatine, Maynard Amerine, and Bob Thompson (Berkeley: University of California Press, 1984).

11 Thomas Pinney, *A History of Wine in America: From Prohibition to the Present* (Berkeley: University of California Press, 2005), p. 2.

12 "Prohibition," in *The Oxford Companion to Wine*, p. 552.

13 Cyril Penn, "What Is Quality?" *Wine Business Monthly* 8 (May 2001): 11.

14 Ibid., p. 12.

15 Ibid., p. 13.

16 Ibid.

17 Ibid.

18 Ibid., p. 13.

19 Kermit Lynch, *Adventures on the Wine Route: A Wine Buyer's Tour of France* (New York: North Point Press, 1990), p. 117.

20 Interview, March 22, 2003, Domaine Tempier.

21 Penn, "What Is Quality?" p. 12.

22 Elin McCoy, *The Emperor of Wine: The Rise of Robert M. Parker, Jr.* (New York: HarperCollins, 2005), pp. 35–37.

23 Ibid.

24 Ibid. Balzer was also an early champion of the new boutique wines emerging from the Napa Valley and other locales in the early 1970s.

25 Ibid.

26 Interview with Robert Parker, *The Charlie Rose Show*, broadcast February 14, 2005, on Vermont Public Television.

27 Ibid.

28 The Wine Institute, "California Wine Industry Statistical Highlights," www .wineinstitute.org/industry/statistics/2004/ca_industry_highlights.php (accessed December 2004).

29 Ibid.

30 The Wine Institute, "Strong Sales Growth in 2004 for California Wine as Shipments Reach New Heights," www.wineinstitute.org (accessed April 5, 2005).

31 Paul Lukacs, *The Great Wines of America: The Top Forty Vintners, Vineyards, and Vintages* (New York: Norton, 2005), p. 298.

32 Tour and interview at Barelli Creek Vineyards, November 27, 2005.

33 Karen MacNeil, "Is Terroir Dead? It's Man vs. Mother Nature in Shaping California Wines," *San Francisco Chronicle*, September 18, 2002.

34 Ibid.

35 The Rhone Ranger, http://rhoneranger.blogspot.com/ (accessed February 28, 2001).

36 http://wine.appellationamerica.com/wine-review/136/Randall-Grahm-on-Terroir .html (accessed June 16, 2007).

37 The Rhone Ranger, http://rhoneranger.blogspot.com/ (accessed February 28, 2001).

38 Interview with Randall Grahm, November 16, 2004, Santa Cruz, California.

39 Interview with John Locke, November 16, 2004, Santa Cruz, California.

40 Ibid.

41 Interview with Nicole Walsh, November 16, 2004, Santa Cruz, California.

42 Interview with Randall Grahm, November 16, 2004, Santa Cruz, California.

43 Interview with John Locke, November 16, 2004, Santa Cruz, California.

44 Interview with Randall Grahm, November 16, 2004, Santa Cruz, California.

45 Ibid.

46 Ferry Building Marketplace, "History and Renovation," www.ferrybuilding marketplace.com/history.php (accessed November 29, 2005).

47 Karola Saekel, "Ferry Tales Do Come True," *San Francisco Chronicle*, May 19, 2004, www.sfgate.com (accessed January 2006).

48 Interview with Fran Gage, November 30, 2005, San Francisco, California.

49 In his recent memoir, Jeremiah Tower disputes this claim directly. See his *California Dish: What I Saw (and Cooked) at the American Culinary Revolution* (New York: Free Press, 2003).

50 Interview with Sylvan Brackett, November 28, 2005, Berkeley, California.

51 Ibid.

52 Interview with Fran Gage, November 30, 2005, San Francisco, California.

53 Ibid.

54 Interview with Sylvan Brackett, November 28, 2005, Berkeley, California.

55 Ibid.

56 Margaret Rigoglioso, "The Accidental Epicure," *Stanford Magazine*, May/June 2003, www.stanfordalumni.org/news/magazine/2003/mayjun/showcase/cuisine.html.

57 Judy Rodgers, *The Zuni Café Cookbook* (New York: W. W. Norton & Company, 2002).

58 Olivia Wu, "The Zen Masters of Zuni Are In for the Long Run," *San Francisco Chronicle*, September 7, 2005, www.sfgate.com (accessed January 2006).

59 Daniel Patterson, "To the Moon, Alice?" *New York Times Sunday Magazine*, November 6, 2005, pp. 56–59.

FOUR. TASTING WISCONSIN

1 National Restaurant Association, "Restaurant Spending 2003," www.restaurant.org/research/consumer/spending.cfm (accessed May 30, 2006).

2 See Jürgen Habermas, *The Structural Transformation of the Public Sphere* (Cambridge, MA: MIT Press, 1989); Pierre Bourdieu, *Distinction* (Cambridge, MA: Harvard University Press, 1990); Rebecca Spang, *The Invention of the Restaurant: Paris and Modern Gastronomic Culture* (Cambridge, MA: Harvard University Press, 2000).

3 See Gary Alan Fine, *Restaurants* (Berkeley: University of California Press, 1996); Amy B. Trubek, *Haute Cuisine: How the French Invented the Culinary Profession* (Philadelphia: University of Pennsylvania Press, 2000).

4 Dana Hoag, *Agricultural Crisis in America* (Denver: ABC-CLIO, 1999), p. 4.

5 William Heffernan and Mary Hendrickson, "Concentration of Agricultural Markets Report," 2007.

6 The majority of restaurants also rely on big food distributors to source their ingredients.

7 See Warren Belasco, *Appetite for Change* (New York: Pantheon Books, 1989); Harvey Levenstein, *The Paradox of Plenty: A History of Eating in Modern America* (Berkeley: University of California Press, 2003); Krishnendu Ray, *The Migrant's Table* (Philadelphia: Temple University Press, 2004); Wendell Berry, *The Art of the Commonplace* (Washington, DC: Counterpoint, 2002).

8 The idea of "purity" plays an important role in both values and practices related to the American food system. Many regulations related to food safety created in the twentieth century imagine a "pure" food supply.

9 Gustavo Esteva and Madhu Suri Prakash, *Grassroots Post-Modernism: Remaking the Soil of Cultures* (New York: Zed Books, 1998), p. 10.

10 These analytic frameworks are deeply influenced by the work of Fernand Braudel, Immanuel Wallerstein, Eric Hobsbawm, and Pierre Bourdieu. Even though I am both familiar with and sympathetic to these approaches, my research into *terroir* and *goût du terroir* has led me to consider analyses that provide an even more dynamic interaction between larger capitalist and nationalist structures and individual and group agency.

11 See Gretel H. Pelto and Pertti J. Pelto, "Diet and Delocalization: Dietary Changes since 1750," *Journal of Interdisciplinary History* 14 (1983): 507–28.

12 Distribution networks were correspondingly regional and, until the advent of steam-powered boats and trains, necessarily so for any perishable items.

13 Warren Belasco, *Appetite for Change* (New York: Pantheon, 1989), pp. 230–32.

14 Ibid.

15 Ibid., p. 248.

16 All of the remarks by Odessa Piper were recorded during October 2003 in Madison, Wisconsin, unless otherwise noted.

17 Priscilla Clark, "Thoughts for Food, I: French Cuisine and French Culture," *French Review* 49 (1975): 32–41.

18 Telephone interview with Odessa Piper, September 20, 2005.

19 Helen Nearing and Scott Nearing, *The Good Life* (New York: Schocken Books, 1989), p. 3.

20 Telephone interview with Odessa Piper, September 20, 2005.

21 Nearing and Nearing, *The Good Life*, pp. 148–49.

22 Waverly Root, *The Food of France* (New York: Vintage Books, 1992).

23 Telephone interview with Odessa Piper, October 2005.

24 What likely will always remain missing from any new *cuisine du terroir* is a group of dishes commonly known in the area, as in a traditional cuisine.

25 Mapping ingredients—making the link between locale and food—may appear to be simply a decorative element in American restaurants, but such maps have a long French history. *Le cours gastronomique*, first published in 1809, includes a map of France that highlights regional products. Included are the wines of regions such as Bordeaux and the Rhône; Roquefort and Brie, accompanied by drawings of cheeses; and many charcuterie items, such as sausages and cured hams. Modern versions of the 1809 map also exist in France. Maps distributed by the Institut National des Appellations d'Origine, for example, specify all the AOC regions and their products. There is also an online map that shows the "100 Sites Remarquables de Goût," places considered unusual for the aesthetic and taste experiences they offer, which can be used along with the contact information provided to organize a visit.

26 Telephone interview with Odessa Piper, September 20, 2005.

27 The narrative continues:

> Our menus are primarily composed from local ingredients all year round and achieved through our partnership with a large network of small-scale farms. They provide most of our meats, freshwater fish, poultry, dairy, and produce, including cellared root crops and greens harvests from solar hoop houses throughout the winter months. Combined with the restaurant's strategy of putting up quantities of local produce throughout the growing season, L'Etoile's culinary options remain creative, delicious and regionally reliant even in the coldest months. We do not seek to be regionally exclusive, though. Our exceptional local ingredients are in best context when combined with artisan products from all over the world, each expressing a unique spirit of place.

28 Interview with Tory Miller, November 16, 2005, Madison, Wisconsin.

29 Ibid.

30 Elizabeth David, *French Provincial Cooking* (New York: Penguin Books, 1960), p. xi.

31 Ibid., p. x.

32 Ibid., p. xi.

33 Esteva and Prakash, *Grassroots Post-Modernism*, p. 53.

FIVE. CONNECTING FARMERS AND CHEFS IN VERMONT

1   Christopher McGrory Klyza and Stephen C. Trombulak, *The Story of Vermont: A Natural and Cultural History* (Hanover, NH: Middlebury College Press, 1999), p. 33.

2   Ibid., pp. 45–49.

3   Ibid., p. 69.

4   Harold Fisher Wilson, *The Hill Country of Northern New England: Its Social and Economic History, 1790–1930* (New York: AMS Press, 1967).

5   Ibid.

6   Howard Russell, *A Long, Deep Furrow* (Hanover, NH: University Press of New England, 1976).

7   Jan Albers, *Hands on the Land: A History of the Vermont Landscape* (Cambridge, MA: MIT Press, 2000), p. 202.

8   Ibid.

9   Ibid.

10 Vermont Agency of Agriculture Food and Markets, www.vermontagriculture.com (accessed November 7, 2005).

11 Nancy Graff, ed., *Celebrating Vermont: Myths and Realities* (Hanover, NH: University Press of New England, 1991), p. 57.

12 Ibid.

13 Klyza and Trombulak, *The Story of Vermont*, p. 89.

14 Northeast Sustainable Agriculture Working Group, *Northeast Farms to Food: Understanding Our Region's Food System* (NESAWG/New England Small Farm Institute, September 2002).

15 Ibid., p. 18.

16 Rebecca Kneale Gould, *At Home in Nature: Modern Homesteading and Spiritual Practice in America* (Berkeley: University of California Press, 2005).

17 Northeast Sustainable Agriculture Working Group, *Northeast Farms to Food*, p. 68.

18 William Cronon, *Changes in the Land: Indians, Colonists, and the Ecology of New England* (New York: Hill and Wang, 1983), p. 35.

19 Ibid.

20 Gould, *At Home in Nature*, p. 229.

21 Ibid., p. 87.

22 Northeast Sustainable Agriculture Working Group, *Northeast Farms to Food*, p. 4.

23 Ibid.

24 Interview with Enid Wonnacott, executive director of NOFA-VT, November 3, 2005, Burlington, Vermont.

25 Ibid.

26 Press release, New England Culinary Institute, January 1996.

27 Chefs Collaborative, www.chefscollaborative.org/ (accessed November 2005).

28 Roger Clapp, personal communication, December 2005.

29 Ibid.

30 Susan Carol Rogers, "Farming Visions: Agriculture in French Culture," *French Politics, Culture and Society* 18, no. 1 (2000): 51.

31 Ibid.

32 David Hale, personal communication, October 2004, Montpelier, Vermont.

33 Interview with Laini Fondiller, October 2004, Westfield, Vermont.

34 Ibid.

35 Ibid.

36 Ibid.

37 Ibid.

38 David Hale, personal communication, October 2004.

39 Interview with Tod Murphy, January 2003, Barre, Vermont.

40 Interview with Larry Tempesta, January 2003, Barre, Vermont.

41 Interview with Tod Murphy, June 2005, Barre, Vermont.

42 Wendell Berry, "The Agrarian Standard," in *The Essential Agrarian Reader: The Future of Culture, Community, and the Land*, ed. Norman Wirzba (Louisville: University of Kentucky Press, 2003), p. 33.

43 Steve Zind interviewing Tod Murphy, "New Farmer's Diner to Open in Quechee," Vermont Public Radio, November 2, 2005.

44   Ibid.

45   Ibid.

46   Ibid.

SIX. THE NEXT PHASE

1   He made this comment in a presentation he delivered at a meeting at the Vermont Fresh Network Annual Forum in August 2005.

2   Jager Di Paola Kemp Design in fact did a pro bono strategic branding exercise with Vermont Fresh Network.

3   David Donath, "Report on the Governor's Summit on the Vermont Destination," unpublished paper.

4   Introductory materials, Governor's Summit on the Vermont Destination, July 2005.

5   Governer's Summit on the Vermont Destination Report, September 2005, Woodstock Foundation.

6   Vermont Maple Sugar Makers' Association, "Maple Facts," www.vermont maple.org/MapleFacts.html (accessed May 2006).

7   Helen Nearing and Scott Nearing, *The Maple Sugar Book*, 3rd ed. (White River Junction, VT: Chelsea Green Publishing, 2000), pp. 13–14.

8   Ibid., p. 14.

9   Vermont Agency of Agriculture, Food, and Markets, "Vermont's Maple Laws and Regulations," www.vermontagriculture.com/mapleregs.PDF (accessed June 2, 2006).

10   Ibid., p. 3.

11   Ibid., p. 6.

12   Leslie Wright, "New Rules for Maple Syrup Labels Announced," *Burlington Free Press*, February 7, 2006.

13   Ibid.

14   Nearing and Nearing, *The Maple Sugar Book*, p. 14.

15   From John Burroughs, *Signs and Seasons* (Syracuse, NY: Syracuse University Press, 1886), quoted in Nearing and Nearing, *The Maple Sugar Book*, p. 4.

16   The Leader Evaporator Company, www.leaderevaporator.com (accessed June 2006).

17   Interview with John Elder, March 2006, Starksboro, Vermont.

18   Ibid.

19 Ibid.

20 "Le Rocamadour: Petite Histoire d'un Grand Fromage," AOC promotional pamphlet.

21 "Le Rocamadour: La Poids Economique de la Filière," AOC Promotional pamphlet.

22 Castelnaud Castle, www.castelnaud.com/castelnaud/htmgb/sommaire.html (accessed May 2006).

23 Interview, March 2000, Castelnaud-la-Chapelle.

24 Carlo Petrini, *Slow Food: The Case for Taste* (New York: Columbia University Press, 2003), pp. 7–8.

25 Ibid., p. 2.

26 Ibid., p. 12.

27 Meghan Sheradin, personal communication, December 2005.

28 Petrini, *Slow Food*, p. xxiv.

29 Ibid., p. xxiv. The manifesto begins with "Our century, which began and has developed under the insignia of industrial civilization, first invented the machine and then took it as its life model."

30 Ibid., p. 69.

31 Adapted by Ronnie Richards, "Terrific Terroir," *La Stampa*, February 27, 2006, www.slowfood.com/eng/sf_sloweb/sf_sloweb_dettaglio.lasso?passaswe=SW_02254 (accessed April 2006).

32 Ibid.

33 Ibid.

34 Ibid.

35 Ibid.

EPILOGUE

1 Steven Shapin, "Paradise Sold: What Are You Buying When You Buy Organic?" *The New Yorker*, May 22, 2006. I was struck by the author's use of this quotation at the very end of the article, which demonstrates the cultural dimensions of the American embrace of organic foods by describing the striking consumer interest in obtaining them. It was as if the author were uncomfortable concluding the piece without undercutting the possibility that Americans do care more about their food than they used to, especially about how it is grown and how it tastes.

If he didn't take away the power of this cultural embrace, I wondered, would he be un-American?

2   Sarah Blowen, Marion Demossier, and Jeanine Picard, *Recollections of France: Memories, Identities and Heritage in Contemporary France* (New York: Berghahn Books, 2002).

3   Randall Grahm, "The Phenomenology of Terroir," *Da Vino Commedia: Bonny Doon Vineyards Newsletter,* Spring 2006.

4   Ibid.

BIBLIOGRAPHY

Ableman, Michael. *From the Good Earth: A Celebration of Growing Food around the World*. New York: HNA Books, 1993.

Adanson, Aglae. *La cuisinière de la campagne et de la ville*. Paris: Audot, 1827.

Albers, Jan. *Hands on the Land: A History of the Vermont Landscape*. Cambridge, MA: MIT Press, 2000.

Anderson, E. N. *Everyone Eats: Understanding Food and Culture*. New York: New York University Press, 2005.

Appadurai, Arjun. *Modernity at Large: Cultural Dimensions of Globalization*. Minneapolis: University of Minnesota Press, 1996.

Association des Amis de Curnonsky. *Curnonsky et ses amis*. Paris: Librairie Edgar Soete, 1979.

Aveyron Tourism. "Aimé Guibert, Owner and Founder of Daumas Gassac." www.aveyron.com/accueil/daumas.html (accessed August 2003).

Barham, Elizabeth. "Translating Terroir: The Global Challenge of French AOC Labeling." *Journal of Rural Studies* 19 (2003): 127–38.

Belasco, Warren. *Appetite for Change*. New York: Pantheon, 1989.

Bérard, L., M. Hirczak, P. Marchenay, A. Mollard, and B. Pecqueur. "Le panier de biens: Une construction patrimoniale et territoriale. L'example de la Bresse." *Communication pour le Symposium International* (2005): 1–17.

Bérard, Laurence, et al. *Biodiversity and Local Knowledge in France*. Paris: INRA, 2005.

Berry, Wendell. "The Agrarian Standard." In *The Essential Agrarian Reader: The Future of Culture, Community, and the Land,* edited by Norman Wirzba. Louisville: University of Kentucky Press, 2003.

——. *The Art of the Commonplace.* Washington, DC: Counterpoint, 2002.

Bestor, Theodore. *Tsukiji: The Fish Market at the Center of the World.* Berkeley: University of California Press, 2005.

Blowen, Sarah, Marion Demossier, and Jeanine Picard. *Recollections of France: Memories, Identities, and Heritage in Contemporary France.* New York: Berghahn Books, 2002.

Bourdieu, Pierre. *Distinction.* Cambridge, MA: Harvard University Press, 1990.

Boutonnet, J., M. Napoléone, M. Rio, and F. Monod. "AOC pélardon, filiére en émergence?" *Communication pour le Symposium International* (2005): 1–12.

Brackett, Sylvan, Wendy Downing, and Sue Moore, eds. *The Slow Food Guide to San Francisco and the Bay Area: Restaurants, Markets, Bars.* White River Junction, VT: Chelsea Green Publishing Company, 2005.

Brillat-Savarin, Jean Anthelme. *The Physiology of Taste, or Meditations on Transcendental Gastronomy.* Translated by M. F. K. Fisher. New York: Harcourt, Brace and Jovanovich, 1978.

Bruni, Frank. "Having Your Ethics and Eating Them, Too." *New York Times,* November 30, 2005, D12.

Burroughs, John. *Signs and Seasons.* Syracuse, NY: Syracuse University Press, 1886.

Butchart, Josie. "Depardieu Resisted in the Languedoc," February 5, 2002. www.decanter.com (accessed August 2003).

Cadet de Gassicourt, Charles-Louis. *Cours gastronomique.* Paris: Capelle et Renand, 1809.

Casabianca, F., B. Sylvander, Y. Noël, C. Béranger, J. Coulon, and F. Roncin. "Terroir et typicité: Deux concepts-clés des Appellations d'Origine Contrôlée: Essai de définitions scientifiques et opérationnelles." *Communication pour le Symposium International* (2005): 1–18.

Castelnaud Castle. www.castelnaud.com/castelnaud/htmgb/sommaire.html (accessed December 2005).

Chaptal, Jean-Antoine. *L'art de faire le vin.* Marseille: Jeanne Laffitte, 1819.

Chefs Collaborative. www.chefscollaborative.org/ (accessed September 2003).

Chen, Jim. "A Sober Look at Appellations of Origin: How the United States Will

Crash France's Wine and Cheese Party." *Minnesota Journal of Global Trade* 5, no. 1 (1996): 19–32.

Claflin, Kyri Watson. "A Cuisine High and Low: Charles Fourier's Gastrosophy as an Interpretation of the Past and Vision for the Future." Unpublished paper presented at the Brillat-Savarin Revisited Conference, April 2005.

———. "Culture, Politics and Modernization in Paris Provisioning, 1880–1920." Ph.D. diss., Boston University, 2006.

Clark, Priscilla. "Thoughts for Food, I: French Cuisine and French Culture." *French Review* 49 (1975): 32–41.

Cleary, M. C. *Peasants, Politicians, and Producers: The Organisation of Agriculture in France since 1918.* Cambridge: Cambridge University Press, 1989.

Cohen, Roger. "Heartburn; Fearful over the Future, Europe Seizes on Food." *New York Times*, August 29, 1999.

Concise Oxford French Dictionary. Oxford: Oxford University Press, 1980.

Cronon, William. *Changes in the Land: Indians, Colonists, and the Ecology of New England.* New York: Hill and Wang, 1983.

Csergo, Julia. "The Regionalization of Cuisines." In *Food: A Culinary History*, edited by J. L. Flandrin and M. Montanari. New York: Columbia University Press, 1999.

Curnonsky. *Recettes de provinces de France.* Paris: Productions de Paris, 1953.

———. *Traditional Recipes of the Provinces of France.* New York: Doubleday, 1961.

Curnonsky and de Croze, Austin. *Le trésor gastronomique.* Paris: Librairie Delagrave, 1933.

David, Elizabeth. *French Provincial Cooking.* New York: Penguin Books, 1960.

De Certeau, Michel, and Luce Giard. *Culture in the Plural.* Minneapolis: University of Minnesota Press, 1998.

De Serres, Olivier. *Le théâtre d'agriculture et mesnage des champs.* Paris: Publiée par la Société d'Agriculture de la Seine, 1805.

Douglas, Mary. *Purity and Danger: An Analysis of the Concepts of Pollution and Taboo.* Boston: Ark Paperbacks, 1985.

Esteva, Gustavo, and Madhu Suri Prakash. *Grassroots Post-Modernism: Remaking the Soil of Cultures.* New York: Zed Books, 1998.

Ferguson, Priscilla Parkhurst. *Accounting for Taste: The Triumph of French Cuisine.* Chicago: University of Chicago Press, 2004.

Ferry Building Marketplace. "History and Renovation." www.ferrybuildingmarketplace
.com/history.php (accessed February 2006).

Fine, Gary Alan. *Restaurants.* Berkeley: University of California Press, 1996.

Fischler, Claude. *L'homnivore.* Paris: Odile Jacob, 2000.

Fremont, Armand. "The Land." In *Realms of Memory: Rethinking the French Past,* edited by Pierre Nora. New York: Columbia University Press, 1996.

Fulbert-Dumonteil, Jean. *Le Perigord gourmand.* Castelnaud: L'Hydre, 1996.

Gordon, Philip H., and Sophie Meunier. *The French Challenge.* Washington, DC: Brookings Institute Press, 2001.

Gould, Rebecca Kneale. *At Home in Nature: Modern Homesteading and Spiritual Practice in America.* Berkeley: University of California Press, 2005.

Graff, Nancy, ed. *Celebrating Vermont: Myths and Realities.* Hanover, NH: University Press of New England, 1991.

Grahm, Randall. "The Phenomenology of Terroir." *Da Vino Commedia: Bonny Doon Vineyards Newsletter,* Spring 2006.

Guiomar, Jean-Yves. "Vidal de la Blache's Geography of France." In *Realms of Memory: Rethinking the French Past,* edited by Pierre Nora. New York: Columbia University Press, 1996.

Guthman, Amy. *Agrarian Dreams: The Paradox of Organic Farming in California.* Berkeley: University of California Press, 2004.

Guy, Kolleen. *When Champagne Became French.* Baltimore, MD: Johns Hopkins University Press, 2003.

Habermas, Jürgen. *The Structural Transformation of the Public Sphere.* Cambridge, MA: MIT Press, 1989.

Harp, Stephen. *Marketing Michelin: Advertising and Cultural Identity in Twentieth-Century France.* Baltimore, MD: Johns Hopkins University Press, 2001.

Heffernan, William, and Mary Hendrickson. "Concentration of Agricultural Markets Report." Report for National Farmers Union, www.nfu.org/wp-content/2007 -heffernanreport.pdf (accessed May 2007).

Henley, Jon. "Villagers Rebel against Sale of Vineyard to Depardieu." *The Guardian,* February 8, 2003.

Hoag, Dana. *Agricultural Crisis in America.* Denver: ABC-CLIO, 1999.

Howes, David. *Sensual Relations: Engaging the Senses in Culture and Social Theory.* Ann Arbor: University of Michigan Press, 2003.

Hufton, Olwen. "Social Conflict and the Grain Supply in Eighteenth-Century France." In *Hunger and History*, edited by Robert Rothberg and Theodore Rabb. Cambridge: Cambridge University Press, 1985.

Husmann, George. *American Grape Growing and Wine Making*. New York: Orange Judd Co., 1880.

Hutchinson, John. "Northern California from Haraszthy to the Beginnings of Prohibition." In *The Book of California Wine*, edited by Davis Muscatine, Maynard Amerine, and Bob Thompson. Berkeley: University of California Press, 1984.

Institut National des Appellations d'Origine. "Les fondements de l'appellation." www.inao.gouv.fr/public/home.php (accessed March 2006).

Jackson, Michael, ed. *Things as They Are: New Directions in Phenomenological Anthropology*. Bloomington: Indiana University Press, 1996.

Jeganathan, Pradeep. "A Space for Violence." In *Community, Gender, and Violence: Subaltern Studies XI*, edited by Partha Chatterjee and Pradeep Jeganathan. New York: Columbia University Press.

Jullien, B., and A. Smith. "Comment analyser les indications géographiques protégées sans préjuger de leurs singularités?" *Communication pour le Symposium International* (2005): 1–32.

Kearney, M. "The Local and the Global: The Anthropology of Globalization and Transnationalism." *Annual Review of Anthropology* 24 (1995): 547–65.

Klyza, Christopher McGrory, and Stephen C. Trombulak. *The Story of Vermont: A Natural and Cultural History*. Hanover, VT: Middlebury College Press, 1999.

Korsmeyer, Carolyn. *Making Sense of Taste: Food and Philosophy*. Ithaca, NY: Cornell University Press, 2002.

———, ed. *The Taste/Culture Reader: Experiencing Food and Drink*. New York: Berg, 2005.

"La notion complexe de terroir." *Progrès agricole et viticole* 2 (1995): 118–25.

L'appellation d'origine contrôlée: Vins et eaux de vie. Paris: Réalisation Euro-Impressions, 1998.

La Semaine du Goût. www.legout.com (accessed February 2006).

Le Grand d'Aussy, Pierre J. B. *Histoire de la vie privée des français*. Paris: P. D. Pierres, 1815.

Lehning, James R. *Peasant and French: Cultural Contact in Rural France during the Nineteenth Century*. Cambridge: Cambridge University Press, 1995.

Leitch, Alison. "The Social Life of Lardo: Slow Food in Fast Times." *The Asia Pacific Journal of Anthropology* 1, no. 1 (2000): 103–18.

"Le Rocamadour: La poids economique de la filière." AOC promotional pamphlet, 2000.

"Le Rocamadour: Petite histoire d'un grand fromage." AOC promotional pamphlet, 2000.

Levenstein, Harvey. *The Paradox of Plenty: A History of Eating in Modern America.* Berkeley: University of California Press, 2003.

Lewellen, Ted. *The Anthropology of Globalization: Cultural Anthropology Enters the Twenty-first Century.* Westport, CT: Bergin & Garvey, 2002.

Lukacs, Paul. *The Great Wines of America: The Top Forty Vintners, Vineyards, and Vintages.* New York: Norton, 2005.

Lynch, Kermit. *Adventures on the Wine Route: A Wine Buyer's Tour of France.* New York: North Point Press, 1990.

MacNeil, Karen. "Is Terroir Dead? It's Man vs. Mother Nature in Shaping California Wines." *San Francisco Chronicle,* September 18, 2002.

Maison de la France. "Association nationale des Sites remarquables du goût." http://uk.franceguide.com/adherents/fiche_atf.asp?idatf=1949.

Mas de Daumas Gassac. Promotional brochure of vineyard, March 2003.

McCoy, Elin. *The Emperor of Wine: The Rise of Robert M. Parker, Jr.* New York: HarperCollins, 2005.

Mennell, Stephen. *All Manners of Food: England and France from the Middle Ages to the Present.* Champaign: University of Illinois Press, 1995.

Moskin, Dana. "Maine Is Busy Praising the Potato." *New York Times,* November 30, 2005, D6.

National Restaurant Association. "Restaurant Spending 2003." www.restaurant.org/research/consumer/spending.cfm (accessed December 2005).

Nearing, Helen, and Scott Nearing. *The Good Life.* New York: Schocken Books, 1989.

———. *The Maple Sugar Book,* 3rd ed. White River Junction, VT: Chelsea Green Publishing, 2000.

Northeast Sustainable Agriculture Working Group. *Northeast Farms to Food: Understanding Our Region's Food System.* NESAWG/New England Small Farm Institute, September 2002.

Pampille, Madame. *Les bons plats de France: Cuisine régionale.* Paris: Fayard, 1918.

Patterson, Daniel. "To the Moon, Alice?" *New York Times Sunday Magazine*, November 6, 2005.

Pelto, Gretel H., and Pertti J. Pelto. "Diet and Delocalization: Dietary Changes since 1750." *Journal of Interdisciplinary History* 14 (1983): 507–28.

Penn, Cyril. "What Is Quality?" *Wine Business Monthly* 8 (May 23, 2001). www.wine business.com/html/MonthlyArticle.cfm?dataId=24592 (accessed September 2005).

Petrini, Carlo. *Slow Food: The Case for Taste.* New York: Columbia University Press, 2003.

Peynaud, Emile. *The Taste of Wine: The Art and Science of Wine Appreciation.* New York: John Wiley & Sons, 1996.

Pinney, Thomas. *A History of Wine in America: From Prohibition to the Present.* Berkeley: University of California Press, 2005.

Pollan, Michael. *The Omnivore's Dilemma: A Natural History of Four Meals.* New York: Penguin, 2005.

Pomerol, Charles, ed. *The Wines and Winelands of France: Geological Journeys.* London: Robertson McCarta, 1989.

Ray, Krishnendu. *The Migrant's Table.* Philadelphia: Temple University Press, 2004.

Reed-Danahy, Deborah, and Susan Carol Rogers. "Introduction." Special Issue, *Anthropological Quarterly* 60 (1987): 51.

The Rhone Ranger. http://rhoneranger.blogspot.com/ (accessed November 2003).

Richardin, Edmond. *La cuisine française du XIVe au XXe siècle.* Paris: Editions de l'Art et Littérature, 1913.

Richards, Ronnie, adapter. "Terrific Terroir." *La Stampa*, February 27, 2006. www.slowfood.com/eng/sf_sloweb/sf_sloweb_dettaglio.lasso?passaswe=SW _02254 (accessed April 2006).

Ridgway, Judy. *The Little Red Wine Guide.* (Paris: Les Arenes, 2000).

Rigoglioso, Margaret. "The Accidental Epicure." *Stanford Magazine*, May/June 2003.

Robert Mondavi Winery. www.mondavi.com (accessed August 2003).

Robinson, Jancis, ed. *The Oxford Companion to Wine*, 2nd ed. Oxford: Oxford University Press, 1999.

Rodgers, Judy. *The Zuni Café Cookbook.* New York: W. W. Norton & Company, 2002.

Rogers, Susan Carol. "Farming Visions: Agriculture in French Culture." *French Politics, Culture and Society* 18, no. 1 (Spring 2000): 50–67.

———. "Good to Think: The 'Peasant' in Contemporary France." *Anthropological Quarterly* 60, no. 2 (1987): 56–63.

Root, Waverly. *The Food of France.* New York: Vintage Books, 1992.

Russell, Howard. *A Long, Deep Furrow.* Hanover, NH: University Press of New England, 1976.

Saekel, Karola. "Ferry Tales Do Come True." *San Francisco Chronicle,* May 19, 2004.

Shapin, Steven. "Paradise Sold: What Are You Buying When You Buy Organic?" *The New Yorker,* May 22, 2006.

Sotte, Franco. "European Rural Development Policy and Territorial Diversity in Europe." *Symposium International: "Territoires et enjeux du développement regional"* (2005): 1–18.

Spang, Rebecca. *The Invention of the Restaurant: Paris and Modern Gastronomic Culture.* Cambridge, MA: Harvard University Press, 2000.

Sutton, David. *Remembrance of Repasts: An Anthropology of Food and Memory.* Oxford: Berg Publishers, 2001.

"A Tale of Two Frances." *The Economist,* March 30, 2006.

Tauzin, Hèléne. "Pourquoi ils ont bouté l'américain hors d'Aniane." *La Gazette,* no. 680, May 18–24, 2001.

Tomasik, Timothy J. "Certeau à la Carte: Translating Discursive Terroir in the Practice of Everyday Life: Living and Cooking." *South Atlantic Quarterly* 100 (Spring 2001): 519–42.

Tower, Jeremiah. *California Dish: What I Saw (and Cooked) at the American Culinary Revolution.* New York: Free Press, 2003.

Trubek, Amy B. *Haute Cuisine: How the French Invented the Culinary Profession.* Philadelphia: University of Pennsylvania Press, 2000.

Ulin, Robert C. *Vintages and Traditions: An Ethnohistory of Southwest French Wine Cooperatives.* Washington, DC: Smithsonian Press, 1996.

Vaudour, Emmanuelle. "The Quality of Grapes and Wine in Relation to Geography: Notions of Terroir at Various Scales." *Journal of Wine Research* 13 (August 2002): 117–41.

Vermont Agency of Agriculture, Food, and Markets. www.vermontagriculture.com (accessed May 2006).

———. "Vermont's Maple Laws and Regulations." www.vermontagriculture.com/mapleregs.PDF (accessed May 2006).

Vermont Maple Sugar Makers' Association. "Maple Facts." www.vermontmaple.org/ MapleFacts.html (accessed May 2006).

Weber, Eugen. *Peasants into Frenchmen: The Modernization of Rural France, 1870–1914*. Stanford, CA: Stanford University Press, 1976.

Wheaton, Barbara Ketcham. *Savoring the Past: The French Kitchen and Table from 1300 to 1789*. New York: Scribners, 1996.

Wilk, Richard. *Home Cooking in the Global Village: Caribbean Food from Buccaneers to Ecotourists*. New York: Berg, 2006.

———, ed. *Fast Food/Slow Food: The Cultural Economy of the Global Food System*. Lanham, NY: Altamira Press, 2006.

Wilson, Harold Fisher. *The Hill Country of Northern New England: Its Social and Economic History, 1790–1930*. New York: AMS Press, 1967.

Wilson, James. *Terroir: The Role of Geology, Climate, and Culture in the Making of French Wines*. Berkeley: University of California Press, 1999.

Wine Institute. "California Wine Industry Statistical Highlights." www.wineinstitute .org/industry/statistics/2004/ca_industry_highlights.php (accessed December 2005).

———. "Strong Sales Growth in 2004 for California Wine as Shipments Reach New Heights." www.wineinstitute.org (accessed December 2005).

Woodstock Foundation. Introductory materials, Vermont as a Destination Summit, July 2005.

Woodstock Foundation. "Vermont as Destination Report." September 2005.

Wright, Leslie. "New Rules for Maple Syrup Labels Announced." *Burlington Free Press*, February 7, 2006.

Wu, Olivia. "The Zen Masters of Zuni Are in for the Long Run." *San Francisco Chronicle*, September 7, 2005.

INDEX

Page numbers in italics refer to figures.

CALIFORNIA STUDIES IN FOOD AND CULTURE

DARRA GOLDSTEIN, EDITOR

DESIGNER
J. G. BRAUN

TEXT
9.5/14.75 SCALA

DISPLAY
AKZIDENZ GROTESK

COMPOSITOR
BINGHAMTON VALLEY COMPOSITION, LLC

PRINTER AND BINDER
MAPLE-VAIL MANUFACTURING GROUP